'A beautiful and moving story that brings to life a fascinating part of Jewish history.'

Claudia Roden

'With his latest book, *Loving Strangers*, Jay Prosser brings a fascinating new geography to the map of Jewish roots memoirs. This odyssey to reclaim his Jewish identity through the memorabilia of his mother's complex family history is both moving and compelling. A shimmering memoir of love's work, healing for our fractured times.'

Nancy K. Miller, Author of *What They Saved: Pieces of a Jewish Past*

'Jay's story is rich and fascinating. Through the prism of a family memoir, he shines a light on interracial marriage and its legacy, stories that have been previously taboo. He's written a beautiful book that will resonate with anyone who is interested in under-represented cultures, and he is bold enough to rewrite history as we know it.'

Lily Dunn, Author of *Sins of My Father: A Daughter, A Cult, A Wild Unravelling*, co-founder London Lit Lab

'What is most moving to me in this gripping family memoir and diasporic Asian-European history is the account of how three generations in Jay Prosser's family actively choose Jewishness. Love and historical circumstances create a hybrid, affiliative form of Jewishness that remains strange and contingent, yet also affirming in a sense of belonging that is neither territorial nor identitarian.'

Marianne Hirsch, Author of *The Generation of Postmemory: Narrative and Visual Culture After the Holocaust*

Loving Strangers

Loving Strangers:

A Camphorwood Chest, a Legacy, a Son Returns

Jay Prosser

This first edition published June 2024
By The Black Spring Press
An imprint of The Black Spring Press Group
Eyewear Publishing Ltd
Maida Vale, London, UK

Cover design by Matt Broughton
Cover and book photographs by Leslie Hakim-Dowek
Typeset by Subash Raghu

ISBN 9781915406804

www.blackspringpressgroup.com

You shall love the stranger as yourself, for you were a stranger in the land of Egypt.

– Torah

The word קֶדֶם (*cadem*) means 'front', 'east', but also 'past'. It reflects the ancient Hebrew concept of time. They thought of the past as in front of their eyes because they could see it; but the future was behind them because they didn't know what would happen.

– Biblical Hebrew Course

CONTENTS

Asia, early twentieth century

OPENING

1. THE CHEST

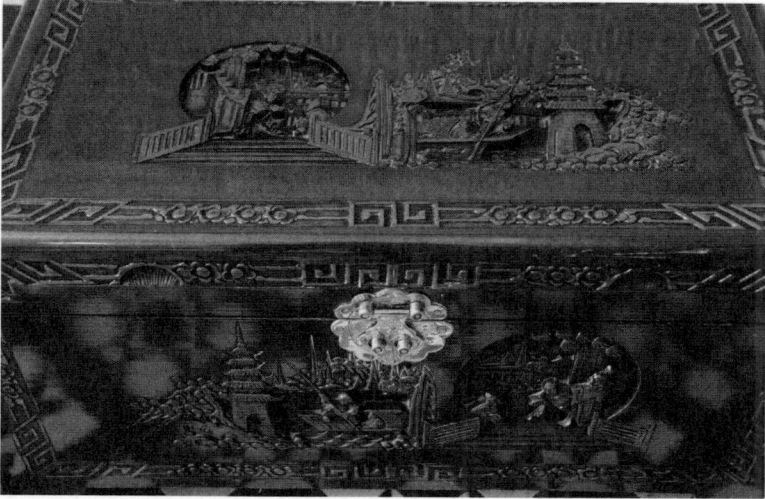

I am sitting before the camphorwood chest, perhaps kneeling. I am ten, seven, five, younger. It is a scene repeated.

From this position, I can't see the top panel easily. So I concentrate my attention, a child's undistracted focus, on the front.

With hands that are still discovering the world, I feel my way into the carvings. Tracing the pictures, I caress the figures. I want to know these strangers from the inside. I try to work out how one scene moves into another, the sequence. I unfreeze the images. I give the characters speech, motives, bringing them to life. I make the story move.

Two strangers are travelling in a boat, a narrow, low, covered sampan, like the ones I've seen in Malaysia and Singapore.

One seated figure – I can't see if anyone is a man or a woman – wears robes and a pigtail. The other, in a Chinese straw hat, poles the boat along. The waters are choppy. The poler has to lean into the action. I run my fingers into the grooves and feel the waves. They are crossing an ocean and there is a storm. What miracle will save them?

This panel melts into another on the left. I figure out that this tale goes from right to left, not left to right. It's another order of story, a reverse way of reading from the one I'm used to.

The two figures glide past a forest, and I glimpse a cave through the trees. The trees thin out, and spires spring up in their place. One ends in a pagoda, like the one my parents, brother and I have walked round in Kew Gardens. One, two, three, four, five, six: I count the tiers. A large arch frames the ground floor. The strangers are passing pavilions and palaces, temples and domes. This is an ancient land, perhaps that in my favourite picture book which Mum has given me, the stories of Jewish kings and heroes from the Bible that I read nightly. But as I look at the carvings closely, the buildings at the water's edge also remind me of the skyscrapers of modern Singapore. I have no clue how often we've visited my mother's home city, but I sense the heat and spice of Singapore all around me: in my mother, in her stories, and in this chest.

Is the journey on the chest also one in time? Are the strangers going backwards, into a mythic past? Or are they travelling forwards, to meet me, here and now?

'Here again? What are you doing, *abdalek*?' My mother's tone is neither accusatory, nor surprised to find me in this no-room, in the hall by the camphorwood chest. 'I just want to check that you're happy.' Her arrival is barely an interruption,

4

and she doesn't expect an answer. Her presence bathes me in gentle sunshine.

Right to left, I continue, with my hands and my imagination.

A wall comes into view. The strangers are approaching the city. In a large open-air house, a third figure is already waiting, cross-legged, on a stone-tiled floor. Hanging over the sitter and extending over the entire scene, a tree casts its shade. The canopy and bark of the tree are, like the waves, carved into the surface of the chest. Even the grain of the depicted wood is etched into our wood. The detail and cleverness of this amazes me. I linger over the knots in the trunk. The bobbly foliage makes me think of the tree on the Chinese bamboo scroll hanging in my mother's bedroom, which I know belonged to my grandmother from China. The waiting figure is receiving a gift from the voyagers, who have now arrived. I can't yet see what their gift is, but I'm desperate to find out.

I need to know the full story.

I catch the figures up. With my fingers, I climb the stairs, perfectly sized for my finger-steps. I push past the wooden gates. And now, in my imagination, I shrink to their size. I blend into their world, and step onto the stone-tiled floor with my characters. They are no longer strangers. I cross over a threshold and find myself inside the chest.

Yes, Mum, I'm happy. I'm the happiest I'll ever be. I am by your camphorwood chest. I am telling stories.

*

In the thirteen homes we lived in when I was a child, the camphorwood chest stood in the hall. My family was uprooted, the chest put down temporary roots, always on the threshold. It was as if my mother's magical container was still travelling, either having just arrived, or just on its way out.

In my child's head, the exotic carvings merged both with my mother's mesmerising tales about her family and with the objects that were in the chest. I seem to have been born with this association of the chest with my mother. For the chest held the heirlooms from her world before she became our mother. I knew that this was the one piece of furniture she brought with her when she migrated from Singapore to England. I also knew that the camphorwood chest was the place where she kept pretty much everything that was valuable to her family past: birth and marriage certificates; expired identity cards and passports; bundles of fading letters written on flimsy airmail forms; piles of tiny, ancient black-and-white photographs.

But also, fairy-tale objects. An unfinished Chinese quilt, and heavy, antique sewing scissors. One of the first audiocassettes ever made. Delicate Chinese and Indian baby jewellery. An anklet with silver bells, one broken off, which still tinkled.

Opening the chest would inspire my mother's storytelling.

She'd take all the letters that she and my father wrote to each other before they were married, following their courtship in Singapore, at the tail end of the British Empire. With their religious, cultural and racial differences, they were loving strangers, whose love drew them across the colonial divide. She'd take albums of her time as an enigmatically beautiful model and the cosmopolitan, mixed-race 'face of Lancôme, Singapore', or of the First Minister of Singapore, an Iraqi Jew like her, dancing at her twenty-first birthday at the Menorah Club. Juxtaposed with these were images of her in charity-donated dresses as a child in a Jewish refugee camp in India, in a Muslim area of Bombay, and she'd tell me of her last-minute escape from the Japanese invasion before the fall of Singapore. 'We left, on the very last boat. It was a miracle.'

She'd tell me of her parents, who also met in Singapore and loved across the chasm of their different languages, countries and cultures. There was my Chinese grandmother –

'My mother was abandoned as a baby by the side of a river in China. A fisherman or a farmer found her.'

Then there was my spice-trading grandfather –

'My father was a spice trader, he was born in India – they called him "Jacob *Bumbai-Wallah*", that Jacob from Bombay. But his own parents came to Singapore from Iraq, Baghdadi Jews, when Iraq was Mesopotamia, a country that doesn't exist anymore.'

And we'd examine a decaying handbag stuffed full of documents, and we'd listen to a tape of my grandfather singing sad songs in many languages I couldn't understand, and my mother would cry.

We'd sit by the side of the camphorwood chest – only she and I; no one else was interested – and she'd tell me stories, one story melting into another. She was Scheherazade, the bottomless treasure chest was Aladdin's Cave, and I was transported into the worlds of my mother's stories.

And I really did feel as though, for the duration of her telling, through the chest's documents, objects and photographs, my mother and I travelled together to the far-off cities, villages and oceans of the family past. We were in China, in a city with three walls, the fourth boundary being a river. We were in India, in a refugee camp with crumbling colonial architecture.

We were trading spices in a market in Singapore. We were in Baghdad, outside a great synagogue, in a white land between two rivers. Sometimes the details varied, or new bits would be remembered and previous particulars left out. So even though this was a repeated activity, repeated at my prompting, there was always something to discover.

The deeper we went into the chest, the older were the contents, and the more distant in time and place the family history became. Although it always seemed already to be packed full, every corner crammed, my mother kept adding to its store, stuffing in parts of our own familiar, family lives: my brother's stellar school reports, my more mixed achievements ('lacks motivation and direction'), and the homemade birthday and mother's day cards that we produced as children. It was an additional wonder to me that my mother – and only she – could arrange everything so that it all fitted back in.

The chest gave me an early lesson in family memory. Nothing should ever be forgotten, but history is still alive. Those who collect it determine what's handed down of the past.

'I'm ¼ Chinese, ¼ Jewish, ¼ Welsh, ¼ English', I would chant to other children, if we got onto the subject of where we were from, which was a key question if you grew up, as I did with a military father and a non-European mother, in different parts of the world. But I didn't know how this fractional, very muddled identity added up, or how these parts, especially the first two, fit together. I was a stranger to myself. The Iraqi and Indian associations never even got a mention. The camphorwood chest gave me clues, but I hadn't yet pulled them together into a story. What was the connection between these people and places that seemed so exotic and far removed from my Western, rootless life? And what brought them to each other, and to and from their distant parts of Asia, and, from there, to make me?

And then came the moment about ten years ago, when my mother issued me with what turned out to be both a gift and an ultimatum. And from that point on, I knew I had to write this book.

2. The Ark

My mother is taking me to her synagogue in south London. It is 2013 and the fortieth anniversary of her father's death. We have come to mark my grandfather's yahrzeit, the ceremony which involves the reading of Jewish prayers in his memory.

I am no stranger to synagogues, and yet I feel like one. I've been in this gem secreted away in a Chelsea back street many times before, and in other synagogues, but always in support of my mother. Of my own place, I've been uncertain. Jewish and not, British and Asian, Iraqi, English, Welsh, Chinese: my mixed ancestry, and my moving every year and a half as a child, has given me a sense of belonging everywhere, and yet being at home nowhere. And in these Jewish airy spaces, dedicated to celebrating an identity handed down without rupture over aeons, from one generation to the next, nowhere do I feel both more peripheral, and yet with a greater yearning to belong. What must it feel like to be this secure in your lineage? Up until today, I've remained on the verge – both of the congregation and of participating.

We pass the metal security gates and enter a welcoming hall, much larger than the outside of the building suggests should exist. My mother introduces me to a woman I've not met before – Leah, a Holocaust survivor. We get chatting, and Leah asks me if I'm Jewish.

As always with this question, I hesitate. For the past twenty years, most of my adult life, I have been a Buddhist. I turned to meditation when my mother was diagnosed with cancer, first as a way of dealing with the black wave of panic that would threaten to drown me at the idea of her impending loss. Then I found a sangha, my Buddhist community, in a Buddhist centre that had taken over an abandoned country estate in Yorkshire near my home. I meditated on impermanence and the equivalence of all relationships. Loss was inevitable. At the same time, according to Buddhism, *all* living beings were my mother, and I was to learn to regard them as such. I worked on my attachment to my mother. I calmed down. Lately I had even been contemplating becoming a monk.

So I don't know how to reply to Leah. If I'm not Jewish, what am I doing in a synagogue? If I am Jewish, what am I doing with Buddhism? I hesitate too long. 'Don't tell me you're Buddhist', she frowns, leaning on her walking stick. Is it my short hair or my floaty calm that gives it away? There are so many Jews turning Buddhist, we even have a name: 'BuJew'. Or as I usually mock my own ultimate failure to commit, 'Bijou'.

'What is it with Jews who become Buddhist?' Leah sighs, not unkindly but with humour, and she moves off into the prayer hall. My mother and I follow her. We take our seats – me, sheepishly, in my customary place at the back of the synagogue.

I could have said to Leah that Buddhism doesn't care about whether I belong or where I'm from. That it doesn't care about legacy. The only past lives that matter are your own past lives; the only sense of continuity, how your present actions will determine your future. I could have said these things, but I didn't. Not here, not in a synagogue. But I have said these words to my mother. I have told her that, with Buddhism, I don't feel like an imposter. That the solitariness of a Buddhist monk's life chimes with my own rootlessness. My mother is not hostile to Buddhism, but at such moments she gets defensive. She senses that I'm rejecting her faith, family, herself. I'm cutting myself off from her and her parents. She tells me that traditions are not so black and white, that I don't know enough and don't understand what it is to be Jewish. And on this last point, I have to agree.

Even with Buddhism, I have to admit, I haven't been able to throw off my sticky attachments: falling in love, food, drink and other bodily pleasures, the energy of a doubting and questioning mind. Unlike my Buddhist friends, I've never been able to take on board the Buddhist precept of reincarnation: that we've all been here before and we'll all be here again. Or rather, the past lives I feel I still carry within me – unprocessed, though; not even fully known – are those of my ancestors. The ancestors who came alive through my mother's stories in my childhood. The past of my mother, who has made me who I am, who is still here. Who beat cancer. And the life of my grandfather, whom we're memorialising in my mother's synagogue today.

The service is well under way by this point. As usual, I have zoned out, unable to follow along fully. But suddenly from my inconspicuous spot at the back, I hear my name said by the rabbi. I am being called to read Torah. I must go to the front and read out loud from the sacred text. I must perform the act that only Jews can once they come of age, normally at thirteen. I'm in my mid forties, never bar-mitzvah-ed. But I've started learning Hebrew, and my mother has told the rabbi I can read. And so now I must take my position at the bimah, the raised platform from which the service is led.

Whether deliberately or not, my mother has brought my identity, 'midway upon the journey of my life' (like Dante), to a crisis. Buddhist, or Jewish? Religious, or nothing? Monk, or family? It feels like a challenge: I must see if I can speak as my mother's Jewish son.

As I climb the stairs, I see my mother watching, wondering how I'm going to measure up. I feel both fulfilment – this is my destiny – but also a large dose of horror. I've been learning Hebrew for only a year and, as I soon discover, deciphering the ink-inscribed Torah scroll is nothing like following the neatly printed handouts that my teachers provide. I don't even pretend I know how to cantillate – to chant the Hebrew according to the liturgy.

Yet sunshine flooding through the windowed dome warms me, and the men at the bimah huddle around me in a collective embrace. The rabbi guides my reading, pointing the yad, the silver symbol for the hand that must not touch the scroll, to where my eyes should follow. My heart swells. It is my mouth pronouncing the holy language of my ancestors. It is my body swaying and reading from the same book they must have read from countless times. Five thousand years of Jewish history course through me. I feel as though I've been plugged into an ancient power source.

Who was the last in the family line to do this? My grandfather, whose memory we are marking today? Or was my great-grandfather my predecessor? Certainly it wasn't my mother, since women in the Orthodox tradition are never called to read the Torah. Here the women sit separately. My mother is among them, and I look to her for reassurance. Her eyes shine, her smile is broad, and her face is a beacon of hope in what she thinks I can do. She doesn't doubt me. I'm reciting the words familiar to her. *She* doesn't think I'm a broken link in the chain.

But as I stumble through the Hebrew, I become conscious that – probably alone among all these men and many of the women – I lack a Jewish education. I do so because my Jewish mother married a non-Jew, as my grandfather also, as my great-grandfather took a non-Jewish common-law wife. Jewish identity descends in the Orthodox tradition through the maternal line, so, by right, through my mother, the lineage is mine. I've long sensed this venerable heritage as a gift: a deep and known way of being, handed down from generation to generation. But how is it truly my inheritance, and in what ways is it a gift for me? What can my mother's legacy bring to my identity?

The one non-white woman in the audience, my mother is still head-turningly beautiful, her ethnicity and geographical provenance unfathomable. Yet she is now well into her seventies. As I look down on the congregation, with the sun streaming in from the glass dome like a spotlight on her face, I see – as if for the first time, as if in a photograph – my mother's actual age. The creases in her skin. Her age spots. Her thinning hair. These days, she tells me on the phone, 'I get tired; I can no longer go to the synagogue so often.' When she's no longer alive, I realise that these words I'm fudging my way through now, these traditions of hers that I'm mimicking, will be my way of sustaining my bond with her, and the bond from her to previous generations of her family. This feels deeper than what Buddhists call the 'attachment' we must rid ourselves of. This feels historical, timeless even. A legacy. If I'm going to find my belonging here, I must do it while she's alive. I realise that in arranging for me to read, my mother is passing me the baton.

I finish my reading and feel some accomplishment, but mainly relief that I can return to my place at the back of the synagogue. I watch the men replace the Torah scroll in the ark, the sacred wooden chest in which the scroll is stored.

And involuntarily, I think of another ark, one that has always held sacred memories for me.

3. The Commission

'You should write these stories down,' I told my mother as I was growing up. We were sitting by the camphorwood chest as she led me through its enchanted portal to her ancestral lands.

'When you're grown up, *abdalek*,' she'd reply.

Then, 'When I retire.'

'When I am well again.'

Then (now retired and well again), when I'm not practising French, Italian, ballet, the piano – travelling.

When I have time. (She never has time.)

And then finally she said to me, 'You do it.' And this led me to learn Hebrew, which in turn led to that moment when I'm reading in the synagogue, where I feel like my mother has issued me with an ultimatum.

'You do it. You've always been interested in my story. You're the writer, after all.'

And so this book began as a kind of commission. I started the research intensely, but without fully understanding my personal investment, thinking of it more as a book for my mother, a book solely about her family – nothing to do with me, really.

But once I began writing the stories of what was held inside the chest – an adult version of my childhood self trying to enter the pictures on the front of the chest – that *commission for* my mother increasingly became, during the course of this book, a *transmission from* my mother. Not only the story, but now the role of the teller, was passed on from my mother to me, and I found myself transformed by the experience. As I had been summoned by the rabbi to read the Torah, I was now summoned by my mother to enter the family archive and narrate its contents, from where I sat, a grown man, beside a much smaller camphorwood chest, and to figure out finally what these materials meant to me: to spend time with them, to inhabit them, to bring them to life to such an extent that these materials, in turn, would lead me to a different life. The call to me in the synagogue became, in the course of this book, a call from my mother that required me to respond with answers that would affect my own spiritual and emotional journey.

I didn't know whether piecing together the legacy of the chest would help me resolve my anxiety about belonging. I didn't know about the chest's darker contents or history, and nor, in truth, did my mother. We had yet to see how killing and my father's role in a jungle war in Malaya lay behind the love of my parents, May and Keith. How loss and repeated abandonment in the lives of my grandparents, Jacob Isaac Hyeem Ezekiel Elias and Sim Koh-wei (renamed Esther), joined them, like the entwined trees they'd visit in the Singapore Botanic Gardens. We didn't know why this was a family tree you had to turn upside down to understand; why I would have to go backwards rather than forwards through the generations and in my chronicling of them. We were ignorant of how, in my great-grandfather Isaac's plot, brother turned against brother; how this almost biblical fable created a family that learned to love those most unlike themselves. Above all, we didn't know the meaning of loving strangers – what this paradox really was, how far back it went, or how fundamental it was to Jewishness, and to my return to our family's Judaism.

But I knew – *I always knew* – that the camphorwood chest was the only thing I really wanted to inherit in my mother's house.

And so once again, my mother and I begin unpacking the camphorwood chest, this time with me selecting the items and trying to steer the story. Now it's up to me to use the contents as talismans to bring back past lives, to meditate, not on absence, but instead on how these presences touch mine. My mother is my indispensable interlocutor, the curator of the chest and the source of my stories. But as we progress, I take up her position. I'm the one who lifts out the heavy objects, while my mother rests, directing me on how to replace them. During the years of our story-journey, I watch as my beloved mother shrinks and becomes frail. Before too long, the camphorwood chest will move to my house, where it will become part of my own legacy to pass on.

Now, as a middle-aged man, I run my hands over the panel, not on the front of the chest but on the top, now easily reached. This second set of carvings reverses the direction of the previous journey. The two figures are travelling not right to left but left to right. Yet while I recognise these characters, this depiction is not a simple inversion, because there are detailed differences from the first story. Their boat is an alternative model. The base is a quilted, basket-woven pattern, and the whole design is more angular. The strangers (no longer strangers) themselves appear older and thinner. The scene must be many years on from their first voyage. The punting pilot is bent double, as if now struggling to bring the boat back. And as they near the shore, the two companions cling to each other, for support or perhaps inseparable after their exploits.

And now I see what their gift is, which they are bringing back. It, also, is a chest, a sacred archive.

It is the end of their story, and the beginning of mine.

READING THE WORDS

4. Some Enchanted Evening

A memory and a recurrent dream.

A boarding school in England, for Army children; for children whose parents are always on the move.

The scene is in the bathroom. Bath-time is collective but also partly private. The children are separated from each other by thin wooden screens, which fall just short of floors and ceiling. Ancient, cavernous cast-iron baths and the steam help the children's voices carry. They can chat across their separate cubicles.

One child is answering the question of where he is from. He is one of only three students of not all-white heritage in this school of 400, along with one Black Jamaican and one half-Chinese child – both of whom are already his friends. He started at the school just a few weeks ago, only ten years old. He recites proudly what he has always been told: that he is part Jewish, part Chinese and part British. He is telling his origin story, the story of his parents' meeting.

After he finishes, there is a moment's silence. Then the disembodied voice comes through the wall. 'So,' it says, authoritatively, disdainfully. 'You're a half-caste, then.'

The child has never heard this term, but he knows it is bad. He is an outcast. He is speechless.

*

Two days after meeting him for the very first time, my mother wrote a note to my father. She was completing the words of a song he had spoken to her which he hadn't quite been able to remember fully. The song, 'You Do Something to Me', is all about the mystification and 'voodoo' of love, the speaker being spellbound and hypnotised by the lover.

Over the next two months my parents saw each other every day, sometimes twice a day, and talked on the phone every evening. Then they were separated for another nine months, during which time they wrote to each other several times a week, sometimes several times a day, across several thousand miles.

It was the end of the era of ocean-liner intercontinental travel. It was the last point in history when letters were the main

24

form of communication between parted lovers. It was the finale of the great romantic songbook. And it was the last moment – mythologised in a popular song, musical and film – when, though born on opposite sides of the sea, strangers could meet across a crowded room, and instantaneously fall in love.

'Some enchanted evening', my parents would say of that Saturday night when they first met. The magic of two people coming together for the first time who are just about to become partners for life has been the refrain of our little family's origin story. My mother especially would regale me with the opener. *Some enchanted evening . . .*

My parents' song, 'Some Enchanted Evening' seems to have been written for them. It's the song they ask to get played if there's a live piano player. It's the one they proper ballroom dance to, propelling me at once into embarrassment and envy. If they hear even a snatch, they get all misty-eyed.

Some of the stardust must have been sprinkled on me, for as a child I was spellbound in my mother's recounting of their courtship. Freud says that the first spell we fall under is that of our parents' coming together, which he calls the 'family romance'. After all, we owe our existence to this encounter. You could say that *some enchanted evening* was my necessary prelude.

Yet what was this magic? What the reason for the enchantment? And what was the meaning of the music?

I hold my parents' letters from the camphorwood chest, feeling their words come alive in my hands. They play out my first love story, my origin story. My parents' enchantment occupies my heart, their music inspiring and becoming my own words.

*

'Some Enchanted Evening' comes from Rodgers and Hammerstein's *South Pacific*. The musical is resonant for my parents' meeting and for the specific coordinates of their relationship. *South Pacific* is set in the islands of the Asian-American Pacific. The historical backdrop is the American military defence against the Japanese advance during the Second World War. The trigger for the Americans entering the war is the Japanese bombing, in December 1941, of Pearl Harbor in Hawaii, where the film was actually made.

The plot entails different cultures coming together to become a love story, with the theme of racial prejudice acknowledged and overcome. For us now, the narrative may seem naïve and patronising, a romanticisation of 'tropical island' mentality and colonial days. But this tale of love across difference and resulting mixed-race children – of love overcoming divisions – was revolutionary, both in 1949, the time of the stage musical, and in 1958, the moment of the film.

South Pacific is a perfect rhyme for my parents, because Singapore was another tropical island, west of the Asian-American Pacific; it had also suffered bombardment like Hawaii and had fallen to the Japanese, in February 1942; and this was immediately after the bombing of Pearl Harbor. Like one of the main characters of the show, Joseph Cable, my father had been sent on a mission as a young lieutenant, similarly acting on intelligence to play his part. He was as handsome as Cable and certainly *'younger than springtime'* (my father just twenty-one). My mother was a Singaporean. While she was not simply a 'native' island girl like Liat, the 'Tonkinese' woman with whom Cable falls in love, she was definitely not white. She had discernible mixed Asian ancestry, with a Chinese mother and an Iraqi Jewish father.

I think my parents are definitely better looking, even than the delectable Cable and Liat. Photographs from 1960 show them as both gorgeous, the electricity between them obvious. One photograph, taken at a picnic, has them locked in a gaze. He, as my mother rightly says now, was 'bleary-eyed' around her, almost visibly spellbound. But really that's not surprising. My mother, apparently Eurasian and with her pacific smile, comes across as tranquil, self-contained, and wrapped in mystique. My father, especially in his service dress uniform with his Sam Browne belt strapped across his chest, has a strong, military bearing. He seems equally self-assured. It's easy to see how they could have fallen under each other's spell.

My parents not only crossed the chasms of culture and race. They also challenged divisions between ruler and ruled, and those fast separating empire and colony. My father was told quite early on in the courtship by his senior officers that his career would be severely jeopardised if he ever married my mother. In the well-meant words of his colonel (who eventually paid for their wedding and who became their greatest supporter), writing in a letter to my father when he had missed out on a job because of his connection to my mother: 'Keith, that sort of situation is likely to occur and recur throughout your career if you marry May.'

But my parents' story would turn out to be the successful plotline of *South Pacific*, and more romantic and significant than the musical could imagine.

*

The date of my mother's first note was 21st May 1960. The sun was rapidly setting on the reaches of the British Empire, particularly on its Asian shores. India, the jewel in the imperial crown, had been lost in 1947. The following year the British had quit Burma and Ceylon. In 1932 the British Mandate in Iraq had ended; the same in Palestine in 1948. Malaya attained independence in 1957; and Singapore itself became self-governing in 1959. The British retained a governmental and military foothold in Asia. Singapore was the capital for its East Asian forces: the 'eastern bastion', counterpart to the western bastion of Britain herself. But by the 1960s London would start to question the viability of even the small presence that remained in Singapore.

It was in July 1957 that Keith had 'come up' to Singapore, as they used to say of British Army officers' service abroad, as if this were a form of self-improvement or development, as in 'going up' to university. He was commissioned as a young lieutenant to serve in the Malayan Emergency, the British war against Malayan communists. The Emergency was also, by 1957-60, at its tail end. Keith's role for three years had been to root out the last of the communist terrorists from the Malayan jungle. In early 1958, he had won the Military Cross for bravery in action. Eighteen months later he became an instructor at the Jungle Warfare School in Johor in the Malayan Southern Federation.

With the additional salary he bought himself a dashing, early 1950s Armstrong Siddeley, a classic luxury British motor car. Singapore was one hour's drive from Johor, just across the Causeway, the bridge connecting Singapore Island to the Malay Peninsula. After his years of fighting in the jungle, the city was now beckoning. He was a young man who had just received a military honour; he had two months left to enjoy the East before he returned to England; he was kicking up his heels. It was at this point that Keith met May, and the spell of love was cast.

On that enchanted evening, the host of the party was someone whom Keith used to play rugby with – not a strong connection. And May was only at the party because a girlfriend had asked her along last minute, and May happened, unusually for her, not to have a date that Saturday night. It was fate, my mother would say, in her retelling. And I understood fate in that double sense: sheer chance, the slimmest accident; but also unavoidable destiny, as if the encounter was written in runes or in the stars.

They saw each other across a crowded room. May could tell he was in the military, though Keith was in his 'civvies' that night, an understated grey suit that didn't hide his height, intensity or commanding ways. She wore a chiffon dress in a blue as bright as the Singapore sky, with pale embroidery on its sleeves and a full-skirted hem. She looked like a model, a film star: Hedy Lamarr meets Anna Mae Wong. (Keith and May both loved films.) Their eyes met. He moved towards her, and he didn't leave her side for the rest of the evening. They spoke about Singapore, about his time there, and also about her life growing up there. But most of the evening, they simply danced.

*

That night he escorted her home, and they arranged to meet the next day to see a film. Before their first date, he came to her home for tea and to meet her family. It was her baby sister Julie's tenth birthday, and May had baked a Singapore speciality, a golden-yellow coconut cake. There were six – or was it seven? Keith had a hard time keeping track – sisters, and one brother. Her home was a flat on Short Street: small, concrete-floored and barely furnished. But Keith also came from a cramped home where the family practically lived in one room, and he tuned in to the intimacy. He felt the joy radiating particularly from the old man, Jacob, May's father.

May's mother, Esther, kept topping up Keith's tea, which was served sweet with condensed milk in a glass. She was trying to read Keith, observing the effect of this tall white stranger on her daughter. But Esther couldn't follow the conversation. She was Chinese and spoke little English. So mostly she sat quietly at her daughter's side, her handbag in her lap. She watched as if she knew how the story would unfold.

Fluent in English and voluble, Jacob commanded the scene. He was a small, coffee-skinned man, with May's eyes and the booming voice of a giant. He took Keith aside and quizzed him, already testing the young man's worthiness of his daughter. Keith felt totally at ease. He was British, officer class now, used to winning wars and medals. But the following day, Jacob told May he wasn't sure about this new beau of hers. He thought Keith seemed 'very English', and he didn't think this non-Jew had a sense of humour – a vital quality in Jacob's eyes.

May knew her father expected her to 'marry in', to marry Jewish.

But Jacob can't have been surprised about how his daughter lit up in the presence of this British officer. He had always called May, not without ruefulness, 'the English one' of all his daughters. He had long recognised that she was different in the family, that she would probably look beyond Singapore, and perhaps even the Jewish community eventually.

And if she aspired to a world without limits, well, Jacob must have known that he was hardly himself blameless.

*

After tea, the couple went to the Cathay Cinema, which was just around the corner from her home. Back then the cinema was one of the few air-conditioned places where you could escape the Singapore heat – and where, also, it was acceptable to sit in semi-public and hold a lover's hand. When she got home from work the following day, May found a huge basket of flowers and a card from him. It was then she sat down and wrote that first note in reply.

In response, Keith releases a barrage of invitations, drawing up a list. This is the next item I come across in their correspondence, which I unwrap like an excited child opening a package at my birthday party. He provides her with dates, alongside dress codes, for parades, balls, curry lunches, swimming and barbecues; and for his send-off party from Singapore, aboard the troopship *SS Oxfordshire*, at the end of July. The list finishes: 'Then, at some point in the next six months – anywhere in England or Europe.'

Keith is clearly smitten. But May plays hard to get. I note that she takes weeks to reply. She refuses to commit herself to any but one of the functions ('there's many a slip 'twixt the cup and the lip', she writes coyly). It was early days, she tells me now when I ask her why she held herself back. And she makes no comment at all on his last, potentially life-transforming proposal. She does accept the cocktail party, to be held at his barracks in Singapore after a military parade.

But she also can't resist joshing him: 'I am sure I could not very well decline so kind an invitation, especially as it has come through the courtesy of an admirable Military Cross holder!' Keith had written on the back of the printed invitation card, 'with the compliments of Lieutenant W. K. L. Prosser, M.C.' He was proud of his merits. She was showing him she wasn't going to fall for accolades.

Despite my mother's initial reserve, my parents saw each other every day during that two-month courtship. That first note is perfectly typed and likely written by May during her lunchtime, while she was working as a personal assistant to the boss of Alcan Aluminium, near Raffles Place, at the hub of Singapore city life. Keith came to these offices and took May out for a *gado-gado,* a salad with peanut sauce, at the Pavilion restaurant around the corner from Raffles Place. If he couldn't get away from work to see her at lunchtime, he would be sure to come later in the afternoon, and they went to Mont d'Or, a little tea-and-ice-cream place on Orchard Road. Keith would then whizz back to his barracks, miles away near Changi, swiftly bathe and change, then drive all the way back to the city in the evening, collecting May from Short Street, in his chariot of the Armstrong Siddeley.

My parents had dinner at one of the smart hotels. Prince's or Raffles was their favourite, the most sophisticated, since there was dancing at dinner. The couple went on to the Golden Dragon, a little night club, where their dancing could resume. They held each other close until long after every other patron had left, and the pianist played for them alone. Keith escorted May home, crawled back to barracks – it could be 4 a.m. by this stage – and both of them were at work by 8 a.m. Part of me wonders how they managed to function, even if this taxing schedule continued for just two months. But then I remember (I know because I have loved, and I promise to tell) that enchantment really does endow lovers with superpowers, especially the young. And you simply don't feel tired, or anything except the infatuation.

They spent their weekends together. Keith played rugby on the Padang, the central field in Singapore outside the Supreme Court and City Hall, and May came to be close to him and watch. Keith's letters remember that, as he scored a try, he looked at May and felt 'like the matador presenting the bull's ear to his lady.' And they went for those bleary-eyed picnics on the Nee Soon ranges, or for walks around Kallang Park, another place where they were allowed to hold hands.

*

Keith and May are finally separated from each other for more than just a few hours only on the last day of July 1960 – the day of his boat journey away from Singapore and back to England with his regiment. And it's this day when the correspondence between them really takes off.

The prior two months of intense dating, and also Keith's impending departure, seem to be making all the difference. May is demonstrably reciprocating his feelings now. On note-paper from Mont d'Or, headed at 1 p.m. on the day he is leaving, she writes to him:

> Dearest Keith,
>
> One last message before you sail away from me. My thoughts are now full of you; we parted this morning so abruptly that it seems to me like an unfinished song – that must someday be completed. Who knows, perhaps someday, in this case, it might. . . .
>
> Au Revoir, until we meet again, someday.

On his ship 'a mere 5 minutes' from her, he sits with her photo-graph, which she had made especially for his journey, 'on the writing table in my cabin. The soldiers are coming aboard, all terribly excited to be going home, whilst I am so terribly sad. . . . Doris Day is singing *"When I fall in love it will be forever"* –

35

and never have words been so true.' In a 'PS' he tells her he has discovered a writing room stacked with masses of 'SS Oxfordshire, Bibby Line' paper. 'I have a golden opportunity to write long letters to you.' He gives her the details of his first port of call, praying that she will write to him there.

And indeed, she does. At his first port of call, Aden, he finds this:

Wednesday, 3rd August 1960 (5.15 p.m.)

My Dearest Keith,

The most wonderful thing has happened to me. My thoughts and feelings as I awoke on Sunday morning last were so mixed and confused. I suppose I really could not grasp the fact that you were going and that we had said good-bye for the last time that morning.

All morning I had been terribly miserable, looking back over the lovely times we had spent together, and feeling sad that they had to be stopped short so. But then, during the afternoon, and especially later that evening when I went to bed, the realisation came that you were really part of me, and that although you had gone away, you were in spirit still with me, and here now, close beside me, whilst I write these words. I cannot describe the beauty and magnitude of the sensation that filled me that night as I lay in bed. I thought – 'I love Keith, I love him, and I feel so big for it that I want to hug the whole wide world. I want to do things for him, and I want him to be happy, because the happiness I feel at this moment is the greatest I have ever known.' From that time onwards, I have never looked back; I look forward to the great future ahead of us.

I want to come to England to see you and to be with you. I need you, just as much as you have said you needed me. I have never felt this way before. Am I being terribly forward? If I am, I don't care. I want to make you happy, Keith – that's all that matters to me now.

She 'comes down to earth' with some practical arrangements, about where he should send his letters – to her office, not her home. She responds to his request – he had noticed journalists on board his ship: could she please send him any newspaper clippings about his regiment's departure?

Into my lap falls the clipping she sent him. 'As the Federation [of independent Malaya] today began its victory celebrations, the 1st Battalion, 22nd Cheshire Regiment – one of the British battalions that helped end the Emergency – bid a quiet goodbye to Singapore.' Since its arrival in July 1957, 'the battalion killed 11 terrorists, captured and wounded many more and won several awards for gallantry.' Commenting briefly on the enclosure, May is soon climbing the dizzy heights of love again. She's now planning to take an extra job so that she can save enough to follow him to England as quickly as possible: 'At this rate, Keith, you are going to have me on your hands before a year is over. Is it, to you, a hateful or dreaded thought?'

As the distance and feelings between them grow, so does the correspondence.

> You should find another letter, an extremely lengthy one, awaiting your arrival at Colombo, so I'm really not doing too badly, am I? Similarly, I should feel acutely disappointed if, during the next few days, there is no sign of mail from you.
>
> Keith, my dear, I am beginning to miss you terribly. Very often these days I find myself transported in a wave of depression to the time when you were here. The memories come crowding back, and I feel an almost overwhelming desire to feel your warm hand holding mine. Of course this does not mean that I am not still hopeful; on the contrary, now that I am free from the shackles of doubt, I feel the memories we share have a fortifying effect on my determination to leave Singapore.

It's 1.30 p.m. on a Saturday, and she's writing before she leaves her office. I note that, as she is working five and a half days, my mother is not keeping Shabbat.

*

When I ask to read their correspondence, my parents are remarkably generous. They haven't looked at the letters again themselves, probably not since the time of their lovesick court-ship separation, and they let them go even before knowing the contents. Maybe my parents' casualness stems from the fact that it was all so long ago, over half a century, and they no lon-ger identify with those young people. Certainly, when I read out parts of their letters over the phone, they express surprise. Did I really write that? Are you sure you're not making this up? And I agree. This Keith and May are indeed unlike the parents I know.

And yet, I also find notes of continuity.

My mother, not yet my mother, is tougher, more strong-willed than I've known her in my life. She seems older than her twenty-one years: fearless, planning to leave the island home she has always known; determining her future. She is beautiful, and a beautiful letter-writer. Who *wouldn't* fall in love with her? I think. But I also recognise in her letters the same strength with which she cares for my father today, now that they're both in old age. She is 'tough as old boot', she assures me, as her arthritic hands hoick a giant wok from a cupboard below. Her mind is still sharp and brilliant. She sits at the kitchen table most nights having cleared away supper, pencil in hand, as focused as a studious child on her French homework or on completing *The Times* crossword. May today is the same diamond who dazzled my father.

My father in the letters is an odd mixture of discipline and waywardness, of courage and softness. I feel tender towards this soldier's vulnerability, wanting to protect his head-long-rushing spirit from disappointment. Keith's extremes have now reconciled themselves into his easy-going companionability. In old age, he is, by necessity, accepting of whatever comes his way.

It may sound odd, but I feel parental towards the young lovers I meet in the letters. Many of us experience this reversed relationship as we care for our parents struggling into old age, and I feel this increasingly. But reading my parents' love letters pitches me into a nurturing and protective role towards who they *were*. Digging into my parents' past, I realise that I'm now a generation older than these young letter-writers. Which means that I could be the parent of my parents' letter selves, and they, their own grandparents.

And as I read their words, I'm overwhelmed by the love between my parents all over again, now as an adult. The letters reveal as true the fable I grew up on; that love between strangers really is an enchanted story.

From the camphorwood chest and the family home, my parents allow me to take their correspondence, which I pack into a small suitcase and order into a chronology. When my brother visits my house and sees my careful organisation of their weighty exchange, he shudders, almost visibly. 'Don't you feel strange reading this stuff?', he asks. Dave is a psychiatrist. He has always seemed to have preserved more distance from my parents, perhaps because he was the older child, and also because, unlike me, he went on to have his own children. He explained to me that when he became a father, it changed his relationship to our parents. Tending to Rosa and Sam, especially when they were young, now became his priority. Whereas my parents have remained my primary family. Indeed, over the years, they've become my best friends.

So on some level, Dave is right: to believe even now in the power of my parents' romance, that their love letters have something to teach me as an adult, is, Freud might say, an abnormal attachment to my parents. Not only because it idealises my parents' courtship. But also because, through reading their letters and using them as my first link to my family history, I become the author of my parents' story, the progenitor of their love.

*

My parents carefully specify time: the time at which letters are begun and sometimes ended. Their time-logging is a measure of the rapid rate of the letters between them – sometimes two or three per day; and also of the minutes, hours – days – weeks – months, of their separation, which they will, together, now chart. As a couple, they are marking time: the time they were last together; the time they are apart; the time when they will be together again.

Bibby Line
S. S. Oxfordshire
Saturday 6th August
12.15 p.m.
May, My Dearest
The days go by so slowly & yet it seems so long since we parted. It is in fact only a week since we were shopping together, & then that very sad lunch, culminating with the realisation that we were soon to part. The best we can hope for before we meet again is another 51 weeks. It makes life so difficult, because to me they

are wasted weeks of my life. I simply wish them to pass as quickly as possible, so that we can be together again and really live life as it should be lived, enjoying it to its fullest.

It is strange, but even in this small intimate ship I feel very lonely, and I seem to spend hours gazing vacantly over the side of the ship, looking back towards Singapore, and wondering what you are doing at this moment. It is Saturday, and I wonder how you will spend this evening; will it be in the Golden Dragon or will it be spent in solitary thought? It is not easy for me to know how I want you to spend this next year. I can only hope that through the medium of our letters we will be brought close together.

Time extends in part because he hasn't docked at Colombo, so he hasn't picked up her letters recently. Being on the boat also means *longueur*. His ship's captain has just announced the daily run of the ship – 'she has covered 450 miles in the last 24 hours, and that is 450 miles further away from you – a horrible thought.' Even the nights and days are extended. He is sleeping enormous amounts – '9 hours at night and another two sometimes during the day. It is a considerable difference to the average of 3-4 hours' sleep during those last few days in Singapore.'

In their stop-over at Colombo, he is not impressed, contrasting the post-independent island capital city with settlements that were still run by the empire. It had been over a decade since the British had pulled out of Ceylon. The 'town was depressingly poor, and typical of the many Indian towns without the British administration services.' He breaks off his account when he hears 'the lunch gong sounding down below.' Meals punctuate the long days. In the evening, in the 'hour before I dress for dinner', he continues writing to her, a string of memories, associations, hopes: the cufflinks she gave him 'that last Saturday'; 'that sad lunch with a note, "Lest you forget." Unkind, how could I forget.' 'The cufflinks are only used on special occasions – for it would be unforgiveable to lose them. I must be wearing them when we meet again.' He's looking forward to being at home in Bath: 'I shall walk so very far doing all the things I did as a child, and hoping all the time that one day I will be doing it with you. Remember your "flatties" when you eventually pack your suitcase.' He is very proud of her photograph: 'I show it to everyone, from the boy who draws my bath to the young girls at our meal table.'

She, too, finds time dragging. Since he left she has not had an evening out – 'I am completely out of circulation. . . I find I would rather settle down in a cozy corner of my huge bed with a book, or sit out on the verandah' – even on Saturday nights which, for her too, no longer have the 'air of expectancy which the Saturdays whilst you were here never failed to bring with them. The days themselves seem to run into one another.' Life in Singapore remains 'a torment. To catch a glimpse of some place we went to together, or hear snatches of any of our own songs, or the recurrence of any little incident resembling one of these we encountered together', keeps her lying awake for hours with memories, such as of dining at the Tanglin Club with him, their 'long, self-interrupted walks' around Kallang Park, 'holding hands for the whole world to see.' 'I feel that strange sensation that arose within me that night as we dined at the Adelphi. It's the same indescribable yearning, a calling out feeling, or rather reaching out, from the very depths of soul, with every fibre of my being. It is a feeling so overpowering and so acute, that it is almost physical.'

Alongside the texturing of time, the references to music accelerate, amplify – *accelerando*. At one point, as the winter draws in, May writes: 'it's a cold, dark and wet evening.' She is listening to Nat King Cole on the radio singing '"Love Letters" (so appropriately)', as the love letter she writes *straight from her heart* keeps her *near to Keith even while they're apart*. She's *not alone in the night*.

When May does finally go out without Keith ('with an old girlfriend'), it is to see *All the Fine Young Cannibals,* a film meant to have been inspired by the life of the angelically beautiful jazz trumpeter and singer Chet Baker. Afterwards, as May and her friend drive down Orchard Road,

I caught glimpses of so many places to remind me of you. There was first of all the Rose d'Or and 'Le Magnifique'; then the Mont d'Or, with our teas and my sad note; Tang's; Prince's, and our very first Saturday date; the Pavilion, and that heart-breaking lunch – lest you forget; and then, last of all, but not least, the Dragon, the pianist, 'To Love Again' and 'My Foolish Heart'.

'My Foolish Heart' was recorded by Chet Baker, in that strangely haunting, slurred, bewitching voice of his, in which the *night is like a tune,* and the *white moon is ever constant*, a warning to the singer *to take care his foolish heart.*

On that constant moon, as he approaches Suez through the neck of water that is the Red Sea, Keith writes in return: 'It is far hotter than Singapore but the nights are so beautiful. The sea is as calm as a millpond and the moon so big & close to us.' He looks at the moon and, knowing it is the same moon she is seeing, talks to her through this constancy in their changing landscape. May, too, sleepless as she now is, communicates to him through the moon: 'Remember the times you asked about the state of the moon, and in particular, that evening by the sea? We were comparative strangers then, having known each other just over a week, and yet in many ways, we were not.' The moon is witness to their pact; they speak of 'the moon, our friend'.

*

My parents write the story of their love through songs. But the songs also become a way of enchanting the other and falling to the enchantment.

The songs Keith and May dance to, quote, then listen to all over again, come from the great romantic songbook. This is the

45

zenith of the love song, of passionate romance. One of the handful of records my mother would bring with her from Singapore was Nat King Cole's *Love is the Thing*. I remember her playing it over and again in my childhood, and I too learned to sing along to it, with her, and then in my own time. My mother gave me her old record player which packed into its own hard pink case, all 1950s curves, that she had in turn packed into the camphorwood chest for her journey. On it I listened to most of my parents' – my mother's, for the records showed they were really hers – songs, imbibing their story word for word even before I'd read these letters. Cole's album is the apogee of romantic love. It includes 'When I fall in Love' (Keith cites the Doris Day version); 'Where Can I go without You?', 'Love Letters' (May quotes); and 'Stardust' – allusions all the way through their letters – and is there a more bewitching song than Hoagy Carmichael's 'Stardust'?

A series of postcards, uninscribed, from Singapore in the 1950s spills out from amongst the letters. Raffles Place, where May used to work. The Cathay Cinema, showing an appropriately named film: *The Passionate Summer* (1956). The ever beautiful, ever colonial Raffles Hotel. My parents' 1960 is unapologetically nostalgic, archaic, classic. The moon would not be landed on, walked on, for another nine years, and so, instead, the cosmos still made sense to some people in the magical terms of 'Stardust', rendered in Nat King Cole's velvet voice, in which the *purple dusk descends on the meadows of the singer's heart,* and the stars exist only to *remind him of his parted lover.*

If the songs are a medium for the enchantment, it's because they transform that 'almost physical' feeling my mother writes of when she thinks of my father. May writes to Keith that, in her letters, she is no longer 'the same May you used to know – reticent and reserved', although 'there are certain things which cannot be written on paper, things I want to say which I would rather say to you in person.' A good part of the power of the letters is in their hedging 'need' with stardust.

Calendar time might indicate the 1960s, the decade we have come to identify with sexual liberation. But my parents' letters express a traditional ideal from a previous age when the only way to have a relationship was to fall in love and get married, particularly if you lived continents and cultures apart. It's all or nothing for my parents; so as Keith leaves her world, May is already planning to come to his.

The second half of the century would usher in not only sexual liberation and the more upfront music (Elvis, the Beatles, the Stones) to go with it. It would also produce new, independent nations, including Singapore, in Britain's former Southeast Asian colonies. The films, music and musicals loved by my parents depict the lead-up to these changes as an innocent period.

Keith and May fall in love to stories of a loving encounter between East and West. But this was the very moment when the Western nations depicted were at war in Asia. The British were fighting in Malaya, in the Emergency. The French in Vietnam (Indochina), soon to be followed there by the Americans. And the Americans were in Korea. Worlds were splitting apart, even as cinematic representations and songs focused on the romantic currents that pulled these poles – and my parents – together.

*

As a teenager, I fell dramatically out of love with my parents' love story. At fifteen I was expelled from the boarding school where I was called a 'half-caste', for not fitting into any of their divisive boxes. Until they chucked me out, the school authorities 'gated' me, that is, ordered me to stay on the grounds for longer and longer periods. I couldn't toe the line. Each of my successive misdemeanours ramped up a gear. I left off bits of my uniform, hating the constriction. I refused to go to 'chapel' every morning, numbed and appalled at the expectation of shared, dispassionate ritual. I laced the fruit punch with vodka at a school social, leading to some amusing and anarchic scenes. I locked a bullying teacher out of the classroom. I shaved my hair. I wouldn't stop hanging out with the town punks, drinking with them in local parks as we also experimented with magic mushrooms and weed.

I was furious with the world and with what I identified as the conformity around me. I held that falling in love amounted to falling prey to false ideology. My parents' love story, their musical backdrop – my parents themselves – seemed conventional and old-fashioned.

Was I also reacting to that label of 'half-caste'? I wanted to belong, but I wasn't sure to what, to whom.

Punk music – hanging around punks, getting into trouble with punks, going on my first dates with punks – became my route out of commitment and my mode of survival. Punk rock subverted love songs, without wholly rejecting them. The sexy gothic of Echo and the Bunnymen's 'The Killing Moon' (*'unwillingly mine'*). The frenetic protest of Buzzcocks' 'Ever Fallen in Love with Someone' (*'you shouldn't have fallen in love with'*). The whacky cut-ups of Johnny Lydon's 'This is Not a Love Song' (*'Happy to have, not to have not'*). Captain Sensible of The Damned even did a deliberately naff cover version of *South Pacific*'s 'Happy Talk'. My parents' tropical island happiness couldn't be seen except ironically.

Needless to say, these were difficult years – years in which I must have been difficult to live with and to love. I grew my antipathy. I embodied it. One particular moment that will remain forever with me: passing my mother, my face turned away, furious and unspeaking, for what reason I cannot now remember, right next to the camphorwood chest. A spotty teenager with dyed, spiked hair and ripped clothes, I headed up the stairs. Floating down the stairs in all her feminine elegance, my mother tried to reach out to me. To my shame now as I return to this past here in this writing and to my mother's story – as I rekindle my romance with my parents' romance – I rejected her. The camphorwood chest was witness to my scorn.

Freud claims that if our first love is our parents, social progress rests on figuring out how to oppose those who have come before us. We each have to question our parents' romance, in order to attempt to find a love of our own.

And yet, my first sexual relationship turned out to be with a woman who was not white, and who convinced me she was a singer.

I was by then in my first year of university in London, after my parents had found another school to take me to finish my secondary education. Beyond a love of soul music and jazz, Delilah and I had almost nothing in common. When we weren't having sex, we listened to music or went clubbing. Our time together coincided with the rise of Rare Groove in the capital, the revival of 1970s American soul sampled with early house music. The best clubs, like the best radio stations, were unlicensed. Parties were held in warehouses or other abandoned buildings. This scene in the mid-1980s was truly interracial. We saw Soul II Soul at the Africa Centre, we boogied to Jay Strongman at the Fridge, we marvelled at Norman Jay spinning discs at the Warehouse. Kiss FM radio, where Norman Jay was the main man, was still a pirate station. The things Delilah and I listened to, the places we went to – our relationship itself – were on the edge, almost illicit. We were fans of the hot sweaty basement of the Bass Clef when it opened in Hoxton. We danced well together.

I don't remember what Delilah was doing when I was a student. Did she work? Was she also at college? She lived with her mother and sister in south London, in Dulwich, and, though she was more likely to visit me in my student flat in north London, I sometimes stayed overnight with her. Asking me kind questions of myself, her Jamaican mother showed no prejudice towards our relationship. Her twin sister, who also had huge eyes and amazing bone structure and who was more suspicious, dated only black guys. Delilah was into white. I don't know how much my mixed ancestry played a role for this young black woman. Delilah made much of my dark hair and eyes against a paler skin.

Delilah had a confident, soulful voice, and she gave me a tape, though it didn't seem anything as sophisticated as a demo recording. There was no band; just her solo singing. The tapes got better, and I asked her if I could come and watch her rehearse with her band. She always found an excuse. Then she gave me a tape that amazed me. I was shocked at the range and control of the singer, how polished the production. 'I can't believe that's you', I said to her over and again, in a way I didn't mean literally but that was expressing my admiration.

It took my flatmate to enlighten me. 'It's not Delilah', he said. He knew the record, which had just been released by an up-and-coming soul group from Manchester. 'Tell me (How it Feels)', by 52nd Street. *Tell me, how it feels. Does it feel for you, like it feels for me?'*

When I confronted her, Delilah put up no defence. She didn't even seem embarrassed. 'Why did you lie?', I asked, hurt, dumbfounded. I couldn't understand such extreme deception. She shrugged. 'I couldn't help it. It seemed to be what you almost wanted. You wanted me to fit an image.' I ended the relationship straightaway. Furious, I gave no thought at the time as to whether she had a point.

Now I wonder. Was my parents' relationship secretly behind what I wanted? While I had thought I was rebelling against them, was the template of *loving strangers* lodged somewhere deep in my unconscious? Did my denial of this pattern lead to my failure really to see my first lover?

Whatever music I had with Delilah had no depth, resonated only with itself. *Tell me, how it feels. Does it feel for you, like it feels for me?'* The question hopes that the lover will reflect the speaker's feelings. Lacking even enough self-reflection then, I never truly answered her.

*

Legacy is history catching up with us. The past finds us in the present and steers us into a different future. It can feel like an ambush, as remembering that moment at the bottom of the camphorwood chest does to me. The gift or command of legacy – a summoning that we re-evaluate the past – may necessitate many volte-faces of self, as we turn and as we return. We revisit scenes and stories we thought we had closed the files on years ago. We properly examine what lurks at the bottom of those family archives – chests, cupboards, etcetera. Our discoveries can make us hear, as if for the first time, the background music to our childhood. This is why, even after years of rejection, and youths of rebellion, we can end up not only really liking our parents again, as friends, but realising that we have become them.

Taking up the piano I had abandoned in childhood, I have even learned to play 'Some Enchanted Evening'. I play it for my parents in their house now, as I collect and bring back their letters. They hum and sing along, encouragingly. As I listen in turn to their story of *some enchanted evening* for the umpteenth time my piano playing inevitably sets off, I grasp for the first time how utterly radical my parents' love is. Their letters spur me to set their story against the backdrop of their very different provenances: Asia and Europe; the Far East and England; colony and empire. These geographical coordinates resonate strongly in the music they most often quoted to each other, and of course in 'their song'. In 'Some Enchanted Evening' and in *South Pacific,* it's love that crosses the cultural divide, and it's because of the music. In my parents' case, the love would go beyond the music.

The music is an incantation about, and weaves a spell from, strangeness. You could say that the music would be nothing without the strangeness; and the strangeness nothing without the mystifying charms of the music. But neither would be worth anything without the love.

The letters give me my response, now, to the invisible voice through the wall – 'half-caste' – as I attempted, in a non-accepting school, to place myself in my family narrative. My voice rings out, loud and clear. Let me tell you a story, or sing you a song. *Some enchanted evening. . .*

How do strangers become lovers? In part, in good part at this moment, with the perfect soundtrack.

Of course, they had yet to broach the topic of how to manage the practicalities, once the evening turned to morning.

5. MC; CT

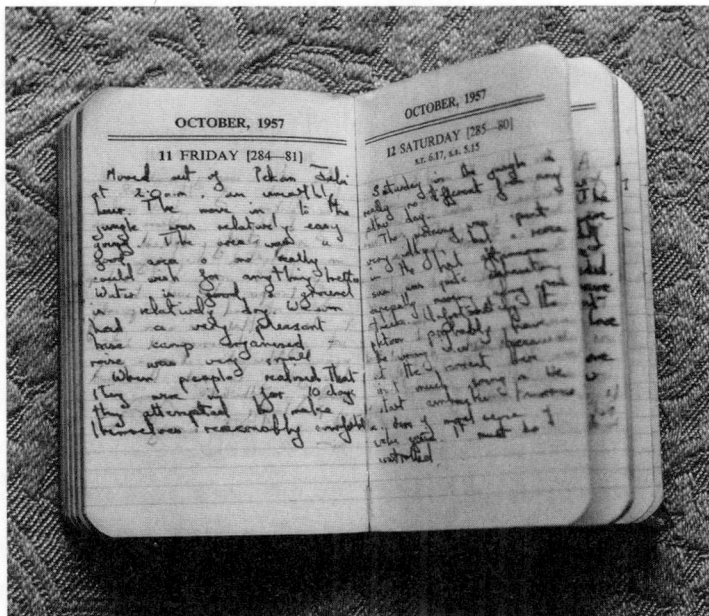

From between my parents' letters, something the size of a cig-arette carton, but heavier, plops to the floor. It seems too small for a book. I pick it up. The brown leather of its binding is as cracked as elephant skin. On its front cover, inscribed in sil-ver lettering: 'Diary. 1957.' I let it fall open to a random page and immediately recognise the neat, minute handwriting of my father. He has pressed hard with his pen and the blue ink has, over time, worn through to the reverse page. But the diary is still legible.

My parents are as surprised as me. They also had thought that this particular part of the camphorwood chest contained only their letters.

1957. Three years before Keith met May. The year that Keith arrived in Malaya to begin his role in the Malayan Emergency. 1957 includes the lead-up to his action, the one that won Keith the MC, the Military Cross.

The journal proves an extraordinary find for me. In it, my father records his first experiences of the Malayan Emergency, in what would turn out to be one of the most controversial and pivotal wars in Asia in the twentieth century, as the British Empire fell apart.

The journal leads me to a father I don't know. When he was present in my childhood, he was forceful and generous: teaching us to play sports and ride bikes; taking us camping. But my father also felt like a stranger to me. He was often away on military exercises, or serving in some trouble spot where wives and children were not allowed. My memories are mostly of my mother, my brother and myself; and then, when Dave preceded me to boarding school, just my mother and me, a cosy couple in whatever provisional home we were then based. Big parts of my father's life have remained buried and hidden from us, as hidden and buried as the journal has been in the camphorwood chest.

*

Keith's diary recounts his experience of the Far East from the very beginning, in August, of his journey out there. His flight to Singapore from England takes place in 'stages' over five days, requiring eight stops for refuelling the aircraft, which is heavy with its cargo of troops along with their gear. Flying over Burma prompts Keith to think about a war not so distant in time or place: 'A most interesting stage – saw the jungle of Burma including the Burma Rly [Railway]. It must have been absolute hell fighting there.' He is right to sense the Second World War as connected to his own war. The British and Allies' defeat in Asia by the Japanese in the Second World War, and the forced labour of the British prisoners of war in the building of the Thai-Burma 'Death' Railway in that jungle, will prove influential in the Malayan Emergency.

Keith travels to regimental headquarters in Segamat, north Johor, Malaya, by way of Nee Soon, the huge camp in Singapore used by all military in transit from and to England. He has been sent in the advance party of his regiment. A second lieutenant, an infantryman, his first task is to train his platoon of thirty-five soldiers to fight with him in the jungle. This band consists not of professional soldiers like Keith, but rather of conscripts, who have been forced by National Service to spend two years in the Army, before they go on to whatever it is they really want to do back in England: plumbing, building, or, as Keith writes in his diary as he meets the men, 'go up to' university, etcetera. The platoon makes for an unlikely, uneven bunch. Most of them are just eighteen years old. Before the trip to Malaya, virtually none of them has set foot outside the county of Cheshire – the home base of the eponymous regiment – let alone England. The responsibility of Keith as platoon commander is huge.

From Segamat, Keith and his platoon are sent into the jungle in Kota Tinggi. Here they receive a few weeks' training at the Jungle Warfare School. The men have been uprooted from their homes in England: from pretty villages, gentle countryside and industrial cities. Keith is from Bath, a beautiful Georgian-Roman city surrounded by idyllic Somerset pastures. Now they are instructed how to survive their inhospitable new home. They are taught how to check their sleeping area for snakes the size of lampposts and scorpions the size of lobsters. They practise crossing swamps. They learn how to remove the leeches that crawl through the eyelets of their boots: how to burn the engorged body so as to ensure that the insect's head doesn't remain buried in their flesh and thus start a deadly infection. Used to the dappled light and temperate weather of England, they struggle to acclimatise to the humidity and darkness of the jungle. Almost no sunlight penetrates the canopy of trees. The relentless rain on top of the steaming heat leaves them struggling ever to get dry.

They are shown how to move about at night. Their eyes develop new powers – an ability to pick out trees from men, targets they must shoot at that are not other recruits or their own shadows. They learn how to avoid booby traps. They disarm hand grenades set to explode at the mere brushing of a shirt on a branch. They step over bamboo sticks buried in the ground with edges sharpened to razors to pierce their unsuspecting feet.

And they learn about the enemy who wants to kill them, who has set these traps. They learn a new concept of enemy, one who first has to be tracked and spotted before he is killed. They learn how, in order to prevent him killing you before you're even aware of his presence, you need to become invisible yourself. In the most ubiquitous instance of all the military jargon they must also get to grips with, they learn the term for this enemy: 'CTs', communist terrorists. It's a term seared into their everyday use and their sleep. At night, they dream about this unseen enemy.

As soon as they graduate from the school, Keith and his platoon are posted twenty miles north to Pekan Jabi. They have been sent straight into notorious enemy-infiltrated territory. Their base is a company camp, overlooking a coconut plantation, at the edge of the jungle. It is makeshift but comfortable. Soldiers sleep six-to-eight to a tent, officers two to a tent. There is even a 'mess dinner tent' with Indian cooks, Keith writes; a man who relishes food that burns your tongue even in tropical heat.

From base camp, Keith takes his platoon on repeated missions into the jungle. In response to intelligence reports, they search designated areas for the enemy. For stints of a few days, the soldiers head out carrying a change of clothes, all food and medicines, weather protection, and their substantial weaponry. For any period over a week, the men are resupplied with food and ammunition parachuted in by helicopter into a 'DZ', a dropping zone. Keith's platoon has attached to it two trackers: 'Ibans', local residents of the jungle, on whose skills and loyalty the British soldiers depend. These *Orang Asli* – or aboriginal peoples of the Malay Peninsula – are able not only to follow tracks, they can tell which tracks were made by CTs, and when.

Mostly, Keith's diary entries are made on the spot. His handwriting – always tiny anyway – can be frustratingly hard to read. The ink is smudged and the paper mottled, as if the diary has been in contact with the rain. Poor lighting and other conditions must have hampered his notetaking. Sometimes the conditions are so bad, or Keith is so occupied, that, although the diary maintains an entry for every day of that year, an account of events has to be made over a week after they happened: after Keith has returned to base camp from his up-to-ten days in the jungle. Examining this record from the time, I realise how, from the very start of his service, Keith faced a situation that – if not exactly the 'absolute hell' of the previous war – was certainly far removed from the tropical paradise idealised in my parents' love letters and *South Pacific*.

*

One of the most immediate challenges for the platoon consists of moving through the jungle. The density of the vegetation makes the task of tracking the enemy CTs difficult as well as dangerous. Many of the diary's entries mention the obstacles in the terrain. 'A very hard and exhausting day spent bashing through jungle on a navigation exercise. It was very difficult to map read correctly and all we could go on were the streams. The going was absolutely bloody, no other word for it and it was absolutely hopeless to try to bash through it, the vine creepers were worse.' The rain in the jungle is itself an enemy: 'it rained today in a way I have never seen rain before; quite incredible.' Other than their ponchos and hammocks, the men have no protection. 'We were forced to spend the night sopping wet', one early entry notes. Mosquitoes, plentiful in the damp and the rubber trees, assault them: 'The first part of the night I spent in scratching, & the second part it was too cold. 2 things are essential in the jungle – 1. get off the ground. Stringing a hammock is improvement on floor. 2. Something to cover one.'

At the same time the troops can find themselves – ironically, with so much rain above them – looking for a supply of drinking water. For this reason they tend to camp near streams: 'move into the jungle – one hell of a flog – very hilly country & full of huge ferns. Water supply is bad – fortunate that we are here only for 5 days.' Keith soon thinks he has a 'touch of dysentery'. Much of the time he, along with the rest of the platoon, is exhausted – 'apart from the Iban who seem tireless'.

Still, Keith finds time to be reflective on the different involvements in the conflict. He comes into contact with a range of communities and interests: indigenous peoples (such as the Ibans); Malays, Malayan Chinese and Malayan Indians in villages and towns; and, of course, British colonials. On the Iban guides he writes: 'The work of the Ibans is invaluable – they are real experts with the parang [Malay machete used for cutting through the jungle]. Very likeable chaps as well.' Of other Malayans and the country as a whole he writes: 'I am growing to like Malaya and even some of the people. They are very easy going. I suppose there will be trouble soon out there. We are here at an interesting time.'

I'm struck that he seems to identify more with the capable Iban 'chaps' than with the conscripts he was having to train. With his platoon of soldiers he struggles even to get them to use their weapons, the 'FNs', a French acronym for the Fusil Automatique Léger, one of the first semi-automatic rifles. 'They are very bad at it and need to practise. Teaching the FN to shoot. Hard work as they are even scared of the weapon.' To Keith – and I have to keep reminding myself that my father was only twenty-one himself – his soldiers 'are very raw and all seem very young. It means a lot of hard training for them before they are fit for manual operations.'

I already see Keith's difference from the men he is training. My father was a career soldier and later competitive rifleman. Whenever he anticipates or is sent on an actual mission into the jungle, Keith is motivated and driven: 'Sooner I go north on operations the better. Hard work but it eases one's frustration to hack down huge trees, some go down with a mighty thump.' Trees were cut down in order to create that 'DZ' for re-supplies. Even when the platoon has to wake up at 2 or 3 a.m. in complete darkness in order to carry out night ambushes, Keith writes that he finds the early morning risings 'so beautiful'.

'Had my first look at Singapore this morning. It looked pretty good and no doubt we will have a good time here.' His first encounters with Singapore and Malayan colonial towns provide an escape from the harshness of the jungle. After a few weeks in Malaya, an old friend from Sandhurst, the officers' training college in England, takes Keith to the Singapore Golf Club: 'it was very like England, very enjoyable morning'; then on to 'Singapore swimming club'. Another weekend that early autumn in Singapore Keith takes himself to a Jerry Lewis film: 'it was a great drinking and eating day – I don't think I really stopped. A film & then dancing taxi girls & then good old drinking songs. Very like an English Saturday.' A 'taxi girl' was a local woman with whom men paid to dance, giving her a fee proportional to her time, hence the analogy with a taxi fare. And Keith was clearly enjoying the ride. He wakes up the next day with 'such a foul head which cleared very slowly after an excellent breakfast.'

I can't help feeling uncomfortable about how, being abroad, being in the Far East, being at war – and then being set loose in colonial towns – afforded my father indulgences and privileges not discontinuous with white male imperialists of old. Was there something of this too in my parents' meeting? My mother, of the East; my father, of the West. My mother among the colonised; my father, the colonisers.

Visiting the colonial town of Port Dickson in Malaya, for swimming 'with the planters', Keith notes: 'It is a beautiful tropical paradise – a wonderful place & I'm sure we will enjoy ourselves.' 'Back via Malacca an excellent weekend'; 'some very attractive Eurasian girls about.' When Keith comes down with 'suspected malaria' and finds he is not allowed back to camp, he spends his time in hospital reading a recently published account of the Allied recapture of Burma, written by British Field Marshal William Slim: 'been absorbed with Slim's book Defeat into Victory – fascinating.'

Equally fascinating to me, my father's time in Malaya was both classic British Empire in Asia, and yet also represented a very new kind of war, as I discover when I read up about it.

*

The Malay – really, British – Emergency is one of the most confusing and disputed of Britain's colonial wars. Firstly, who exactly were these 'CTs', were they really terrorists, and what was the role of communism in their uprising? Secondly, was the Emergency a terrorist insurgency, or a legitimate war of independence? Thirdly and consequently, what did the Emergency mean for British imperialism? Was it 'the end of empire', or a further entrenchment of imperialism? Next, how do you actually win a war when the battleground consists less in physical terrain than in 'the hearts and minds' of the Malayan people? At least in the policy shared with the public, the Malayan Emergency sought to use minimal military force and soft power to cut the terrorists off from popular support, promising to reward the people with 'freedom'. On the ground, as we shall see, the reality was very different. The Malayan Emergency is a turning point in military history, and something of a touchstone for all subsequent attempts to counter terrorism. The final and most material difficulty posed by the Malayan Emergency lay in the jungle itself, as already suggested by my father's diary.

Officially, the Emergency ran from 1948 until 1960 – that is, for the British, who were still effectively governing Malaya. But the dates are not so neat. The situation that would require the declaration of an Emergency had been set in motion well before 1948, during the Second World War. After US defences at Pearl Harbor had been taken out and the Malay Peninsula and Singapore had been occupied by the Japanese, the British had relied on the Malayan Chinese population as the main resistance. In particular, the British had looked to the Chinese communists, who saw themselves as continuing, in their adopted homeland of Malaya, the defence against the Japanese invasion on motherland China, embodied in their hero Mao.

During the Second World War, the British had sent their officers into the jungle to train Chinese members of the Malayan Communist Party (MCP) in guerrilla tactics. It was these very same Chinese MCPs who now turned against their former allies. The new enemy, the 'CTs', were in this sense created by the British. The British called them 'terrorists', as the war had begun with the killing of three rubber planters; but that action had been reprisal for the killing of left-wing activists by colonial forces. The Chinese fighters did not think of themselves as terrorists, but instead as engaged in a war against British colonialism. In their eyes, they were fighting what they called the 'Anti-British National Liberation War'.

The war was therefore also one around naming. The communist guerrillas were the military wing, simply the army, of the political organisation of the MCP. In their successive name changes, you can hear their shifts in their sense of their own identity and that of the enemy. Initially, the guerrillas were called the 'Malayan People's Anti-Japanese Army'. Then, in the early years of the Emergency, they were known as the 'Malayan People's Anti-British Army'. Finally, they became the 'Malayan Races Liberation Army'. The transitions say everything about identity origins, desired destination, and about the difference between where you come from and where you end up. I'll find that, in my family, particularly in the case of my Chinese grandmother, name changes similarly distanced past beginnings from eventual becoming.

As with calling their enemy 'terrorists' rather than recognising them as an 'army', in using the term 'Emergency' rather than 'war', the British presented the events in Malaya and Singapore as an insurrection of extremist left-wing ideologues, part of a pernicious spread of communism worldwide. Keith had arrived in Malaya from Berlin. He went straight from that increasingly tense site of the Iron Curtain between communism and the 'free world' in the West, to Malaya, which must have seemed at the time like the Asian edge of this same Cold War. But in Asian, South American and African countries, communist uprisings were intertwined with independence movements, as colonies threw off the yoke of Western imperialism.

On the question of whether the Emergency marked a 'retreat or revival' of the British Empire, I sense that it was both. My family shows that the British Empire brought strangers together. But the history shows that it worked predominantly to set them against each other – in Keith's war too.

*

Lieutenant Keith Prosser (with a recent Communist kill to his credit!) sits in the centre of a guard circle as this Cheshire patrol rests in a jungle clearing.

Alongside Keith's diary in the camphorwood chest, there are public records of my father's time in Malaya. One of these is a third-party eyewitness account of his regiment's tour, in which Keith plays a prominent role. Appearing first as a series of articles in the *Chester Chronicle*, the reports were later collected and published as a single pamphlet, 'The Jungle War, With the First Battalion, The Cheshire Regiment'. I find Keith identified as a sharpshooter on the Battalion Rifle Team in the Army championships. He also appears in connection with his battle action. A photograph places him centre stage: 'Prosser, a determined young officer who revels in jungle operations, already has a Communist kill to his credit.' This efficient soldier-assassin, I have to remind myself, is the same father I have just met as the tender letter-writer, pining to the soundtrack of Doris Day and fussing over his cufflinks and May's shoes.

The report compares the regimental camp to 'a Hollywood film set'. The analogy strikes me in bad taste, but I try to work it out. Is it because the camp's makeshift quality calls to mind a hastily constructed film set? Or is it because the camp's orderliness gives the sense that there is someone behind the stage, directing? The reporter was an observer of the regiment's war. With restrictions about what he could see and say, he would have been directed to specific scenes. Writing for readers back home, he also has to tell a good story. The tale he tells romanticises the war and celebrates virtuous British masculinity. As well as tracking terrorists, the troops had to contend with snakes, tigers and elephants. The article ends addressed to the men, like my father, whom the reporter met during his tour: 'by God, you are all gentlemen!'

How could this ideal of the masculine hero *not* be part of May's enchantment?

*

The filmset backdrop makes sense as I resume reading my father's diary. When back in camp – the regimental camp in Segamat, not the platoon base camp – Keith spends most of his time when he is not working, and presumably when not writing in his diary, going to see films. Segamat has, of all things in the middle of a jungle war, an outdoor cinema, and Keith finds watching films 'very enjoyable sitting out here in the open.' He gets so absorbed in them that he can 'almost forget the existence of the jungle.' At the same time, in their themes, plots and settings, the films dovetail so much with the events of the diary that, as I read, I can't help wondering if the films were shown to the troops in Malaya, if not as some form of propaganda (which seems too strong), at least for morale-boosting ends.

For example, Keith considers 'rather a good film' that he saw in the camp cinema to be *Beyond Mombasa*. Released in 1957 with the tagline 'Deep in the jungle, and into secret human passions!', *Beyond Mombasa* was an adventure film, in which the Western hero is *engaged on a mission in the jungle* to find his brother's killers. He ends up being *guided* and rescued (in the company of his love interest) by *native tribesman*, whom he had at first suspected of the murder. Putative *killers become guides* and helpers. This, in essence, is Keith's plot with the Iban.

Also showing at the camp cinema was *The Pride and the Passion*, another 1957 war film, starring Cary Grant, Frank Sinatra and Sophia Loren. The hero here is a British naval captain, whose mission is to retrieve a huge cannon from Spain, but who first has to cooperate with the Spanish guerrillas in their fight against the French to liberate an occupied city. Male hero on a mission, in difficult terrain abroad, struggling against a difficult and sometimes unidentifiable or off-scene enemy: I couldn't create a stronger parallel to Keith's situation.

Not all of the films Keith saw in Malaya were recent releases either. This makes me think even more that there was an element of screening before the screenings, so to speak; that the troops were meant to learn from these films. *From Here to Eternity* came out in 1953. Set in Pearl Harbor just before the Japanese attack on Hawaii, this film centres on high tensions among American soldiers (Burt Lancaster, Montgomery Clift, Frank Sinatra), created mainly by the conflict of attraction to women (Deborah Kerr and Donna Reed) and fealty to army brothers. The film climaxes in the attack on Pearl Harbor, the precedent to the Japanese incursion into Singapore and Malaya and also into Burma (which would result in the battle for Burma, Slim's book – and the entire situation in Malaya that Keith now faces). My head spins with these concordances between films, books, history and Keith's circumstances.

From Here to Eternity, about American soldiers, takes its title from Rudyard Kipling's 'Gentlemen-Rankers'. This 1892 poem, about soldiers of the British Empire, showed the brutalisation of war, on the enemy, and on the British soldiers, underlying empire. Kipling's soldiers are 'out on the spree, Damned from here to Eternity'. The poem unpicked the myth of 'by God you are gentleman!'

Even a film as early as 1952, the Western *High Noon* was screened at the camp cinema. With very little shooting of weaponry and instead the whole set-up resting on anticipation of 'encounter with the enemy', this film proves of keen interest to Keith, who was waiting for his own encounter. As he notes in his diary, after seeing Gary Cooper's steely, steadfast performance: 'great psychological build up to a great state of tension.'

The build-up to tension also comes for me as I read on in Keith's diary, looking for the 'encounter with the enemy' I know it must be heading towards.

*

Keith's platoon begins ambushing in earnest towards the end of that year. He moves his soldiers through the jungle by stealth, trying not to warn the enemy of their approach. 'Our main lesson is to learn how to move quietly. . . which means moving more slowly. It requires great concentration of body and mind to try not to beat everything out of the way.' They have to cut back the Lalang grass, which can be almost double a man's height. Their progress is painstaking.

Malaya's topography made war extremely difficult. A range of mountains and dense tropical forest run vertically through the centre of the peninsula. In the early 1980s, having finished school and desperate to get away from England and all that was familiar, I made my first trip to Asia without my mother. With a friend, I backpacked in Malaysia and throughout Southeast Asia. We discovered that even intrepid tourists didn't travel across or in the middle of the Malaysian peninsula. So we hitchhiked up one coast and down the other. In the 1950s, there were fewer roads and much more jungle. Keith was in the centre of the peninsula, in the centre of a jungle. The jungle gave way to miles and miles of rubber plantations, tin mines, and occasional villages, which could be infiltrated by CTs.

I think about how my father was in the area of deepest enemy concentration and also fighting during some of the fiercest years of the campaign. His diary shows no fear about being on the frontline of the war at its climax, only eagerness and a recognition of the importance of history. Even after thirty years of postcolonialism in Malaysia, I sensed that the fact that my friend and I both appeared to be British (she was half Irish) was not a great hit with the Malays. In more remote areas, people were not as friendly or open as they had been in the Thailand we had just left behind us. In the final years of the Emergency, CTs were seeking to cause maximum disruption to the colonial infrastructure: blowing up bridges, roads and railways; ambushing soldiers; and killing British rubber planters. After Malaya obtained independence on 31 August 1957, the Emergency was officially meant to wind down. I find Keith's diary entry which records the transition and speculates about its significance:

The Federation of Malaya is now independent. The handover of power from Britain took place at midnight. Thousands of young members of the Malay, Chinese and Indian parties, which form the government, stood in darkness for two minutes at midnight to mark the official handover. The raising of the Federation flag was met with cries of 'Merdeka' [Malay for 'freedom']. I wonder if it will work and last.

Independence was supposed to signal transfer of sovereignty from the British. The CTs should have had little justification to continue their struggle. But the fact that the troops were still here seemed to prove to some Malayans that independence was in reality some way off. Rather than giving up, the CTs withdrew deeper into the jungle and became even harder to track. Their leader was Chin Peng, the handsome anti-imperialist who had previously been awarded the Order of the British Empire for his resistance against the Japanese in the Second World War. Keith was charged with tracking, and capturing, or killing Chin, this former friend now considered enemy.

'Contacts' with the CTs, as such captures or kills were known, were highly prized by the British government. I note that Keith is disappointed at losing the possibility of any 'contact', and conversely excited at its chance. 'We are having no luck at all, no contact, and not even a sign of a solitary CT.' He wishes the platoon would 'meet with some success. A contact. It would really boost morale.' I feel his impatience, his sense of urgency. He really couldn't wait for that euphemistic contact.

As 'contacts' with CTs began to outnumber the anti-imperialist 'incidents' produced by the CTs, the end of the campaign was thought to be in sight. The next eighteen months focused on the 'mopping-up operation', with key military breakthroughs taking place over the six months following independence. This was the period, I realise, checking the dates of my father's diary, leading up to Keith's action. Here were more euphemisms and renamings. 'Mopping up' meant cleaning out or 'eliminating' the remaining CTs: in other words, assassinating them. The *Chester Chronicle* notes the contribution of Keith's regiment to 'mopping up', as they followed the official policy: 'shoot first and ask questions afterwards.' 'Eliminations' were conducted by 'hunter-killer platoons', made up of 'tough, aggressive soldiers well trained in jungle warfare and marksmanship'. Marksmen like my father.

The goal of Military Operations 'Shoe' and 'Tiger' that ran over Keith's mission was to 'mop up' hardcore MCP districts. The area of Johor where Keith was working was considered 'black', meaning still in the control of the CTs, not yet made safe or 'white', with Pekan Jabi 'blackest' – in other words, having the strongest Communist organisation. When the platoon was working in a 'black' area, my father and his soldiers had permission to shoot on sight. In 1958, the year of Keith's action, there was a tally of 153 'guerrillas eliminated' by the British.

In the US and UK's recent interventions in Asia, in Afghanistan, Iraq and Syria for instance, we have become used to how terminology fogs the realities of war ('collateral damage', for example). Behind the clinical lingo in the Malayan Emergency of 'elimination' and 'mopping up', these with their metaphorical register of having a good spring clean or pest control treatment, lay hunting and killing. And if 'white' was the trustworthy designation and 'black' had to be cleaned up, the racist overtones of the British military intervention in Malaya cannot be ignored. Fifty years later in 2008, my father exchanged some friendly, admiring letters in *The Times* with Chin Peng. My father wrote that he was glad Peng was 'still alive that he could pay tribute to his former enemies with such elegance.'

In 1958, my father – of his times, professional solider – did not question Britain's imperialist divisions, at least consciously. He was set only on his mission, to kill or capture Chin Peng and his compadres. My father's desire for my mother, however, and the points in his diary when he identifies with Malayans, suggest to me that his unconscious pulled against the rules, towards those on the other side of the colonial divide.

'Colonel very pleased. I only wish we could get those very elusive CTs', Keith writes. Sergeant Evans, his platoon sergeant, has found tracks. A few days later: 'CT tracks were found – I got quite excited getting near to them once again. One only hopes that we can get nearer to them. It will be a great achievement. I will be very frustrated if we don't get something at the end of it all.'

*

Jungle Capture Gains Bath Man M.C.

BRAVERY AGAINST TERRORISTS

Malaya, Cyprus awards

Gallantry in service against terrorists in Malaya and Cyprus is recognised by awards announced in the "London Gazette."

The Military Cross goes to Second-Lieutenant William Keith Lloyd Prosser, the Cheshire Regiment, of Bath, and to Major Henry Arthur Irwin Thompson, Royal Scots Fusiliers, attached to 22 Special Air Service Regiment, of Portrush, Northern Ireland.

Second-Lieutenant Prosser displayed skill, leadership, and courage in command of a patrol which destroyed a party of terrorists deep in the jungle. He achieved the single-handed capture of a desperate armed man." Major Thompson "consistently displayed skill, courage and determined leadership in command of a squadron operating against Communist terrorists in jungle swamps." The water level in the swamp where Major Thompson and his men were operating varied from ankle deep to shoulder height, "with very occasional dry patches."

The D.S.O. is awarded to Lieutenant-Colonel Arthur William Neville Langston Vickers, 2nd King Edward VII's Own Gurkha Rifles (the Sirmoor Rifles) who four times went into the jungle accompanied only by two police officers to negotiate the surrender of six terrorists.

The Military Medal goes to three British N.C.O.s for courage in anti-terrorist operations. They are Acting Corporal Alan Bond, Royal Lincolnshire Regiment, of Lincoln, Acting Sergeant Harry Sandiford, Royal Artillery, attached 22 Special Air Service Regiment, of Rochdale; and Corporal Douglas Swindells, Middlesex Regiment, also attached to 22 S.A.S., of Congleton.

Six British Empire Medals are awarded to British N.C.O.s for courage and devotion to duty or gallantry in Cyprus.

AN Old Sulian, 2nd Lieut. Keith Prosser, of the Cheshire Regiment, whose home is at 12 East Close, Weston, Bath, has been awarded the Military Cross. The award announced in the London Gazette, is for "skill, leadership and courage" while commanding a patrol in the Malayan jungle.

The citation says that on Feb. 18 last, Lieut. William Keith Lloyd Prosser led a combined military and police patrol whose orders were to capture or kill terrorists believed hiding in a cultivated area amid deep jungle.

"During the approach march a surrendered Communist terrorist guiding the patrol was incapacitated and had to be evacuated. In consequence 2nd Lieut. Prosser had to split his force and continue his approach march with considerably reduced strength.

GALLANTRY

"Having successfully located the cultivation and personally reconnoitred it with considerable gallantry, 2nd Lieut. Prosser decided that an attempt to induce the terrorists occupying it to surrender would not succeed and might result in their escape.

"At this point, in the face of the enemy and without waiting for the remainder of his force to come up, 2nd Lieut. Prosser followed by his Iban tracker, chased two armed terrorists who tried to escape.

"One was shot by the tracker, but 2nd Lieut. Prosser, knowing the importance of making a capture, continued to chase the remaining terrorist until he overtook and physically overpowered him.

"The success of this operation was mainly due to 2nd Lieut. Prosser's skilful planning and determined leadership, culminating in his most brave and dashing single-handed capture of a desperate armed man."

SCHOOL PREFECT

A Regular officer, 2nd Lieut. Prosser went to Sandhurst from the City of Bath Boys' School, where he was a prefect and captain of cricket.

When he left Sandhurst in 1956 he was commissioned in the Cheshire Regiment and served in Germany. He went to Malaya in 1957.

He has played rugby for the Old Sulian Seven in the Bath and District Seven-a-Side tournament.

His younger brother is Ivor Prosser, who plays for Swindon Town. Ivor was the Bath City F.C. ring-half and was a Lansdown Club cricketer. For a time he was groundsman for Bath City.

Helicopter men kill Reds

SINGAPORE, Saturday.—A young British lieutenant led a raid on a Communist fort in the Central Malayan jungle, killing two terrorists and capturing a third.

Lieutenant Keith Prosser, aged 22, and 33 picked men from the 1st battalion, the Cheshire Regiment, were dropped by helicopter some miles away.

Halfway in the fort a black bear attacked a guide and severely mauled him. A stretcher party took him back to base.

In the assault Prosser brought down six terrorists with a Bren gun.—Sunday Express Correspondent.

Foot-and-mouth

8
DAILY EXPRESS

The paper that makes politics exciting

OPINION

THE MEN WHO SERVE THE CAUSE

DEEDS to remember! They may be read in the cool, formal words of the London Gazette announcing awards to 226 British soldiers in Malaya and Cyprus.

Men to remember: Second Lieutenant Prosser, M.C., who single-handed caught a desperate terrorist deep in the Malayan jungle.

Lieut. - Colonel Vickers, D.S.O., went into the jungle to negotiate the surrender of six terrorists.

Acting Staff - Sergeant Holcombe, B.E.M., in a fire in Famagusta, Cyprus, pulled out a high explosive bomb and made it safe.

A cause to remember! Holding the Empire against anarchy and murder.

Men serve that cause. Do not take their courage for granted. Do not be patient with those who malign them.

At the point he rightly guesses is close to the 'end of it all', Keith 'gets' the contact that would win him the MC. But in echo of his frustration tracking the CTs leading up to this moment, I'm exasperated to discover the diary stops just before his encounter. My father's Malaya diary is for 1957, and the action that earned him the MC would take place in early 1958. There's no diary in the camphorwood chest for 1958 or any of Keith's subsequent years. My father thinks 1957 is likely to have been the last year he kept any kind of diary. If he stopped writing at the end of that year, it must have been because of the action itself. What, I wonder, would he have written?

In the chest, there's a series of newspaper cuttings about my father's action. The articles are likely to have been clipped by Keith's mother, proud of her honoured son; one of them is from the *Bath Chronicle,* the local paper of my father's home city. Headlined 'Jungle Capture Gains Bath Man M.C.', the account appeared on the occasion of the awarding of Keith's medal: 'the success of the operation was due to his skilful planning and determined leadership, culminating in his most brave and dashing single-handed capture of a desperate armed man.' In language and plotline, I am thrown back into the swashbuckling masculine heroism of the films Keith was seeing and in the romanticised regimental newspaper report. And yet, I remind myself, this was a moment in which one man was killed, and the other man, my father, became a successful soldier by killing.

When I finish reading his diary, I ask my father for his version of what happened, and he explains with some humour and humility, but also with an awareness of the gravity of history. My mother is amazed that I manage to get my father to tell this story at all. She tells me he has never talked about it until now: until I discover the diary and start to ask questions. He received other medals subsequently, and we made sure we were at Buckingham Palace for all those ceremonies. His military regalia festooned our houses. It was part of the ubiquitous décor, and far less interesting to me therefore than the unique camphorwood chest with its hidden treasures and secrets to be discovered. The flags and drums and statues of soldiers also represented the emblems of Britain and its imperialist past that I scorned and rejected.

If the details of my father's Malayan war remained a family secret, it's in good part because his experience was overwhelmed by my mother's narratives: by stories of her family and my parents' meeting, and *my* fascination with *her* stories. I was drawn to the non-British exoticism of her tales, and she was the better – really, the only – storyteller in the family. Yet I suspect that my father was also adhering to the old soldier's rule of not sharing military intelligence secrets. When, instead of my mother, my father takes the place beside me at the camphorwood chest, it's for the very first time. He sits on a chair I drag to the hall from the kitchen, upright but stiff-joined, while my mother crouches with me on the floor, and he begins telling me his story.

At the beginning of 1958, Keith was given information from intelligence HQ about a group of CTs. The platoon set out on an ambush, guided by two Chinese ex-CTs, who claimed to have renounced their side and agreed to lead the British back into the jungle to the camps of their former compadres. As they entered the jungle, the platoon party was attacked by a completely unexpected enemy: a Malayan brown bear, 'of all things', my father says. One of the former CTs went to shoot the bear, but ended up shooting the other ex-CT 'in the backside.' The heroic war film is fast mutating into a Laurel and Hardy farce, I think. (The account of the incident in Keith's regimental magazine from the time, following this skit between the two ex-CTs – 'S.E.P.s – Surrendered Enemy Personnel' – ends the description of the platoon's raid on the CT camp with burlesque: 'The fourth Communist Terrorist managed to escape wearing only a pair of striped underpants.') My father then had to make a quick and difficult decision; and his account reminds me of the brainteaser about the man who has to get a dog, cat and bird across a river, but the challenge is that he can only take one animal at a time, and if he takes the bird the dog will eat the cat, and if he takes the dog the cat will eat the bird, etcetera.

In the brainteaser of my father's situation, he couldn't very well abandon a wounded man; but neither could he fully trust the former CTs alone to get themselves out of the jungle and not betray the platoon's coordinates to their terrorist colleagues. So Keith split the platoon, commanding the track-discovering Sergeant Evans to take some of the men to evacuate the wounded CT, while he went ahead with the mission, together with the other CT and the reduced force, in the continued search for the 'contact'. Just before dusk, this remnant of the platoon, with Keith at the lead, found the terrorist camp; surrounded it; and attacked. They killed three or four men, and captured two or three others.

My father says his MC was less laudation of any singlehanded confrontation, and more recognition of his leadership in straitened circumstances and also of the platoon's successful capturing of CTs. Still very much the professional soldier, my father may be being modest. Even while I find hearing these details for the first time shocking, I can see that there was, surely, bravery and intelligence at work in his decision and action. Indeed, he says – albeit with my mother's prompting – that, at one point in the confrontation, it was either the other man or himself.

My father sits back. But he is not finished. He leans over the camphorwood chest and digs out another hidden part of its archive: a handful of photographs of the confrontation, or rather of the after-effects of the confrontation. The images make for disturbing viewing. They hurl me out of any adventure film.

The larger photographs are of a hut, a form of encampment. Two smaller ones each show a different dead man. Except the bodies are so contorted and swollen or discoloured – I can see this even though the photographs are black and white – that it's hard to recognise these bodies as ever having been anything alive. Although I know that this fact is essential to these photographs and to this story, it's impossible to tell that the dead men were Chinese.

I turn the photographs over. On the back is handwritten, 'PLEASE RETURN TO INTELLIGENCE SECTION FOR SEGAMAT.' The images were taken for the purposes of evidence, to report back to Army command the results of the planned operation. These were intelligence documents. Those who came into contact with them – or who were there – were required to maintain confidentiality. The *Chester Chronicle* reports how 'the Army must have photographic records', but it published very different kinds of photographs – 'Lieutenant Keith Prosser in a guard circle' – cinematic valiant masculinity, not of any kills. Field Marshal Gerald Templer, British High Commissioner and Director of Operations in Malaya who brought the Emergency to an end during my father's years, spoke about the importance of such photographs. Templer said:

It is absolutely essential that the communist dead should be identified. War in the jungle is not a nice thing, but we cannot forgo the necessity for exact identifications . . . . The viewpoint of [critics] who have no possible inkling of an understanding of conditions or terrain . . . is not understandable to the Security Forces who have the task of tracking down armed communist murderers and producing evidence.

Unlike many of the other things the camphorwood chest holds, I hadn't seen these photographs very often, and I'd repressed the details. They are a counterpart to the newly discovered diary. More than the diary's twin, however, the photographs fill in something of the missing bits from the diary and from what I think of as my father's other narratives – the films, the newspaper reports, even his telling. There is no evidence of 'by God, you are all gentleman here'. This is no comedy. They tell me what he has never been able to put into words. They capture the unspoken and, until now, the unspeakable. Here are the bodies of the CTs that underlay the MCs: the dead Chinese underneath the empire's medals.

If I didn't look at the photographs before now, even though I have a memory of having seen them, it's most likely because they hold a scene I didn't think I would find in the chest's cache. For how did these atrocities, these terrible deaths of strangers, fit into my parents' love story? How were the paternal hands that taught me how to mend a bicycle puncture the hands that did this?

I look at my father's hands holding the photographs now. In his mid-eighties, with little strength and dexterity, he can't even figure out how to shoot the water pistol I gave him to keep the marauding squirrels off his birdfeeders. Who is this man who killed – who had to kill or be killed – and how is he connected to the lonely, lovelorn letter-writer?

And yet these brutal deaths in the photographs lie behind my parents' love. It was the war in Malaya that allowed my parents to meet. The MC for the dead CTs brought my father as instructor to the Jungle Warfare School, and to his continued stay in Singapore, and to that enchanted party, to May and the spell.

As well as the moonlight and the music, the camphorwood chest holds these dark and difficult events. They, also, are my inheritance.

*

I was a much more committed diary-keeper than my father.

In a visit home, in a bored moment I pull a drawer out from under my old childhood bed. Amongst the cache (my personal camphorwood chest), I find the journal I kept during that trip at nineteen with a friend to Singapore, Malaysia and Thailand.

The friend and I were tripping in more than one sense, doing a lot of hiking, consuming too many hash cookies, smoking too much weed, even toying with opium gongs. My descriptions of the vegetation could almost be from my father's diary:

> I've never seen so much thick greenness. Everything a lurid, unreal green. A day's trekking. Seven or eight miles on narrow muddy paths, wading across large streams, ankle-deep in mud. Two huge storms forced

us to stop. Became increasingly exhausted, which was evidenced as I slipped and stumbled down slopes into rivers.

Clearly, I didn't have – don't have – my father's soldier competence.

. During our time in Singapore, I recount being taken to the Jewish cemetery by my mother's brother, Uncle Sunny. My grandmother Esther had died the year before. My mother was with Esther when she died, and she had been keen for me to visit the cemetery containing her parents' graves. I remembered her talking to me intensely about it before I left the UK; I hadn't remembered my response to her, or what I'd felt as I accompanied my uncle around the cemetery when I got to Singapore.

> About half of the people buried there, Sunny informed me, were related to us. Although the run-down on the family tree grew rather tedious, I felt as though I'd done my bit. Mum wanted me so much to see Nana's grave: she cracked at the time because I said I was travelling for a holiday and that I was more keen on meeting living relatives rather than dead ones.

My remark makes me 'crack' now. Who was this son who told his mother he didn't want to be around her beloved dead? How could he turn away so brutally from his grandmother, whose real story, Jewish but also Chinese, he then didn't care to know? I barely recognise myself. It was Esther's yahrzeit.

But reading my own discovered diary, I realise I also hold dark and buried histories.

6. Reprise

I decide to find a synagogue of my own. Following that moment when I'm called to read in my mother's synagogue, I make up my mind to learn more about Judaism and Jewishness for myself. I need to see if I can connect to a Jewish community and identity without my mother, although the fact that she is my link and incentive isn't lost on me. I speak to various rabbis who reassure me that mine is a common story. Half Jewish, sort of Jewish, a lost Jew. One term that I particularly like, since it captures what I feel like I'm doing, going back in time with her family history, a returning Jew. I'm going back; backwards.

I spend some time looking for a synagogue close to where I live – not easy in rural Yorkshire. I bounce between places in nearby cities, until I settle on the Liberal Jewish Community in York. York: the British city every Jew in the world knows where Jews are not supposed to live, a city cursed by a shocking episode in which Jews were treated as strangers.

It was one of the worst and earliest medieval pogroms, which expunged the entire local Jewish population. On 16 March 1190, a Friday night coinciding with *Shabbat haGadol*, the 'Great Sabbath' before Passover, 150 Jews were massacred, mainly by non-Jewish York citizens and noblemen, in Clifford's Tower, at the very heart of the city. But Jews are now once again back in York, especially since the founding in 2014 of the city's Liberal Jewish Community. And York's infamous Jewish history appeals to my sense of defiance, of reclaiming a lost legacy. History can be changed. You *can* return. The York Liberal Jews are a youthful and growing community. Jews are coming to the city and re-establishing not only a living presence but demanding that York's full Jewish history be made visible. I join the community and quickly become involved not only with the synagogue, but with discussions about how the restoration of the tower and redevelopment of the site around it should remember and openly present to the public the events of 1190.

There hasn't been a functioning synagogue in York for over half a century, and so we hold services in the Quaker Meeting House. The unadorned Friends' House feels remarkably like a synagogue. High windows channel the light, and benches laid out in friendly three-wall formation allow attendees to kibitz (to chat with each other during the service). I know chatter definitely won't happen here among the silent Quakers. It's a contrast, too, with my quiet Buddhist times.

At my very first Buddhist retreat, I felt myself silenced by the Buddhist nun in saffron robes raised up on her crimson meditation cushion, whose task it was to try to guide us toward love and compassion. I interrupted her flow to ask a question that now I see was not meant to be part of the teaching, at a time that, obviously now, there were not meant to be questions from the floor. She turned her shaven head toward me, her beatific smile unbroken, the personification of compassion for this churl. 'This is not what this course is about. Although fine if you find that helpful.' I felt shut down. I wanted discussion, debate. I wanted intellectual argument. I fled that retreat early, alienated too by the chocolate placed on the shrines before the statues of Buddha, by the fact that all the books in the bookshop were by a single author, the principal guru of this Buddhist school. I was also a bit bored by the silent meditations, during which I could not get my mind to shut up, a fact that I admitted to myself but not to others. I embraced Buddhism as a philosophy. Practising love for all beings and lessening strong attachments couldn't have seemed more reasonable to me. But I never experienced it as faith in the way that those around me on retreats seemed to: faith as in unquestioning belief. Faith as in feeling, rather than thinking.

In our improvised synagogue in York, in contrast, the rabbi throws questions at us constantly in the services – 'why do we block out Haman's name with noise?'– expects us to question him, and sometimes questions the teachings himself ('Why so much attention to the way priests should dress? Why, oh why, should we care about the exact cubit measurements of the

Tabernacle?'). I love the endless back-and-forth, the interpreta-tions, the disagreements. I love the noise and the passion that I missed, and tried to give up but failed, with Buddhism.

York's Quaker Meeting House setting fits the pluralism of our Jewish community, and the multiple ways in which we are Jewish feels liberating, enlightening and reassuring. Over our potluck kiddush (blessing) lunch after the services, along with the food we also share stories of marryings-out and -in, of con-versions to Judaism, and of discoveries of long-buried Jewish family pasts. Geoffrey, an academic in his seventies who didn't receive a Jewish education and who apologises for knowing no Hebrew but who eats all the symbolic foods with gusto, tells me that now his mother has died he wants to find out about her abandoned faith. Moses, formerly Mohammed, a Jordanian Muslim converted because he always felt himself to be Jewish. Vibrant red-haired Rachel rejected her Orthodox upbringing when she found she couldn't reconcile its rules with her fem-inism and desire for tattoos. In its liberal form, she is re-em-bracing Judaism and is bringing her children into our fold. Her eldest son is earnestly attentive in our services. I watch him wrap himself proudly in the most beautiful prayer shawl. When he was bar mitzvah and called to read Torah for the first time, this twelve-year-old's commitments and promises were so seri-ous, so obviously heartfelt, I almost cried. Here was the trans-ference of legacy. Here is what I had missed. But here I am now, in York.

My hunt for a synagogue where I think I might be able to fit makes me realise how hard it is to practise Judaism, if you don't live with a permanent Jewish community around you: friends with whom to pray, mark festivals, share food. This was one reason for my childhood ignorance of Jewishness. We rarely lived anywhere with a community. For May in the '60s, married life with this English officer, in frequent postings all over the world where there were few-to-no functioning synagogues (Cold War Berlin and rural Germany; early independence Malta; Northern Ireland during the Troubles), would not be compatible with remaining part of a Jewish community. Not to say that she wasn't still Jewish and didn't want to remain as such, even though coming to England and being with my father meant deepening a relationship – getting engaged? – with a non-Jew.

So how were my young parents going to negotiate this problem? Keen to see how they work through their significant differences, I pick up the remainder of my parents' letters to continue their story.

*

Despite the enchantment and the fairy tale and the moonlit music, my parents' letters are freighted with the many obstacles to their union, and not only religion.

One obstacle is England. From Singapore May dreams of an England of green fields, art galleries and shops with the latest fashions. England is simply a figment of her imagination at this point. The reality to which Keith returns, in the autumn of 1960, is very different. After his three years in the East, even while on the ship, he charts the shifts in light and anticipates the change in season: 'As we move northwards so the evenings become longer, and it is now most unusual after three years for it still to be light at nine in the evening. It will be equally strange this coming winter for it to be dark at 4.30 p.m.' Once back in

England, his envelopes are stamped with the young Queen's head (as in Singapore, but larger) and postmarked 'Bath', along with the old name of the county, 'Somerset'.

Over a few weeks' leave in Bath, Keith has a routine: walking into town for morning coffee and to read the papers, and to write to May, sometimes in the post office so as not to miss the post; then coming home to spend afternoons '"glued" to the television set watching the Olympic games from Rome', and often to write another letter in reply to one of hers that has arrived while he has been out.

In his parents' council house, he has very little privacy, including for his writing. 12 East Close, the semi-detached in the little cul-de-sac on the hill in Whiteway, is cramped. The two bedrooms are occupied by his parents and sister. When Keith's younger brother returns soon after him from his two years' National Service (somewhere in the UK, not Malaya), the boys, now men, sleep in the front room. Back in England, back in the council house, back on the sofa: Keith is back in the world he was desperate to escape before he left for Malaya.

Keith's father is a builder's labourer. William Prosser works with his hands: digging roads, carrying bricks; then coming home and digging his garden to grow his own veg. Keith's mother, Maud, is a nursing assistant – not qualified or educated enough to be a nurse. Before that she was a maid, in the very boarding school to which her ambitious eldest son, able to rise from his working-class roots to become an exceptionally commissioned officer, would, in future, send his youngest child.

Keith has kind parents, but he doesn't share their values. Unlike him, they accept the place in life to which they feel they've been born; they don't seek to change the status quo.

They do the football pools, collect Co-Op tokens to afford the odd extra (a new fruit bowl, an electric kettle), go on holiday once a year a short train ride away to the coast at Weston-su-per-Mare. William and Maud spend a lot of time talking to Mr and Mrs Wright over the fence next door, with the two women especially hitting it off, since they both come from the mining valleys of South Wales. The Prossers don't have friends over; only, occasionally, family, with whom they play rummy or crib-bage for small betting sums.

And already, Keith writes to May, 'I don't like England. It is so bleak & dismal, so smoky & industrial, the people are so quiet & look so white.' England is thoroughly 'staid'. He finds the weather and the people – particularly the women – along with the (lack of) nightlife, insipid, pallid, disappointing: 'the sallowness of the people, the fact that I was unable to get a glass of beer after 10.30 p.m., the rain, and many girls who were try-ing to look sophisticatedly beautiful.' Then there's what he calls the 'industrial side' of England, which he sees when he travels from Southampton, where he docked, to Carlisle, where his regiment is now based. Like many Southerners in his day, even today, he associates the North of Britain with factories, indus-try and manual work – the manual labour of his father: 'I always feel so depressed in getting as far north as York.' I can't help laughing at this sentence, since the epitome of the North that brings on my young father's misery is the very city I live closest to, which he now so loves to visit.

And if he has problems acclimatising, Keith wonders what May will make of England. He knows she'll like the country-side, the pretty churches, the arts and culture: dream-book England. But what of the realities of winter city-living? 'I must write them all down in preparation for your arrival in England. Snow, frost, fog, escalators, trams, double decker buses.' He wanders around Bath, trying to convince both himself and her that she will fit in: 'you will look wonderful in big furry sweaters and tweed skirts and even fur boots.'

Feeling lost at home, Keith is more aware of what he gained while he was in Singapore. His parents think he has 'become fat, spoilt by the pleasures of the East.' But 'The East did not spoil me; it showed me a new world.' In England, Keith is still inhabiting that world in his mind. Showing a cousin round Bath, with a break in the weather he sees only Singapore: 'The sun is really shining & as I look out of the window I can see the blue sky – almost Singapore blue.' Playing rugby again, he thinks only of seeing May standing behind the touchline, 'as I did in Johore Bahru that day.' Even doing cross-country runs to try to shake off his apathy (and some of the fat), he lacks the purpose he felt in the East: 'particularly in the early part when the Emergency was still strong, one had the sense of doing something worthwhile.' He has become a stranger at home.

Reliving his recent past, Keith sends May another clipping about his military action. He goes out recruiting to encourage more young men to join the Army, showing films and lecturing on his experiences in Malaya and Singapore. Even trying to resurrect the Armstrong Siddeley, he buys a 1950 Jaguar from a fellow officer in the Gurkhas for £25, with the promise of a further £25 later (still owing, he tells me now).

Of course, in missing Singapore, Keith is missing May. The first of September and, beginning another day, he feels autumn coming on. It must be sunny in Singapore, and she will be returning from work – while 'here it is a very wet, miserable grey and dull day, the rain drizzling and showing no signs of abating; so miserably wet that I am not even going to town this morning, instead I will add a few more lines to this letter.' He longs for Singapore heat, to hold her hand. Her hands were always cold – how will she deal with the cold of England? He will have to keep her warm. The songs come back, in simultaneous refrain with his memories: 'The wireless at the moment is playing the "September song – the Autumn Leaves" one of our songs & Dearest May I miss you so very much at this very moment. The music takes me to the Golden Dragon, dancing so slowly with you, holding you so tight, both of us quite oblivious to the remainder of the world.'

Meanwhile, in Singapore, May is also thinking about the adjustments she will have to make when she comes to England. She is looking in shops for warm clothing. She experiences a slight drop in temperature (it has dipped 'below seventy!'), and for the first time ever she has had to wear stockings to keep out the cold. She will 'have to' have central heating in England. She is even – 'don't laugh, Dearest, collecting recipes!'

She was hoping that after some years in England they might come back to Singapore, but she sees an article in the *Straits Times* stating that the War Office in London is considering withdrawing all troops from Malaya and Singapore. The Emergency had ended, and the empire was winding down. She has 'been consulting Boustead's about sailings to the U.K. next year', working out how much she needs to save to come either on the *Corfu*, leaving in March (1961 – it is still only August-September 1960), or the *Carthage*, which sails in April. During her own leave she takes on a temporary job, as personal assistant to Air India's manager, in offices at their old haunt of the Adelphi.

She will earn an extra three thousand Singapore dollars, a lot of money for them, but which will not be handed to her 'until after I produce my passage ticket and convince the authorities that I was leaving for good (?)'

I note that the parenthetical question mark leaves their future commitment patently open.

*

Lack of money poses another obstacle between them. Keith worries how back in England he can make enough for them both to be together, now that his temporary Singapore captain's salary has reverted to that of a lieutenant. His anxiety is palpable: 'My Dearest, you choose to live with a Pauper, & I cannot understand why. It is one of the things which causes me a great deal of worry because I shall never be able to afford to look after you the way you so richly deserve and the way I want to.' 'I come from a very poor home, and I think I know what it is to be poor. I am not prepared to let you know.'

Because he is a 'pauper' – a word Keith repeats – he is also trapped in England during his leave, instead of doing what he really wants to be doing: going with his friend Denis 'as tramps to the Continent (as in the French films)' (a reference perhaps to Godard's *Breathless,* which was released in 1960). He aims to start a 'saving campaign' for when she arrives, so that they can escape together. He regrets her working through her holiday. He doesn't deserve it: 'May I hope you realise what you are doing, because I am so ordinary, so basic & mundane that I can never come up to your standard, and never be good enough for you.'

Keith also repeats the word 'ordinary' a lot. He had used it earlier about his letters ('My letters will be so ordinary'), and now he uses it about himself, his parents, his family, and his background. I detect that *ordinariness* is a synonym – maybe a euphemism – for working class. Eating 'tea'; going to bed before eleven; taking the bus instead of having a car: all these things count as 'ordinary' and are to be avoided. They are the habits of his parents. He worries about what she will make of it all, of this, his, actual, and unromanticised, England; of his family: 'They are such ordinary basic simple folk, their tastes in life are so ordinary, & I hate the suburban way of life, but I am still very fond of them.'

When he goes to Buckingham Palace to receive his Military Cross, his parents don't accept the invitation to accompany him. They are too shy, think themselves far too 'ordinary' to attend anything so grand and *extra*ordinary; to venture to London at the behest of the Queen, even to support their eldest son. That was 'not their place', they told him and he recounts to her. They hand him back the invitation he had asked the Palace to address to them. I find the two unsurrendered tickets in the camphorwood chest among its saddest items. They are a measure of the different purviews, and the growing social distance, between my father and his parents. And that we can't unlearn experience – he is forever changed.

Keith has always felt exceptional in his family, and 'in the process of time it is likely that we will grow even further afield', he writes to May of himself and his parents. He finds his parents' way of life as small as their house. The boxy council house on the estate on the hill above the city hardly justifies his use of 'suburban'. I remember his parents and their welcoming home with great fondness. I spent many half-terms there. I was delighted to be fed, for me, exotic 'teas', such as baked beans on toast or alphabet spaghetti. Accompanying Granny to the Co-Op 'the secret way' through Mrs Wright's garden was an adventure. I'm struck how, even in his apologising for it, Keith idealises his home to May. He wishes it was she who could be there at the Palace with him, for he knows she would fully share in his occasion, and he would not have to go alone, which he ends up having to do.

Keith writes that he is not ashamed of his origins, 'but Dearest May, I don't want you to have any illusions about my family background.' He knows she isn't snobbish either: 'I know you will like them & they will like you.' He imagines her meeting his parents. And he's astute to his own contradictions; that he seeks to escape the 'ordinary' is 'probably because I am very ordinary and I don't face facts.' But in telling her things about his background he hasn't told her before – and, with his continued hedging in his writing, likely that he hasn't told anyone – he shines a light on the English class system. He is insightful about how he managed to become an Army officer in spite of his upbringing:

I come from a very ordinary working class family & by rights I shouldn't be in the Army as an officer. Virtually every one of my friends [in the Army] comes from a wealthy family, they own their own home, have a large car, etc.; well we don't have any one of those things. I suppose I have a chip on my shoulder at times when I see so many fools in the world.

By 'fools in the world', I think Keith means those born with prerogatives and inheritance, especially those who take their legacy for granted and are destined for a life of privilege.

But he needn't have worried, because May chimes with Keith on ordinariness. She, too, worries about money. Saving for her fare (she now has two-thirds and by early December thinks she'll have all of it), she takes on a second and even third job. In the evenings she goes straight from the office now to the Cathay Hotel, in the skyscraper above the cinema where they first held hands, to compile a report 'for an Australian'. And she's busy not only with secretarial work but as a fashion model, modelling among others, L'Oréal and Dior, for the Singapore Model Academy, though she skips over the details.

She plans that, once in England, she wouldn't go out to work, at least not in the first months or years of marriage. She 'wouldn't want to be a failure as a wife', she writes. May was a woman of the pre-sexual revolution 1960s, but my mother would continue always to put family first. Their discussions of money practicalities sound more like the sensible, planning parents I know, though in order to help out financially my mother will end up going out to work, first as a secretary, the very week after her marriage. Much later in life, she will start her own business, which will allow my parents to enjoy in their old age the dreams they'd expressed to each other in their youth. With Keith before marriage, May is even discussing the number of children; three is the ideal. They – we? – would go to school in England. 'I shall be much stricter with our children', Keith writes, disapproving of how quickly his baby sister has grown up.

'The warmth of intimacies shared by two people' must also address 'the coldness of practicality and unpleasantness of having to face facts and accept in good grace the more ordinary, everyday things, mainly problems, in life.' May writes of the necessity of joining up their romance with both of their 'ordinaries'. She also feels split about her background – her family and her culture.

And it's in their ambivalence, also, that my parents are ultimately similar. *Born on opposite sides of the sea*, they are as *alike* as people can be; and their estrangement from what is expected of each of them fuels their coming together. May is also not ashamed of her family, but she feels herself to be – if this doesn't sound too paradoxical – similarly different; also not fully of their world. Of Jacob, she says, 'I know he will disapprove and make things difficult for me', 'my father who is not deep-thinking and accepts everything at face value. And yet because I love my parents, I am to-day still with them.' Her mother is more understanding, but this hurts as she knows that her mother, 'who is so dear to me and who champions my cause, will be made most unhappy by my leaving.'

As I'll discover much later, Koh-wei will have her own tragic backstory which makes her not want this daughter to leave.

*

England; money; class; family. The Army poses another hurdle.

May writes that what bothered her when she worked for the British Army – in what was her first job – was 'the rigid discipline and rank consciousness' of the Army. The Army crystallises the British class system and colonial attitudes. Keith agrees that the Army requires fealty and sacrifice: 'One can never say in the Army that one's life is completely one's own.'

By this stage, Keith has told his colonel about May, and has received that letter in reply warning him about the difficulties he would face in his career if he went ahead with marriage. May, too, is sceptical about whether she would be welcome: 'you know my feelings about the Army, Keith; I have never tried to hide them. But I am willing to learn to like it with you, because you so love it, and perhaps the Army too, would in time grow to accept me, although I'm sure with greater difficulty.' She has reason for these doubts. Not only is there the colonel's letter, but she experienced a difficult episode with some Army officers still in Singapore.

To try to learn more about the Army and to fit into his England, she had agreed to go with two of his friends, who 'went round to my office and practically bullied me into accepting their invitation', to a regimental dinner and gala dance. She 'made a bad mistake in going, Keith. Not that B. and R. did not go out of their way to make the evening as pleasant for me as possible.' And she enjoyed it –

when the trumpeter in the band played the 'Post Horn Gallop' through a rifle barrel. But not to have you there with me – oh, Keith, it was so painful. The sight of B. and R. in their uniform brought memories flooding back to me – memories of a beautiful evening you drove down from Selarang in your mess kit to escort me to the Cheshires' cocktail party. I felt an overwhelming desire, at the dinner this last Thursday, to see you as you looked on the evening of the cocktail party – tall and straight and handsome in mess kit, and later in evening dress, just as handsome.

But alongside the longing for him is the discomfort set off by remarks passed by one of her escorts about 'our association': 'He was of the opinion that it was just as well that you had gone away, and thought that your leaving was the final sequel to our story. He said that the English, not being a widely travelled people and whose general outlook on life was not a particularly broad one, would be loath to accept a non-English bride into their society.'

I spend some time wondering about this remark. Was this narrow-minded tactlessness meant to be kind, or was it outright racial prejudice? Okay to dance with a Eurasian or Asian girl; not okay to marry one? The incident sets off in May a chain of concerns, doubts and questions. She worries that Keith would 'suffer a certain degree of ostracism or perhaps curiosity' because of her. She prompts him to consider 'the disadvantages' of marrying her: 'Would you be willing to suffer the social discomfort of being known to have a wife that is "different"?' She wonders why, after all, as 'deep-rooted an Englishman as you, should, from amongst the countless women you have known, choose for your wife this girl from the East who, although generally Western in many respects, must still possess characteristics born of life-long association with only Eastern customs, traditions and mode of life.' She feels 'trepidation' that she might 'in any way at all come between you and your family, or relatives, friends, your busy career and anything else.'

The anxiety brings May to consider ending the relationship. If she is going to jeopardise his career, she would

> die rather than go on living, but I would force myself to
> break away from you and England and doom myself to a

life of solitude and bitterness at the cruelty of the world. I am so afraid that in your new, or rather back in your old, environment, your three years here will soon fade into the past, and become just a hazy dream, a closed chapter in the book of your life.

She offers him a beating of the retreat: 'no strings attached.'

*

And so to the biggest difference between them, and the reason for the fault line in my own Jewish identity.

For of course my mother is not simply a 'non-English' girl as some of their critics thought – another Liat for Lieutenant Cable; the free island girl. She is not even the generic 'girl from the East' she pins onto the narrative of her relationship with Keith. She is the eldest daughter of Jewish parents, and all her life she has had no intention of marrying outside of the religion passed on from her Baghdadi Jewish father. This explains why May has 'had "words"' with Jacob. She would be leaving not only her home and culture; she would also be tacking away from her faith. Jewish heritage is, I'm learning, absolutely connected with fealty to family. Is this why it takes her a while to raise this obstacle to Keith? Now that they've become more seriously committed to each other, she writes openly of her dilemma: 'should I marry a non-Jew; it would, if I were to do so, bring shame to my parents, who place such importance on being accepted by the Jewish community.' The implication is that marrying Keith would lead to the rejection of both herself and her parents by the Jewish community. This is huge and has far bigger implications for them both than simply a British-Asian marriage.

Keith agrees they need to 'talk religion', for 'it affects & will affect us.' They already knew of the difference, of course. But the two months of whirlwind romance had blurred this dividing line. He sets the scene for her of England's then national, low-key, C of E religion, as if to cool this heated issue: 'It is a beautiful Sunday morning, England is quiet, the shops closed, the streets deserted, church bells ringing, & some people going to church.' He recognises, now she puts it so fully in her letters, that she is not allowed to marry outside her faith. Why, then, he proposes, shouldn't he become Jewish for her – 'it wouldn't mean anything to me, it would be a mere formality because I believe religion to be a personal affair.'

I'm left reeling by this offer. Keith was willing to convert to Judaism? This is the first I've heard of it. During our childhood, my father was quietly C of E. Over the years, he became even more inexpressive in this faith, especially once he accompanied May to her synagogue in London, where he was so welcomed by her new, Orthodox, Jewish community. But young Keith seems to have no idea of the difficulties that conversion to Judaism would entail.

May, however, does. She absolutely cannot allow his conversion. For a start, she is too deep-thinking to accept Judaism as a 'mere formality'. Religion was definitely not a personal affair in 1960, and he hasn't thought through the additional prejudice he would likely face in the Army as Jewish, with yet another insignia of not being the typical, public-school-educated, English-marrying, Christian officer. In any case, to become Jewish would require months, possibly years, of religious preparation. No: his converting to Judaism is out of the question, she writes.

Between them lie not only several thousand miles of sea. And the divisions of England 1960 mirror the divisions of Singapore 1960, for the English, even in social ways, still ruled much of the world, and where they did, there was not much compromise.

When my parents met, in most British places in Singapore there was still stigma around cross-cultural and interracial social mixing, or 'fraternisation', as it was called. Only once did my parents venture to the Tanglin, the prestigious Singapore club set up for British colonials and military. The mixed couple was met by raised eyebrows. 'It was the age of the Sahib', my mother now tells me wryly, by which she means the white colonial master ruled.

Her comment underlines how their commitment to each other challenged the rules and expectations. They never went back to Tanglin. Now, when they return to Singapore for holidays, they delight in staying there. They are welcomed as honoured guests. They never mention their first experience.

*

They say that opposites attract, and clearly there was a good deal of magnetism between my parents. But the differences between them also allowed them to give to the other what, on their own, each couldn't have had. I feel this strongly in their letters. My father gave my mother England. My mother allowed my father both to be of England but also to escape it, through her.

As their relationship matured and as I grew up in its midst, I watched as this mutually giving, even compensatory, structure deepened. Keith gave May a life lived around the world. He gave a Singapore girl mountains and taught her to ski. He gave her caravanning holidays with us children, driving hundreds of miles from where we lived elsewhere in Europe, to Spain, Italy, France. Here she learned to swim, to ride a bike; things she'd never been allowed to do by an overprotective Jewish father.

In return, May gave Keith connections and holidays across Asia, so that he really never had to leave Singapore or the East. She gave him music, especially opera and ballet, along with art, theatre, and the life of the mind. She gave him beauty and glamour, of a non-English (not 'sallow') kind. And she gave him the boundless generosity and compassion she'd inherited from Jacob and his tradition.

Now when I return to my parents' house, I'm struck even more by how much these two poles make a single axis. My father has lost sight in one eye, hearing in one ear, and is becoming forgetful. My mother holds his hand as he negotiates a kerb. She finds lost keys. She remembers his hospital appointments. My father still attempts to make their tea first thing in the morning, cut the melon for breakfast, water the garden and the flowers in the window baskets. I watch them in their ritual of sorting out the pills for the month. As daily medication for each of them runs into double digits, it's a procedure that takes two days of careful teamwork and concentrated focus. My mother empties bottles, counts and makes piles; my father fills the pill organiser. If they're not paying attention to each other (as does sometimes happen), they have to retrace their steps, even start over. But mostly, they get the job done in harmony, an unspoken communion between them, characteristic, but still it seems to me extraordinary, after sixty years of marriage.

*

Despite all the obstacles they reveal, the letters also created the beginning of this bridge between them. Via the letters, they really got to know each other, even through the ups and downs. Over those nine months, the letters were, as my parents both say, the only 'physical contact', after the intense, two-month courtship. 'Our love has survived the most trying of tests, a period of waiting that may well have killed it in frustration.' May is right, but the writing extends, appropriately over a gestation period, to give birth to a new 'something': their love story, soon to be followed by their marriage. Their writing will give birth to me of course, but more to the point, to my writing. And because they had already lived their courtship as a written story, I couldn't fail to begin my story through the camphorwood chest with their letters. They set the first tone, the tuning fork of my legacy.

My parents initiate their departure from themselves to each other – perhaps May especially – with the beginning of their correspondence. As she says, writing letters to him 'has helped me to lose a lot of the rigid reserve with which I used to hold myself.' Keith is also transformed by the exchange: 'I feel so very different after your letters. I experience the same sensational feeling as I experienced after an evening out with you, when I drove home in the early hours of the morning singing to myself so free from the cares of the world.'

Each seeks to inhabit the different world the other is leaving. Keith has sympathy for May's mother; she works very hard, and he knows that she especially will miss her daughter. May writes to him that, now that she has told both her parents of her intention, they have 'given their consent, though somewhat reluctantly.' With the days approaching, they're going through 'a tearful time with the family in this past week; I don't know if it is characteristic of our race but we are a fairly sentimental people', and it takes only a song for her father to speak sadly of her leaving. 'And this, of course, sparks a general tear-shedding session amongst members of my family, including myself.' She writes to him of the Jewish festivals, the Day of Atonement that has just passed. She is clearly meditating on what leaving would mean for her Jewishness. In the synagogue she would have been fasting, listening to the hazan, or cantor, intoning the mournful Yom Kippur prayer, Kol Nidre ('all vows'). The words and music spoke directly to her soul.

More than this, though, in these later letters she seems to be leaving behind some of her Jewish past in order to come to him. For this Day of Atonement she has not been atoning. Instead, she confesses, 'I have spent almost every moment of this day thinking about you', and her evenings listening to 'soft dreamy Nat King Cole numbers', which take her back to her nights with him. There is a competing music now. She has also been spending time with her mother, going together to Chinese street operas, 'wayangs' – 'age-old opera held on a fabulous scale'. While the words and music are impenetrable to her, she finds 'the graceful movements of the actors, the stage setting and the costumes fascinating'. And her mother, 'with her perceptiveness, tells me the only way to chase my blues away is to fly to England right away – so well does she understand me – although breaking her own heart in saying so.'

May is equally magnanimous about *his* mother, encouraging him, when he complains about the tension in his parents' house, to consider the point of view of a woman whose two sons have been away for years and who return having grown away from home.

Try to understand, my Keith, that it is because you are her son, and she loves you, that she is hurt by your apparent loss of interest in family life. She has probably known all along, deep down inside her, that some day, especially now that you have travelled and so widened your horizons, you would look beyond the home that you'd always known for the greater things you seek.

When he buys a 'special frame' for the photograph she had made for him and sent to him on the boat, he finds it's given 'a place of honour in the sitting room. My parents love it.' Remembering that my father's parents left the UK only once in their seventy years of life – William to fight in North Africa during the Second World War, Maud to visit us when my father was posted to Malta in the late '60s – I find this detail deeply moving. Their location of her photograph in the room they practically lived in signals an unquestioning embrace into their home of this girl visibly and culturally so different. Even if I hadn't seen evidence of this for myself, I sense that this elderly couple was not as parochial – 'ordinary' – as some of Keith's letters made his parents out to be. May was right; his mother knew all along, and indeed accepted, that he would 'look beyond home'.

Love allowed them to transcend all the obstacles. They bucked against what they both called the 'narrowness' of their own confines. They shared, fundamentally, the same desire to leave home, which was to break out of the restrictions of nation, class and culture. The estrangement, you could say, began at home.

May expresses an idea of love as freeing, as precisely that which travels. You cannot force or limit love, she writes.

> When we are old and grey, and our children grown, they will, through the sort of love we give them, regard our home, their home, as a haven of peace and not a prison. For the very essence of love, Keith, is the joy one gets in giving and not in taking, and that is how my love for you shall be, strong and open-minded and generous, not demanding and possessive.

How I recognise my mother. In our pasts my brother and I too sought to escape the familiar, an uncanny repetition of our parents' departures. Both Dave and I were keenly drawn to the detachment of Buddhism, me, seriously, extensively. Both of us travelled or lived abroad for periods, again me more committedly, in New York, thinking carefully before I returned to family and the UK. And I've cycled through partners of various nationalities, ethnicities and religions. Yet my parents' home in London, as my mother's vision has created it now that they have settled in one place, has indeed proven a 'haven'. In its centrifugal force the opposite of neediness, my parents' love has provided me, in my different and often difficult guises, with the confidence to explore various religious and other identities. And now indeed to return home.

Because of the divisions of each of their separate worlds, my parents had every reason for transcending. And in their creation of love as that which travels to understand and embrace difference, young Keith and May are not so much old-fashioned, as ahead of their times. And in this, they seem to me still ahead of ours.

*

The last several weeks of their separation returns the correspondence to the magic of the earliest exchanges. All opposing forces discussed and defeated, the current flows freely between them, as they increase the counting down.

Her twenty-second birthday, 25th November 1960, and he sends her orchids from Princess Flower Shop, where he had bought her flowers after that first date. At a time before Interflora not to mention the Internet, this feels like pure conjuring, and May is intrigued at how he has managed it. (In fact he got a friend who lived in Singapore to arrange it. Orchids will remain my mother's favourite flowers and go on to become Singapore's floral emblem.)

As Christmas approaches, May confesses that she is listening to Christmassy crooner tunes over the radio. Again, I sense May feeling her way into a life partnership with this Englishman, this understated Christian. Even as a non-Christian, she writes, 'Christmas never fails to touch and move' her. She has been shopping excitedly for her departure. Envisioning herself 'positively loaded with luggage' when she docks, she has bought 'a short swagger coat in a soft furry material', and three Japanese lamps for his relatives from the market in Change Alley. 'I seem to be having appointments with everyone these days': immigration authorities, and dressmakers for clothes she is designing herself. She encloses a sketch of a suit she plans to wear when she first sees him again, at Tilbury Docks: a tapering skirt, wide-collared jacket, and a hat to match, all in greyish-blue light wool. It looks like it could have been designed by Christian Dior. She is in a mess in her bedroom, 'suitcases, dresses, papers and boxes, scattered all over the place – you'd be horrified.' So she is contemplating buying a single piece of furniture, a trunk or container of some sort, which will hold her most precious things.

And then my chest, perhaps my true protagonist, makes its way onto the stage for the first time: 'There is, among other things, a small camphorwood chest which has caught my eye and I know it will prove useful.'

Little does she know how valuable it will prove. I welcome this chest, which is at once new to me here, through my mother's letters, and yet feels very familiar. My old friend. My childhood story-box.

*

She takes leave of her friends, a few at a time. 'The biggest wrench will, however, be when I bid my final goodbye to my family. This will be my first separation from them, and I shall miss my mother's good guidance and companionship.' Esther is creating every opportunity to spend time with May, leaving Jacob to look after the other children. She wants this time alone with her daughter. They go out at night not only to watch wayang but to walk arm in arm through the night market on their doorstep in Short Street. May inhales the scents of ginger, garlic, chilli and listens to the hawkers' calls, storing the sensations in her memory. Mother and daughter buy *mee goreng*, Chinese fried noodles, and bring it home wrapped in a dried banana leaf to share with the rest of the family.

May is given a farewell party at her club, the Menorah Club. She sends Keith a photo of herself from the evening, 'to lessen the shock of you seeing me for the first time in almost nine months.' She looks forward to her ship's holiday to get some colour in her cheeks – 'I hardly wish to look like a ghost when we meet again' – because other than with her mother she hasn't been spending much time outside, 'or eating with any great enthusiasm'. 'But how I love every moment of it! I am filled with so much excitement that I can hardly bring myself to swallow the food that I eat or shut my eyes in sleep at night.'

She tells him that she has never returned to the Golden Dragon since he left, so sacred is the memory. But

> I intend going there just once more before I leave, for the first time since your departure, to look up our friend the pianist and let him know that I am going to join you in England. I remember, even on our last evening there I was so doubtful of such a thing being possible. And now the dream is to become a reality. We were destined to meet that evening in May – that enchanted evening. We were strangers, yet we looked at each other across the crowded room, and came together. And you are here in my heart to stay.

During her last couple of days, she goes to the Rose d'Or, 'and then to the Golden Dragon to tell the pianist there of our wishes beginning to come true.' She will never forget all their places, 'even the cinema where in the darkness your hand stole out, after an unbearably long time, to hold mine. Oh, how much there is to be re-lived, and in just over 4 weeks' time!'

He is counting down:

> The dream is coming true, slowly but surely, & now increasing its momentum until it will soon burst into realisation. About seven months ago as I steamed away from Singapore, up the channel, Blakan Mati one side, Keppel Harbour the other, I wondered if we would ever meet again. I thought that if we did, it would only be by my coming back to Singapore. Yet in Aden, there was a letter awaiting me saying that you had decided to come to England. I believed the truth in those words. . . yet it is only now in this last month that I really see you stepping onto the gangway.

He speaks of her arrival as '"D" Day': 'Darling Little One, the song is endless, as the wind rushes through the trees.'

Just hours before she boards the *Corfu* and steps on the gangway, she writes to him one last time from her flat in Short Street.

> Yet how sad I am to be saying goodbye to all that I have known here. It's my mother I find it so hard to part from; she watches silently as I go about assembling my things, and I know from the sadness in her eyes that she weeps in her heart. And I have to keep trying to appease her by saying just how much the journey is going to mean

to me, to you and I, and that it will mean the fulfilment
of a long-cherished dream; and then she is happy again.

Yes it's goodbye to Singapore and very soon, hello to
England and you.

Until then, my Dearest,

and ever after,

I am yours.

May

When she boards the boat, he is with her in spirit. He imagines
her 'terrible hour', as she leaves all that is familiar:

soon your lovely home and city will be a mere dot on the
skyline. Darling I felt terrible leaving it after only three
years. I know what you will feel after a lifetime. We do
have the great consolation that with the passing of each
day we are coming closer together. Darling if you only
knew how much I need you, how very very much I need
you it would help you on your way.

Darling do you know that your letter which arrived
this morning was the 50th you have written to me. I
quite often sit down and read them at random, one day
I must read them all through again in their chronologi-
cal order. I have just reread your last note written from
Mont d'Or. . . you wrote an unfinished song – that must
someday be completed – it is being completed, now.

During her boat journey, which makes the same stops as his
did, he writes to her at every port, as she did to him. To Suez,
he writes, 'you are leaving the East behind and entering the

West – although it is not really that different.' To Port Said – 'Soon there will be no need for words – soon it will be possible to look.' At Gibraltar he cables her, the final line in their correspondence, a reprise of the first line: 'YOU DO SOMETHING TO ME VERY MUCH IN LOVE.' The song, at least in their correspondence, is finished.

And the last item I find in the package of my parents' letters? A British Railways ticket, issued at Southampton, for 'Luggage Accompanying Passengers – Weight, 212 lbs' – over double the amount she was allowed free, an excess for which she paid 16 shillings and 6 pence – for a camphorwood chest, which was obviously not so small, and which, once they were married, could come to contain and keep these letters.

*

With this, I, too, am finished with their correspondence. I tie the letters into bundles with string, interleaving his and hers, organised week by week. I secure the flimsy receipt for the chest as the final note in their music. I tuck my father's miniscule diary back where it surprised me, between the piles of airmails; war amidst love. I am meticulous. I realise I'm treating the letters as if they are a special collection in a library.

Then I realise I've engaged with the letters not just for their story. Their materiality has rubbed off on me. The words, the very paper and ink, have affected me deeply. My parents' script leaves an imprint. All that writing, the exchanges. The sheer weight of the communication. Above all, the keeping of these papers, as if my parents knew that they, both the letters and themselves as a couple, would amount to something. That these letters needed to be preserved. For someone to find and read them.

With this final thought, I return everything to the camphor-wood chest.

*

The scent of camphor is nothing like the woods of the other furniture that could be found in our houses. Oak and pine, beech and elm; the earthy woods of Northern Europe that go nowhere, that stay in place for centuries.

With camphor, I inhale travel; the East. I taste nutmeg-sweetness, mixed with fresh, unsmoked tobacco. Tangy clove wipes my mind clean, and warm, rich, winter cinnamon enfolds my body. Camphor alchemises opposites in me. Musty and life-giving. Ancient and new-born. Mysterious, and yet unmistakeable. Camphor breathes distance – ancient times, as well as far-flung places. Whenever my mother raised the lid, the scent pulled me into those other worlds. It coated the objects she took out from the chest that inspired her tales, and her stories became camphor-infused.

The chest has allowed me to relive the magic that started my parents' relationship, interrupting me with my father's diary and the atrocity in his story. It has yet to tell me about the world my mother gave up when she left: to tell me about her Jewishness, and hence help me to understand more about mine.

FOLLOWING THE THREAD

7. THE MENORAH

David Marshall, on his election as Singapore's first Chief Minister in 1955; the Iraqi Jew who led Singapore towards independence. Source: © SPH Media Limited. Permission required for reproduction.

When she met my father, my mother was on the rebound. It was from her one serious relationship. May had been deeply in love. The man in question was from a wealthy Singapore Jewish family.

While May had many cross-cultural dates and friendships, there was a goodly number of Jewish boys who courted her. There was the boxer with the inevitably squashy nose, blue eyes and crinkly hair, who lived in the flat above her family. He way-laid her with his patter on their way up the stairs of their block.

Then there was another boyfriend, dark curly hair and dark eyebrows, who stood below her veranda and sang Dean Martin songs up at her. I imagine May sandwiched between these characters, the boxer upstairs and the crooner below, the chatter and the songs – their courtship tools. There was also a wiry doctor, who had returned to Singapore after having been in England studying for his degrees. Of him, though, May was shy. He was educated and articulate, and his having been abroad – especially to England – in my mother's eyes placed him above her. May seems already to have had a sense of going to England, immersion in the metropolis of empire, as marking a person out.

With none of these Jewish boys was May truly in love, though, as she most certainly was with Edward Maier. I think of Edward Maier as the opposite of my father in every respect. He was quiet, intellectual, spiritual. From the beginning, he and May were on the same wavelength, surely that 'higher plane' that – I'm not surprised to read in some of her later letters – she panicked sometimes that she couldn't attain with Keith. My mother is cerebral in a way that my father is not. She is an intellectual. My father lives in his body and practically, a true soldier. Poring over the handful of photographs in the chest of this ex of my mother's, I wonder what could have been, and why it would not be.

Dark, wide-set eyes. Full lips, caught between smiling and sad. A face that can't hide its sensitivity and appeal. Yet also reserved and shy, giving the sense that he wants to retreat from the camera's spotlight. Jewish looks. The ladies in various synagogues who've measured me against some template of Jewishness would surely agree on this. I realise he looks like he could be family. The olive skin, the deep-brown almond-shaped eyes, the simultaneous unguardedness-and-yet-withdrawal, bear a striking resemblance to Sunny, my mother's retiring only brother, or to my own gentle, home-centred brother, the letter-shy psychiatrist. Edward Maier doesn't have the look of someone who's going to shout from the rooftop of the Cathay Building, win any medals, or ever look far beyond home, even at the cost of losing what he loves. Putting his photographs alongside those of my military-bearing, exquisitely tailored, thrusting, English, gentile father, I see these men as a fork in the road of May's life at around aged twenty: between marrying in, and marrying out.

Far from getting togged up for three occasions per day, Maier looks uncomfortable dressed in anything like formal wear. Here he is at a party, in a wide-lapelled, by then unfashionable, striped suit. Maier also took May out to dinner and dances, to many of those same places that my parents would later go. He looks younger than his twenty-something years, and as though he needed courage just to put on his accompanying, not quite dapper polka-dot bow tie. In another image, he's in a plain white open-necked office shirt, relieved to be back in less showy circumstances. He is most comfortable in the shots where he and May are dressed casually for picnics.

One photograph of my mother and Maier stands out. They're at a dinner, possibly at the Menorah Club, the social club for young Singapore Jews, where David Marshall, the new, Jewish, Chief Minister of Singapore, sometimes showed up. (There's a photograph in the camphorwood chest of Marshall dancing at a party for my mother at the Menorah Club; unfortunately, he has his back to the camera.) The image of May and Maier at the Menorah Club, both directly facing the camera, suggests complementarity: what each might have brought the other.

May is dazzling in a cut-away silk dress with a diaphanous shawl. She smiles confidently. She wears no jewellery, her own glow making it unnecessary. And I think: she must have brought brilliance to Maier's life, as she would do for my father. Maier is dark, handsome, his face sensitive. But his jacket looks too long in the sleeve, as if it has been borrowed from a father or better-built brother. Though he is clearly with her, he is quite happy to be in her background. He is her shadow, a shelter or retreat also for her, perhaps.

Although they're out of view, I can tell his hands must be resting stiffly on his knees. My mother says that Edward played the piano, beautifully, and that he would play 'Fascination' for her. Having become a piano player herself once she had left Singapore, she jokes flippantly that, really, she fell in love with the piano. But I imagine that Meier had beautiful hands, with long, elegant fingers, a gentle touch; again unlike Keith's sharp-shooting, military fists.

And what is my fascination with their being together? What am I looking for in this relationship? There would be no Jewish marriage. My mother would marry my father. I would not be raised Jewish. I would be moved around the world, rootless. I would not know where I belonged. It is hard for me not to feel some regret.

As I recover this road into a Jewish marriage not taken, I learn something new from my mother's cousin Moshe, who is older than her and who was exposed to things she wasn't at the time. Moshe tells me that the relationship was serious enough for May's father to approach Edward's father to discuss a match, in all likelihood, as Jacob was the father of the bride, to request the marriage. In the meeting, Jacob was rebuffed. The Maiers thought her family not 'good enough'; they didn't have sufficient standing in the Jewish community. From then on, Maier's parents refused to allow their son to see May. To break the couple up, Maier was sent to America. May was told that he left to study, but she sensed the truth of his absence, even if she wasn't given the details. In the beginning, Edward wrote her letters. Then the letters stopped, and he never returned to Singapore.

Jacob never told his daughter of his rejection from the Maier family. Lovingly, he sought to protect May from what must have burned in him as shame; a shame that my mother feels newly on learning the story from Moshe as a result of my poking about. She is disbelieving at first. Why didn't her father tell her? But as Edward never explained or even announced the break-up, she accepts that her family was the reason for the rejection. Rather than inherit generations of shame, however, my hackles rise. That others in the wider family, quite possibly wider Jewish community, knew of the drama suggests that a larger deep-rooted convention was enacted, a convention of being judged sufficiently Jewish. It's a convention I want to uncover like a buried bone and gnaw away at, until it disintegrates.

I think my grandfather must also have felt furious at his rebuttal. He was poor and not self-important, but his presence and confidence made him seem a larger man than his small stature. What was it – *what is it* – I wonder, to be 'good enough' within the Jewish community? I suspect that this obstacle in my mother's Jewish story was not only the obvious class difference between the Maiers and the Eliases, but also the fact of May's Chinese, originally non-Jewish mother: a difference of race and lineage. For really what's at stake in a girl being 'good enough' for a Jewish boy but being 'Jewish enough'? And what is the harshness of this legacy, which I find myself stumbling over again here, if such life-determining decisions and divisions can be made over and above the heads of the young people who are expected to take it up?

The story reminds me of when I've felt others measuring up my Jewishness. *You have a Jewish mother but not a Jewish father? Did you receive a Jewish education? Do you go to 'shul'?* – a word that has no resonance for non-Yiddish-speaking, Asian Jews. At these points, I've wanted to cut ties to Jewishness fully; the opposite of the Groucho Marx theory of clubdom. Legacy, or at least how it's judged, can make or break your Jewishness.

I can imagine the pain that May must have felt on Edward's sudden departure was enough. But the lack of an explanation, including from Edward himself, broke her heart even more deeply. Edward Maier was not willing or able, as my hardheaded father was, to swim against the strong current of his times or elders deciding correct matches. The rejection May experienced explains something of her reserve during my parents' months of courtship; as Keith says she maintained, until her letters overflowed the bounds. At the same time, it would have made her impatient to get away from enclosed communities. It would have left her, surely, waiting for someone from the outside.

And the effect on Maier? I have this reason to think it never left him.

About fifteen years ago, his cousin met my mother at a family wedding in London. The cousin said that Maier had only recently got married and – did she know? – he had continued to love my mother for 'a very long time.' Then a few years ago, my mother and Edward Maier themselves met, at a bat mitzvah in Singapore, their first and only encounter since they had been parted almost fifty years previously. At the party everyone was asking her, 'Do you know that Edward Maier is here?' His love for her was common knowledge, they said. My father, who was accompanying my mother, went and found Edward, and the three of them stood together for a short while. 'How life changes everything', my mother said, finally, to Edward. 'Yes', he replied. 'But some things never change.' With her standing before him again finally after half a century, what else could he have meant except his feelings for her?

Ever the social lubricator, or maybe mischief-maker – *you lost, I won* – my father, still standing between them, filled the silence: 'She's learning to play the piano. "Fascination", you know.'

Edward said simply: 'It's in C. Major.' And at that point, he moved off.

Edward Maier is the only character in my mother's family story whose name I have changed.

'At this point,' my mother says to me, 'I gave up the idea that I would marry Jewish. But in no way did I gave up being Jewish.' She tells the story of Edward's long-lived passion for her, her eyes shining with the remembered romance. But she has no regrets now. I'm probably more regretful than her. A Jewish father and Jewish upbringing would, I think, have gifted me a clearcut Jewish legacy. But then, I sense, I might have less reason to dialogue with my mother. There would be fewer questions to ask.

*

The puzzling thing to me in the story of her break-up from Maier is that May did have a place, and even some status, in the Jewish community. The dates she went on with Edward – on picnics together, dancing at the Menorah Club – reveal her at the very hub of the young Jewish community, wholeheartedly engaged with Jewish life.

At the time of dating Edward, in fact, May was Secretary of the Menorah Club, and she was President soon after that. I find her featured in a big commemorative coffee-table book on the Jews of Singapore. In 1959 she is pictured seated and smiling, with six other young Singapore Jews, in a photograph captioned 'Menorah Club office bearers'. May holding two such posts in succession provides me with evidence, even though I know I might be charged with finding what I'm looking for, of how she was valued in the Jewish community and seen, for a time at least, as leading among young Jews. May is frequently in the newspapers as President of the Menorah. One clipping, headlined 'Pretty May, Happy Ray', shows her tying a victor's belt around the Chinese fighter who had just beaten the Jewish boxer upstairs. Many of these matches took place at the Happy World stadium, with Jewishness fitting comfortably into the cosmopolitan space of her childhood.

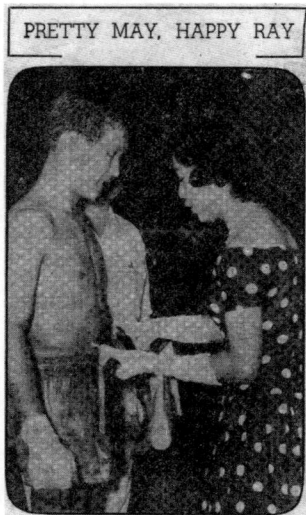

PRETTY MAY, HAPPY RAY

As Club Secretary, May attended meetings and kept minutes at the wealthy synagogue in Singapore, Chesed El. She took tea regularly with Mrs Moselle Nissim, at her big house on the hill, helping her to plan parties for the religious festival of Purim. Mrs Nissim was the daughter of Manesseh Meyer, the grand scion and philanthropist of Singapore's Jewish community, who had built the impressive Chesed El synagogue. Via Mrs Nissim, the Manesseh Meyer Trust had funded and helped to establish the Menorah Club, and this institution had gone on to have a substantial role in Jewish Singapore after the Second World War. May was excited to be a part of this thriving, building moment, both as the Menorah Club's President and Secretary.

The Menorah Club grew out of the Singapore branch of Habonim (*ha-bonim;* meaning literally 'the builders' in Hebrew), an international socialist secular Jewish youth movement, which had been set up to support an independent Jewish homeland in Palestine and to create pride in Jewish identity among the Jewish diaspora worldwide. The club had started off with Habonim-type activities, centring on Jewish identity, especially for adolescents: scouting, sports, Hebrew lessons, Hebrew singing, Jewish dancing. May embraced all these activities.

So far, so Zionist. By the time of her office-holding, the Menorah had become a social club for high-school leavers and those in early years of work: the 1950s equivalent of the village matchmaker. There were parties, dinners and dances. Just months before she met Keith, May held her twenty-first birthday party at the Menorah Club. By this time, Edward had already been sent away from Singapore. She had lots of dates, and yet no specific single date for the evening. But David Marshall showed up, and he danced. She attracted the leading Jewish lights of emerging postcolonial Singapore.

A photograph in the camphorwood chest from this time captures May smiling confidently in front of the oldest and central synagogue in Singapore, her family synagogue, the Maghain Aboth. Caught from a casual sideways angle, she stands before the Magen David on the synagogue wall, itself unapologetically prominent as it absorbs the full sunlight. In many shots, May wears the Magen David (Jewish star, or really, 'Shield of David') on a chain around her neck. I find her with two of her Jewish friends, dressed up for Shabbat. They pose in pretty dresses, white court shoes with matching handbags, forearm-length gloves, and Audrey Hepburn sunglasses. May outshines them in a polka-dot dress, another of those she'd designed and made for herself, along with a headband in the same material. They look like they're going to a party, not to a religious service.

The synagogue was segregated in the traditional Sephardi style, men below, women in the galleries. But this wasn't a restrictive or proscriptive space. My mother tells me that the girls used to take the opportunity of looking down on the scene to spot the boys they liked. And I imagine that the boys – teen-agers, young men as they were – must have struggled not to turn their kippot-covered heads up from their books and return the looks of those dazzling girls. Those boys' cheeks burned, whenever they were called to read at the bimah (don't I know it), and when they became conscious of being watched, wanted.

L'chayim! Jewish life in Singapore was in its element. There was no split between religious observance and love: the life of the soul and the life of the heart.

Another photograph of May, aged about fourteen, shows her in a headscarf, again with her Magen David clearly visible. Her eyes are narrowed against a bright sun. My brother and I both love this image; for years he has hung it in his house. I think we admire the air of optimism and gentle, confident strength, the qualities I most identify with my mother; the things I hope she might yet give me as her child. But now more versed in Jewish history, I can also see that this photograph bears strong resemblance to early Zionist iconography. There's an irony here, since she's actually wearing Malay traditional dress, the *sarong kebaya,* including the 'Muslim' headscarf. But to me she looks like one of the chalutzim (pioneers), a kibbutznik or tiller of the new Israel's soil.

At about the time this photograph was taken, when she was about thirteen or fourteen, May appeared on Radio Singapore, on a programme called *Youth at the Helm.* She was selected as one of the young bright lights, potential future leaders, which was the topic of the programme. She recited Byron's 'All for Love', a poem that rejects age-old wisdom for the 'glory of youth'.

> O talk not to me of a name great in story;
> The days of our youth are the days of our glory;
> And the myrtle and ivy of sweet two-and-twenty
> Are worth all your laurels, though ever so plenty.

Her word-perfect recitation for me now resurrects this confidence, from the days of her own youth, and of Singapore's young times as a nation.

So despite the Maier taint, coming through the stories and photographs, and through the history of the Menorah Club, is that this was really the best time to be Jewish in Singapore. It's as if the Jewish lamp, which is the meaning and symbol of the menorah, cast its light and lent a glow to everything in fifties Singapore.

*

There were geopolitical reasons for Jewish identity to have shone so brightly in 1950s Singapore. Jews worldwide had emerged from a systemised attempt in the previous decade to erase them. In Singapore, they had survived a brutal occupation and internment. Elsewhere in the East, a Jewish state had been created, an apparently Jewish nation finally provided a homeland in Israel. Even for those Jews remaining in the diaspora, including for many of these in the East, Israel served as a beacon of reassurance and an assertion of Jewish strength. Jews in Singapore, Jews everywhere, like May, seemed to have everything to look forward to. These were indeed the days of glory.

But perhaps the principal reason why this was the finest time to be Jewish in Singapore – above and beyond the founding of Jewish organisations such as the Jewish Welfare Board and the Menorah Club – was David Marshall, who had showed up at May's party. Marshall had been 'at the helm' of many of these Jewish organisations. In 1930s Singapore, he had founded a Zionist-inspired Jewish community magazine, *ISRAELIGHT*. With his desire to see a Jewish nation replace British Mandate Palestine, and his own experiences as a Jew in Singapore, not surprisingly he had also been a keen participant in early anti-British imperialist activity on the island.

During the War, however, Marshall had fought, with the Singapore Volunteer Corps, to defend the British colony. When the Japanese invaded Singapore in 1942, he was sent as a prisoner of war to the Japanese island of Hokkaido, to work the coal mines. It was on his return to Singapore and rejoining the Jewish population that Marshall and other leading Jews decided that they were never again going to rely on those outside – especially not the British. The Jewish community must become autonomous and an example to other colonised communities in Singapore. With Marshall serving as its first president, the Jewish Welfare Board was founded. Fired by Zionist and Jewish socialist ideals, its remit was to care for the poor in response to devastations wrought by the war. It would prove essential for the survival of May and her family.

Marshall was pivotal in the island's transition from colonialism to postcolonialism. A great orator, he became a prominent lawyer and then an increasingly important politician. He led Singapore's first political party, the Progressive Party. By 1954, now as leader of the Labour Front, he was demanding immediate self-government for Singapore. In April 1955, he won the island-state's first proper political election to become Chief Minister of Singapore. Though he is invariably sidelined in histories of Singapore, Marshall was, in effect, the country's first prime minister, its first noncolonial, non-British governor.

Marshall was first in another sense: his Jewishness. And his inclusive, questioning form of Jewishness interests me. He was the first Jewish lawyer in Singapore and the first Jewish politician. That his Jewishness was not incidental to these achievements, Marshall himself recognised. Looking back on his life he said:

> I wanted justice. And the fact that I am a Jew is not without significance. There is a Jewish cry for justice which echoes down the corridor of the centuries and that cry for justice has encouraged many social reforms in many parts of the world. . . . If you wear the shoe that pinches, you know exactly where and why it hurts. We [the Jews] have worn the shoe of injustice for centuries.

On winning the election in 1955, he said:

> By electing a member of the smallest domiciled com-
> munity here [the Jews, the people of Singapore] have
> proved that Singapore can work, think and act non-com-
> munally. By electing a stranger to politics in preference
> to the founder President of the longest established party
> in Singapore the people have proved that Singapore has
> a spirit which can be touched by ideals.

There is no coincidence that justice and freedom for Singapore
– a political ideal of loving strangers – were first demanded by
a Jew, a Jew moreover from a poor, immigrant Baghdadi family like May's. Reading the Torah, over and over again in synagogue, then three times by himself, gave him the power of the
word, he said. His *Iraqi* Jewishness in particular, his not being
European or yet natively Singaporean, meant that he was perfectly placed to negotiate tensions between the different political loyalties of his moment. Classified by the British like May
and other Singapore Jews as 'Asiatic', Marshall called himself
'non-white'. But of course he was not Chinese, like the majority
population of Singapore. He was among a group of Singaporeans who were English educated, but who would use that education to overthrow the British. This group included Lee Kuan
Yew, Marshall's arch-rival. Lee is still known as Singapore's
most successful leader and eclipses Marshall.

In his autobiography, which is the canonical story of postcolonial Singapore's rise, Lee has some weird, antisemitic things
to say about Marshall. He calls Marshall 'a mercurial, flamboy-
ant Sephardic Jew', 'a prima donna who loved to be centre stage

and would be uncontrollable', who 'flounced' out of his own dinner parties in tantrums. Yet even Lee has to acknowledge Marshall's greatest and lasting gift to Singapore, the Citizenship Ordinance in 1957, which accorded citizenship of Singapore to all the island's local residents – wherever they had been born. This was an important turning point, both in Singapore's increasing independence from Britain, and in the story of the city's cosmopolitanism. It gave a legal home to Singapore's resident strangers, especially meaningful for the substantial number of China-born immigrants.

Among them, I'll discover, was my Chinese, not Jewish-born, grandmother.

*

It seems to me the paths of Marshall and my mother dovetail in many crucial ways, beyond the fact simply that they were both from poor Baghdadi Jewish families. May was also on the 'road to *Merdeka'*, the route to independence. She, like Marshall, in her growing up, her social circle, had a vision of the cosmopolitan architecture of Singapore, while respecting separate pillars. And as with Marshall, the weight of communal tradition would cause this edifice to tumble. Marshall, too, ended up marrying out, also to a non-Jewish English partner.

May could have ended up a lawyer too, like Marshall. Before she met Keith and around the time that Maier was sent out of bounds, May had the chance to study for a law degree in England, in the footsteps of Marshall. If she had done so, she would have come to England without the incentive of Keith, and she would never have met my father. The Jewish Welfare Board was going to pay for her to attend the University of London, Marshall's alma mater. If she had come, she would have been one of the first women to benefit from the fellowship scheme that Marshall helped to set up, another of his extraordinary liberalising achievements. But May's poor family couldn't afford to sacrifice her salary, which was the main thing keeping them afloat.

When I ask my mother how she felt about the opening and then immediate shutting of this door, she says she was sad, but she accepted she had to work to support her family. She was willing to do it, and she had to do it. She sees no tension between these responses. Life had been a struggle for her family, especially after the war.

Unsatisfied, I continue to wonder what that fifteen-year-old must have felt. Witnessing her embrace whatever difficulty – including me in all my phases – life throws at her, I think my mother probably did just knuckle down to the task at hand. She certainly shows no resentment or regret now. Far from feeling hard done by, she voices thanks daily, including for a childhood which she insists was happy in spite of the poverty. And after we'd grown up, she more than made up for a lack of choice in her childhood, with a career as a successful businesswoman and self-edification.

But what about that passionate and articulate young woman I find in her letters to my father? Was *she* not the smallest bit resentful? Did that girl (not yet mother, not yet wife) not feel the least bit stifled, held back by family and its traditions? These are the feelings I hear when I read those difficult parts of her letters fifty years later. Looking back with me now, my mother is horrified by how at points she felt let down by her life in

Singapore after Edward Maier. She pushed against her family. 'How could I be so cruel?' she says. 'If I could have my life over, I would have behaved differently.'

But would she? Unlike my mother, I don't find her youthful protests the least bit surprising, nor her resulting decision to leave Singapore, her family and come to my father. For if you are kept at home, even by request rather than compulsion, even out of a loving need rather than hateful punishment, aren't you ultimately going to look for the fastest and most radical route out?

Even though I was never kept at home, never needed financially, and got to receive a very privileged education, I left home as fast as I could. I left my family as soon as I'd finished my undergraduate degree. I took up my chance for a postgraduate scholarship in New York. But I left behind, then, any chance to connect to my mother's Jewish story and hence create my own. So I also understand her regrets about her own past now.

*

Too busy at work, May no longer had time to attend Habonim teachings, and she stepped back from leading activities at the Menorah Club. But she remained deeply involved in the Jewish community. And it was because she felt deeply Jewish and identified herself as such, that she has a period during her letters to Keith of expressing her strongest doubts about their relationship. May thought of herself as fully, properly Jewish, and I sense that, during the epistolary relationship, she was very reluctant to give up the expectation of a Jewish marriage.

Marshall intertwined with May's life in one final, consequential sense. For it was Marshall who brought to Singapore the rabbi who was not only one of the city's longest serving, at a quarter of a century, but also one of Singapore's and indeed all Eastern Jewry's most interesting, humane and radical Jewish leaders. Marshall recruited Jacob Shababo from Egypt, but with his fair skin and blue eyes Shababo's origins were likely elsewhere. He said he was born in Palestine to a Romanian mother. Shababo arrived in Singapore with his son and three beautiful daughters – the second of whom would go on to marry May's cousin Moshe. Shababo immediately involved himself in Habonim and the Jewish community broadly. At the same time, he became president of the Inter-Religious Association, a group for cross-faith and cultural community-building in Singapore. And most radically and significantly for our family's Jewishness and the story of Singapore's Jews, he went on to convert those who felt themselves to be Jewish into the Jewish faith, including a large number of Chinese women.

There's a letter in the camphorwood chest from Rabbi Shababo. Dated September 1959, the signed letter is one of validation, stating that May had 'undergone all the necessary rites, according to the laws and customs of Israel, as required of proselytes intending to embrace the Jewish faith.' From the Greek meaning 'person who has come to a place', also 'stranger, sojourner', *proselyte* is the term in English for a convert before the conversion. So, when she was almost twenty-one, May was converted to Judaism, by Shababo.

My mother's memory is that her conversion had happened before this, when she was still in her teens. The letter is a historical document. Its date must be correct. But my mother's memory is in a deeper way more accurate, because it captures how she felt, based on her commitment and belonging to the

Jewish community in Singapore before her conversion. For a short time, she insists, but nevertheless in fact, for others, for her peers, as I've seen in the photographs and clippings in the camphorwood chest, she was not only already Jewish but 'at the helm' in her role at the Menorah Club. She had been attending synagogue and been involved in Jewish activities as long as the photographs go back. She felt that her conversion was a *confirmation of*, not a *conversion to*, Jewish identity. Above all, she arranged it as an official commitment to Judaism the religion; in particular, Halachah, the strict religious laws held sacrosanct by Orthodox Judaism.

The Hebrew word for convert is *ger*. Like *proselyte*, it translates as 'stranger'. One contemporary Orthodox Sephardi rabbi has said that when the Torah commands compassion and equal justice for the *ger*, it is referring not just to strangers but also to converts.

When he converted her, Shababo said to May that any children she had would now be fully Jewish, a detail that was important to her. A detail that involves me.

When I joined my synagogue in York, and before that connected to others in Leeds, I was insecure about whether I 'counted' as Jewish. I had a Jewish mother, but I felt I knew so little, about my family and the traditions. Rabbis and community chairs assured me that I qualified. But for others, including the rabbis in Israel and some more religiously extreme politicians, and without doubt also some in the UK (the Beth Din, the highest authority in the UK on Jewish law), though I count as Jewish for the Law of Return (one Jewish grandparent) which would allow me to live in Israel, I am not properly, that is, religiously, Jewish. And yet, given the rates of marrying out among diaspora Jews, and the rates of immigration to Israel of non-re-ligiously accepted Jews, Jews like me, so-called 'non-Jewish Jews', returning Jews, sort of Jews, will soon be in the majority among those with Jewish heritage worldwide.

*

And so conversion connected love and the stranger in the case of May, but with inadvertent consequences, which for me solve the mystery of why Edward Maier was sent away. For while May was very much accepted as Jewish as a single girl, mar-riage to a Jewish boy of Edward's class was another matter.

May herself had sufficient status in the Jewish community; that much is clear to me. The problem, I think, was her lin-eage: issued and issuing. May's conversion indicated to others that she needed to *become* Jewish, rather than *being* Jewish, by birth. And contra Shababo's own words, in the eyes of some, May's children would therefore be insufficiently Jewish. But if it is the conversion and what required it that ultimately pre-vented marriage to any of those handsome Jewish boys, this also in turn propels my mother's exodus from Singapore, and into the arms of my gentile father, whom she meets just over six months later. The logic seems to me clear and, at least before I began this journey, I agreed with it: if you can't get in, get out.

Now as I write, I feel I have something to reclaim.

Of course, this question of why you couldn't *become* Jewish *enough* needs answering. If my focus in trying to figure out my own identity has to be on May, it's because she provides me with the umbilical cord linking me to all the past lives in the camphorwood chest and to my own Jewish identity. Why the conversion of the apparently already Jewish May was necessary in the first place reveals a convoluted knot in that cord that will need untying. To do this, I'll need to go back into the lineage.

8. The Worlds

After a four-week boat journey from Singapore, she steps onto the gangplank at Tilbury Docks to meet my father. I can easily recognise my mother. She's wearing the outfit she has designed and sewn herself, the sketch of which she sent to Keith just before she left. From a distance, her 'Dior' suit makes her look a bit like Jackie K. The wool is the colour of uncertain English skies. I recognise her because of the exceptional stylishness.

My parents' London house is stuffed with my mother's clothes. Her dresses fight their way out of the wardrobes, looking for air and space. Ball gowns. Little black numbers.

Sequined jackets. Business suits. Don't even get me started on the shoes – as my father says. My mother admits she has a 'penchant' for shoes. They are her literal Achilles' heel.

After decades of moving around the world with the Army, my parents settled in London, just in time for me to come home and live with them, once I was expelled from the boarding school. Free of travel and the Army when Keith retired, May ran a recruitment agency, which she set up in Sloane Street, in the height of a recession in the 1980s. From Sloane Square to Knightsbridge, she walked with her quick, determined pace along the row of designer shops, slowing for the shoe displays. If she saw shoes she liked, she bought several pairs, in assorted colours. Although I joked about my mother's habit ('the Imelda Marcos of southwest London') and called it 'superficial', secretly I was proud always to have the best-dressed mother. She oozed confidence and control, but also warmth and charm.

The business, the walking, the working; the buying, the shoes. I think of May seeking control of her own pace and fate, a life of her own design after she left the community in Singapore. She arrived in London that leaden spring without a winter coat. As even the 'Dior' wool suit wasn't warm enough, a cousin's mother lent her one of her own coats. When you travel, especially far or in hurry, you can't take much.

The last time May had travelled such a long way on a boat she had taken much less – certainly no chest, no coat, no suits. The few precious possessions she and her family had, they wore, or kept close by in the odd bag, or carried hidden, sewn, along with a little money, into a pillow slip. That was a vastly different journey, and May was just a toddler. It was February 1942, and she fled Singapore, hurriedly with her family, on the eve of the Japanese invasion. They scrambled aboard the very last ship to leave the burning city. And for the war period, they were refugees in India.

Journeys are like legacies, I think: driven by a mixture of choice, chance and circumstance. I find it isn't easy to separate these strands. My mother's leaving Singapore cuts our family's physical tie to Asia and to her ancestral past. Her archive is my only route back.

Yet how much did May really map her own design? How much was she compelled by larger patterns? The burning question to ask about my mother's life, and about my relationship to Jewish legacy, I realise, is at what point these threads – choice, chance, circumstance – separate. For if traditionally Jewishness can only be passed on to children by the mother, to keep the legacy alive, every Jewish child has to choose to take on the ancestral story. To be Jewish means to take it in, and to continue to trace the pattern, forward and backward.

*

For much of my life. I absolutely didn't want to continue any pattern. I became particularly (literally) conscious of this when it came to clothes.

Before we were teenagers, my mother often made our clothes. If she had leftover material from sewing an item for herself, she used this to make me something. A coat. A pair of trousers.

I wasn't sure how I felt about this. On the one hand, I liked the association with my mother and the attention. We were intimate. We were connected. On the other hand, I didn't want to be an offshoot, an offcut. It felt too close, too projective. I knew I couldn't be, and therefore didn't want to be, an extension of my mother. I needed to determine my own pattern.

Still, I never stopped admiring my mother's ingenuity, the way she could create clothes that looked not only professionally tailored but absolutely in time with the latest designs.

*

On her steamer departing from Singapore harbour in 1961, May held one end of a roll of actual thread. Esther, who stood on the dockside, held the other end. As the SS *Corfu* pulled away and the thread unspooled, they were still for a while connected: mother and child; May and the island that had been her home. Although my mother can't remember what happened to the thread – whether one of them let go and if so which one – I like to think that the thread pulled in half between them, as gently and inconspicuously as the steamer would have had to wind its way through fishing boats, Malay praus, cargo ships and tankers, to make it out to the open sea.

The thread is an irresistible symbol to me: of connection and conjoining; of the ties that continued to bind her back, even as May couldn't wait to move forward to Keith. I can feel the attraction drawing her to my father. But there's also a huge sense of loss, emanating particularly from Esther, a cavernous ache May comes to share that makes leaving harder. May writes in her letters she found it 'so hard to part from' her mother, who watches her go, with so much silent 'sadness in her eyes', that May knows 'she weeps in her heart.' Esther's sadness holds back a story.

There is also May's attachment to the world she had always known, now to be exchanged for an England only imagined. In her twenty years, May had chosen to leave Singapore only once, on a volunteering trip to a nearby island. She had become almost immediately homesick and had to return home early. The thread that continues to reach out in the wind is also that attachment to Singapore.

It's new hope for May

TWENTY - two - year-old May Elias, who has never been away from Singapore, left for England recently to learn how the other side of the world lives.

An experienced stenographer, she hopes to find employment in London where she will make a temporary home on her own.

Looking at May, petite and utterly feminine, I expected her to have a few misgivings at the prospect of going to a country quite strange and unknown to her.

But on the contrary, she said: "Oh, no. I am not one bit afraid of going alone to stay in London. I hope to find work soon. "In fact it has been my childhood dream to see what that city looks like. I know it will be a hard life, minus the luxuries I have had at home."

May is willing to go through the mill and find out for herself how to live on a budget, make new friends and gain more working experience.

When you leave, even voluntarily, there is always push as well as pull, ties perhaps already run threadbare that departure finally snaps. As my mother and I reread her letters from the eve of her emigration, she is shocked to discover how radical her leaving was, and less the physical departure than her emotional breaking loose. She is taken aback to discover how she began cutting free before she left the island. She is judgemental of the impetuous young woman she was. She regrets how her twenty-year-old self writes about her family, her culture, her religion, especially her father. She realises now what he felt as he sang her songs about leaving, having no home and every country being strange. 'Poor Papa,' she says, 'I broke his heart.' She feels this so strongly as we read and talk, it's almost as though she has become him.

Poised in middle age, I'm more sympathetic. I try to convince her that, at the age she was, everyone speaks harshly about family and home, particularly to lovers and outsiders. I remember how teenage punk me pushed her away. It seems that for both of us the guilt increases over time, so I understand my mother's remorse. Our legacy is also one of guilt towards parents. It's a prickling self-questioning not wholly separable from Jewishness.

Yet still, I wonder. What was the bigger Singapore beyond the Jewish community that May couldn't bear to leave, and at the same time couldn't wait to leave behind?

*

Some months before she left Singapore, and after Keith had already sailed aboard the *SS Oxfordshire*, on his sleepy, food-laden way back to England, May went to have her fortune told. As the only time she ever saw a clairvoyant, May must have had her doubts about this all-or-nothing throw-of-the-dice decision to come to my father. Because of the yawning distance, she would be able to come back to Singapore next only after several years, and after then only ever on fleeting visits; so that she would count the number of times she saw her mother on the fingers of both hands, and her father on those of just one hand.

My mother tells me that she was more secure about coming to England, less sure about my father. After the passion of those two months, and even during the conflagration that was their correspondence, she had time to wonder: were they really so suited? He was a materialist, she an idealist. The fortune-teller didn't make the decision for her. That was already made; her passage was booked; the camphorwood chest bought. But the fortune-teller's prophecy did give May the courage to make the journey.

The fortune-teller was Lebanese and she brought with her to Singapore the ancient Arabic practice of coffee reading, itself adapted from the even more ancient Chinese art of tea reading. These arts of divination – cosmopolitan, exchanged – were pre-Islamic. In her own community, the fortune-teller was a stranger who had to practise her gift in secret.

But across other communities in Singapore, Badriah – for so the fortune-teller was called – was famous. She was so famous for her powers of prophecy that she makes an appearance in a novel written by my mother's cousin, Moshe Elias, about a Jewish childhood in cosmopolitan Singapore set before, during and just after the Second World War. In Moshe's fictional version, 'Rashidah', Badriah is the person whom Singapore Jews go to see when they 'know something is wrong'. One scene in his book describes the ritual of her coffee reading with an evocative characterisation. 'She got up, pulled her skirt out of her rear cleavage, waddled off, and returned with a smell of strong coffee. Drink, she said, and leave a little. . . . More, she said, until your lips feel powder. She covered the cup with the saucer, flipped it, circled a palm three times over it, said a prayer, and let it stand.'

I meet 'Uncle' Moshe to find out more about Badriah. Moshe is really my second cousin, but to show respect I've always called him 'uncle'. His thick beard, now white, and intelligent, blinking eyes used to make me think as a child of the pictures in the book of Bible stories my mother gave me, particularly of Uncle Moshe's Hebrew namesake, Moses. Nicely, over cups of coffee, Moshe tells me about Badriah: 'She'd sit there chatting to you. Then when the feeling was coming on, she would go and brew you a coffee. Even the Jews who had left Singapore would send their coffee cups from abroad back to her for their reading, they thought so much of her.'

To May, Badriah said: 'You will travel a long way from here. You will marry a white man. You'll have two and a half children. You'll never be very rich, but you'll always be comfortable. You don't have to worry about your mother. Worry about your father.'

Everything Badriah said came true.

*

The world Badriah seems to have walked right out of was called – perfectly – the Worlds. The Worlds is the most evocative place my mother describes to me when I ask her about what she left behind in Singapore. She makes it sound like a magical alternative to her daily life. In my mother's memory, the Worlds exists in a frozen moment: before radical change in her family's life and in Singapore.

The Worlds was a mixture of old world's fair, modern-day amusement park, and city entertainment district. Before the Cathay Cinema, before radio ownership, the Worlds provided the main recreation in Singapore, for adults and children alike. Affordable to all classes and permissible to all races, it was popular with Asians and Europeans, locals and overseas visitors.

Multi-world in many senses, the Worlds was accessed through a gateway, via which, according to the *Singapore Free Press*, 'Electric words proclaim you are entering a "Happy", a "Great", and a "New", world, a world bounded by high fencing, inside which can be found laughter and happiness, and the comedies and tragedies of life.' This gateway provided the looking-glass or back-of-the-wardrobe moment you find in children's books. As in the carvings on our camphorwood chest, here were European castles, Middle Eastern palaces topped by domes and minarets, and, by the time of May's visits, a Chinese pagoda towering at the centre of the main world, New World. In amongst this cosmopolitan architecture was a maze of alleyways, lined with hawker stalls, and giving out onto open-air theatre stages, raised dance floors and sideshows.

The Worlds was a tropical snow globe version of Singapore. A miniature city, it shrank, condensed and coated with glitter all that could be found in the real city of May's childhood. A British rubber planter in Malaya wrote of his adventures in the Worlds the year May was born. Each audience member 'was an unselfconscious display of exotic difference to the other, in this cosmopolitan promenade of people from all walks of life.'

Elsewhere in Singapore, social contact between the white rulers and the diverse ruled was controlled. Places of leisure were either for locals or colonials, not both. Even the colonial clubs carefully selected their members according to pedigree. Such was the case with the swimming club Keith visited, the yachting club, and the Tanglin where, as late as 1960, my parents being together was met with disapproval.

In the years of May's childhood, the '30s and '40s, the gap between Asians and Europeans was much wider. The British developed what one historian has dubbed 'Singaporitis': racial arrogance mixed with blindness to historical change. J G Farrell satirises the British in Singapore in this period in his novel *The Singapore Grip*. Farrell shows how it took the war to puncture this imperialist ego. In the novel, the only legitimate meeting place between Asians and Europeans before the war, in the racially compartmentalised Singapore ruled by the British, and the only place to begin an East-West love story, was my mother's Worlds. The Worlds turned upside down the normal imperialist rules, those of ruling by racial division.

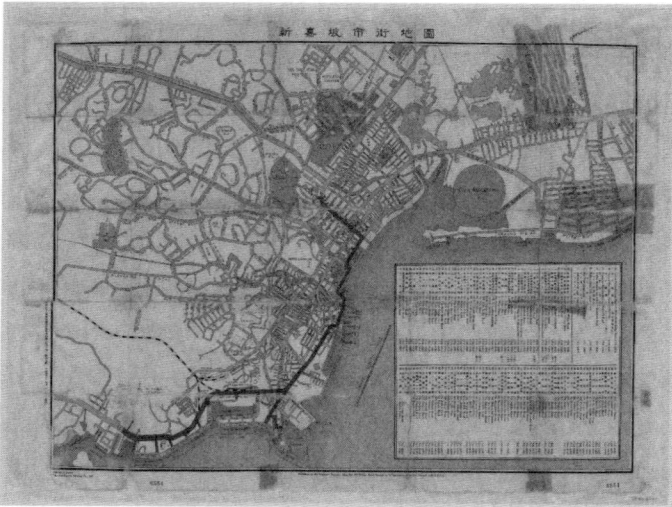

English-Japanese map of Singapore, 1938, the year May was born, showing major roads, rivers, railway, buildings, hospitals, markets – and the Worlds. Published by Singapore Japanese Club. Printed in Japan. Source: Vera Johnson. Courtesy of National Archives of Singapore.

And the Worlds is where I picture May in her early years. Here she is, taking a ride on a ghost train, gripping the hand of an older sibling. Here she is, standing next to my grandmother, in front of a stage showing wayang, the Singapore Chinese opera. I find her transfixed by the actors' gaudy costumes, their reedy high singing, the clashing cymbals. She stops before the swashbuckling heroes advertised on film posters, Errol Flynn, with sword and breeches, or Johnny Weissmuller, near naked and swinging through the trees. She watches *ronggeng,* the traditional Malay *jogget,* or dancing. Circling her hands and lifting her feet, she mimics the elegant choreography of the women.

She isn't yet old enough to visit the tea dances in the New World. But if she was, she would see couples doing the foxtrot, the waltz, the Lambeth Walk, the cha-cha, the rumba, inside dancehalls and under bright lights. Chinese couples, the men in suits, the women in cheongsams; Chinese girls and European men; Eurasian girls and European men. The walls are lined with taxi girls who partner a man on the dance floor, and the rumour is maybe more. For the Malay rubber planter in the '30s, as much as for my soldier father in the '50s, these girls provided the intimate colonial-Asian contact that was otherwise taboo.

The Malay planter notes that the waiving of the colour bar in the Worlds was 'almost complete'. For you wouldn't see a European woman dancing with a local man, as Keith also doesn't find local men at his parties during his weekend leave beyond the Worlds. Nor would you see cross-cultural intimacy in the more reputable sites of entertainment outside the Worlds. And in this permissibility, some British at the time consider the Worlds a little seedy.

May comes with her family only as a rare treat. For the visit May and her sisters are given identical outfits to wear. For days before, she watches Esther cut their dresses from the same pattern, in progressively smaller sizes, then sew them from the same roll of cloth. Sally first, May's impish much older half-sister. Then May. Then June, a year younger than May, pale-skinned and in Western terms more beautiful, who will also go on to do some modelling. Katie next, the joker. Hannah, the most vulnerable, without a bad bone. Julie, the baby. The brother, treasured amongst all these sisters, David – whom they called Sunny – had his clothes bought.

Walking around the shows in her new dress, May feels like a princess. The family walk and talk and laugh, building a moment she will remember seventy years later, passing it to me, as the family passed between them the ten-cent newspaper cone of channa, the chickpeas fried in spice until they are nut-crunchy. May's father buys her *kueh lapis*, the Malay rainbow-coloured cake she loves. She savours the combination of pandan leaf, coconut and sugar. She succumbs to the cake's softness and sweetness, watching its colours disappear, layer by layer.

*

Chacha Haron is on stage! – Jacob's older brother. *Chacha* is Hindi for 'uncle', and he is always 'chacha', never 'uncle'. He's about to perform his one-man show, a riddle in answer to a challenge posed by the audience. Pronounced 'Haroon', the Arabic rather than the Hebrew or English phrasing, 'Aaron', Haron is the most talented of Jacob's three brothers.

Timur, Barat, Utara, Selatan
Inche Kassim punya kekayan
My name is Kassim Bhabha
renowned in North, South, East and West.

Constantinople, Turkey;
Baghdad, Yemen, Aden, Tripoli;
Bombai, Hindustan, Karikal, Pondicherry;
Hyderabad, Lahore, Afghanistan, Delhi.

Haron is a harlequin of Asian difference. His song tells the tale of an Arab trader ('Inche Kassim'), who travels all over the East, from 'Karikal, Pondicherry' in South India ('Hindustan'), to 'Constantinople, Turkey' in the Near East, from Aden and Yemen in the south of the Arabian Peninsula, to Baghdad in the north in the Middle East. While not himself a trader, Chacha Haron makes a living by telling stories about being one. His song moves backwards and forwards between different languages, sometimes translating, sometimes not.

The way my mother describes it, Haron's talent seems to have been for a kind of narrative improvisation. He was given a subject by the audience, and within the hour he was back on stage, ready to perform his one-man riddle, to meet the challenge of his commissioning audience. In May's childhood, he is a star of *bangsawan,* Malay cabaret, and the largest and most well-known *bangsawan*, is here, in the New World. Haron's performances draw the sultans from across Malaya, including the wealthiest and most legendary among them, Sultan Ibrahim of Johor, along with his entourage.

Haron embodies the spirit of this theatre. While its seed was traditional Malay – the Malay word *bangsawan* can also mean 'nobleman' – British colonialism made the art form cosmopolitan. Haron was nothing if not cosmopolitan. He, along with his family, was Jewish from Iraq, brought to Singapore by colonialism, after a stay in India. Chinese, Arabs, Indians,

other Easterners and Westerners too, came to the Straits Settlements and Malaya, drawn to work for the empire. And with
them, they brought their stories and languages. As in Haron's
performance, these cross-pollinated, infused each other and
produced hybrids. In *bangsawan,* you could see an English
version of 'Aladdin and his Wonderful Lamp', morphing into
a Hokkien version in Chinese costumes. You went from the
'Goddess of Thibet: A Tragedy of Exorcism', to 'A Trip to Fairy-
land or Hawaii Majlis'. You were swept up by djins in Nepal,
nights in Shanghai, and a 'scandal' in Bombay. You could even
see *bangsawan* Shakespeare, with a Malay Prince Hamlet taking a steamer to university in Sumatra instead of Denmark, his
mother a saronged Sultana, and his stepfather a baggy-panted
Rajah. When my mother tells me her memories, I think that the
characters of Chacha Haron's Worlds could have stepped right
out of our camphorwood chest carvings.

The gorgeous backdrops in themselves told you stories.
They were not to be ignored. If you saw gardens, you knew it
meant love. Forests and jungle were fighting. Sand meant exile;
blue seas, travel; blue sky, heaven. In *bangsawan,* anything could
happen. Women floated into the air, live snakes danced, soldiers
fought as if they had superpowers. You could be or become anything. You could fall in love and be instantaneously, and with the
help of ropes and scene changes, transported to heaven. In the
nick of time, you would be rescued from disaster. Most wonderfully, the point of all fairy tales, you could be who you have
always dreamed you want to be. I can't help finding my mother's
own story of transformation and passion in these fables.

In a kind of *oompa-oompa* rendition, my mother remembers
most of the words to one of Haron's songs. She laughs at the

memory of Haron's clownish act. But almost every time she sings it to me, she changes the places, not only the order but sometimes the locations themselves.

So I find myself in the reverse position of Chacha Haron's audience. I have the end but not the origin that would resolve the riddle. I will have to reassemble the family trade routes, as my mother and I descend deeper into the camphorwood chest; the *kueh lapis* in reverse.

*

May had been born not far from the Worlds, at Kandang Kerbau hospital, in Malay meaning 'buffalo shed', a remnant of Singapore's recent rural history, in Little India. An English lady doctor delivered her, May's first imprint of Englishness. And so Jacob will always call this daughter 'the English one', which becomes another prophecy. Esther's labour was hard. When the baby finally appeared, she gasped for air, her face blue. Her birth certificate, not issued until 1950 twelve years later – for reasons I myself will only fathom later – left her unnamed.

At first, I'm led to believe that Jacob and Esther had too little time to register her, or maybe they didn't trust the authorities. Or, as my mother herself initially suggests, they had to come up with a name that her non-English-speaking Chinese mother could say and remember. My mother was called May, later children in their turn June and Julie (i.e. July), although none was born during these months. It was as if her parents had found in the English calendar a workable system of naming and were dutifully working through it.

My mother remembers her toddler life in out-of-focus and partial pictures. Objects, places, even some relatives, are only transitory impressions. Their house has a big basket in it. Here they keep the rice. There is a trunk of some sort, a chest. The start of a family archive, I like to dream. Stored in the chest is my grandmother's most precious item. For some reason – again these details will only make sense to me as I come to piece them together with earlier generations and more deeply buried treasures in our camphorwood chest – a scrap of peach-coloured organdie cloth. Her mother was at home all day and quiet. Her father, the joker, singer, talker, went out to work, his voice filling the house on his return.

May was the first of her parents' children, but Jacob already had two daughters, much older than her. They were not her mother's children but the children of her father's first wife. Jacob had become a widower soon after meeting Esther. May found these relationships confusing. The younger of these children, Mimi, had been fostered out after their mother's death. When Mimi's foster mother brings her to visit, May knows Mimi is a sister of sorts, but the visits indicate that she is not fully family. When Jacob went to collect Mimi to bring her to live with them after the war, Mimi was terrified of this stranger, her father whom she barely knew.

The house bustled with visitors. Chacha Haron, with his songs easy for a child to love the best, May knew was her uncle. Poor Windy (he was always 'poor'), a Jewish trishaw-puller, as thin as a stick insect, came for meals. Gomez, who wafted the smells of his Portuguese-Indian curry house into the flat. Abbas and his son Akbar; Muslim and Malay, May understood, but their families were so close they felt related. And then there was Donald, so handsome and regal they called him Prince, who spent so much time at their flat and for whom Jacob always drew up the chair closest to his. May noted the intimacy, more even than between her father and Chacha Haron. But she never called Prince 'uncle'.

Mimi's older sister, Sally, lives with them, and May loves this half-sister dearly. There are ten years between them, and Sally is like a second mother, caring for her when Esther is busy cooking, sewing, shopping. Sally takes May everywhere, carrying her to the side of her young, straight body. My mother is still convinced this is what made her legs go bandy, so that she has never been able to put her knees anywhere near together.

The photographs tell me of the limited means of this family. Here is May, an angelic-faced brown girl, sincere and naïve, but serious and grown up before her time. Here she wears pyjamas and is barefoot in the street; here, simple cotton dresses, probably made by Esther.

So how did May find her way out?

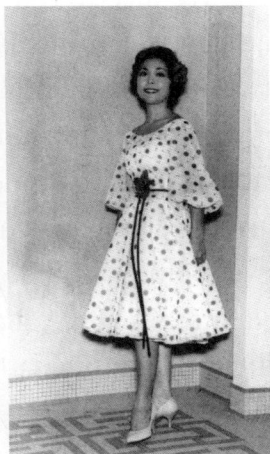

*

In an uncustomary reversal of our usual meet-ups, my mother comes to visit me in Yorkshire. Amazingly, the small country house near my village is putting on an exhibition of fashions of the 1950s. From their modest clothes collection, they have mustered up an exhibition, the 'Age of Glamour'. Touring the displays together, my mother and I admire the 'tea dresses' with their full skirts and bold prints. In the woollen or tweed 'pencil' dresses, we spot a match with her Dior sketch. In the evening dresses, we note how the cutaway necklines gain drama by being worn (to the opera, to the theatre) with matching, over-the-elbow gloves. In the floor-length gowns in taffeta and chiffon, I find an echo of her own glamour outfits in London.

We learn how women's clothes transformed dramatically after the Second World War. Make-do-and-mend, masculinised straight-up-and-down austerity was thrown off. The new decade heralded designs that exhibited the female figure, with an emphasis not seen since the Victorian bustle and music hall. Fashion's newly discovered love of femininity launched star designers, shows, and media spreads. Along came Dior, the New Look: 'Couture'. And this meant models. Real live women, sometimes called 'mannequins', referring not as now to the plastic dummies in shop windows, were in demand to 'perform' the clothes. Dressing was again theatre.

At our exhibition, I find even I, who cares so little about fashion and knows so little about women's clothes, am seduced by the surprising combination of extravagance and sharpness. So much is new to me: the strapless 'swim-dresses'; the back-seamed stockings; the wired corsets. Definitely the cone-shaped 'bullet bras'.

But to my mother these clothes are familiar. Indeed, she had modelled some.

In her letters to Keith, May mentions that she was taking on 'a little modelling' to help towards her passage to England. Below the letters in the chest which contain the Dior sketch, the next layer down, are what my mother calls her 'modelling albums'. She has always been shy of showing these, not taking her role or this moment – her role in this moment in Singapore – seriously. But here, among the photographs, are a number of newspaper clippings, all of which are about my mother the model.

I take them out and examine them carefully, one by one. My mother tries to hurry me along. 'Why are you so interested in these? They're not important. It was just something I did on the side. You're making too much of them.' But I sense that the modelling was transformative, not only bringing May money, but also helping her design her way out of a poor Singapore childhood. The modelling shots perform who my mother ends up becoming.

Here is May as the 'face of Lancôme, Singapore', a recurrent advertisement – 'preferred by the elegant women of the world'. Here she is in *Her World*, 'Singapore's most established monthly women's magazine with the highest readership'. Here she is in the *Straits Times*. She is model for L'Oréal and Dior. She is a popular 'mannequin' at the Singapore Model Academy. And she is a member of 'Joan Booty's Mannequin and Charm/ Glamour Club'.

make-up
by
Lancôme

This blue satin dress from
Janialna shows the new Paris cardinal
collar. And heightening the look of
Parisian chic is make-up by
Lancôme of Paris—the
high-fashion cosmetics
preferred by elegant
women the world over.
There's a colour and
texture specially
planned for you.
Nail Varnish 50
shades • Lipsticks
2 textures Powder
38 blends • Quick
Make-up for all skins

LANCÔME
of Paris

In these shots, May flaunts dresses rather than simply wearing them. Soft silk falls away in folds, or is double-skirted, trumpeting opulence as well as femininity. Tailored suits, neatly tapered to end mid-calf, hug her form. Her tops are low-cut, sleeveless, strapless. Or in stiffened taffeta, they have tightened half-sleeves. Her hats are precarious and outrageous. When modelling evening dress, her hair is worn up, held in place with jewellery such as a rose or a tiara. She is adorned with pearl necklaces and orchid-shaped earrings. And the shoes. Well, don't even get me started on the shoes, I find myself echoing my father. These are absolutely not the 'flatties' Keith in his letters wanted her to bring to hilly old Bath. They are unbearably pinched and dangerously heeled.

At the time May owned a single pair of high-fashion shoes. Although she was the embodiment of Singapore glamour, she couldn't afford to own anything she modelled. She was the main breadwinner in her family and she gave most of what she earned to sustain them. But one pair of shoes May couldn't resist. These were dark green suede and each heel – fantastically, crazily – consisted only of a solid brass hoop. She is often wearing them in model shoots and on the catwalk. Her legs are elegantly arranged. In these shoes, any bow seems to have disappeared.

See how a ragged, poor child is transformed into. . . what? A top Singapore model? A princess looking for her Prince Charming? A poor migrant desperate to come to London, European metropolis of fashion? A girl from a traditional Jewish family to an independent young woman in a secular modern world? Or all of these? Even down to the shoes, it's the story of Cinderella.

Fifties fashions promised to fulfil women's dreams. These clothes transported their wearers to a world of opulence and romance. In some of the modelling shots, May looks to me like the *bangsawan* heroine she would have seen on the Worlds' stages as a child. As the work brought May some necessary cash, modelling helped her to create a route out.

Because she couldn't afford to buy what she was modelling, May copied the designs and sewed her own clothes, or had them made cheaply by local tailors. She was very proud of a spotted dress she sewed for her eighteenth-birthday party. The photograph of May in this dress for me captures her in the moment of transformation. She inhabits the frock, beaming her smile more naturally than in the mannequin shots. But she is already remaking herself as someone else, in another life; no longer the child who could barely afford a visit to the funfair.

May had to use the material that was available in her world. But alongside her clothes, her later journeys mapped her own designs. Such, indeed, was the Dior Jackie K. suit that she was wearing when she arrived at Southampton to meet Keith.

*

Whereas the design of Chacha Haron's life shrank down and he didn't get out.

Haron Elias ended up living in a cage. The Jews built him a corrugated iron and wooden shelter, attached to the Maghain Aboth synagogue. My mother tells me that this way the Jewish community could look after him. But another of my mother's cousins, who was older than her and who stayed in Singapore, tells me that Chacha Haron went mad – that people could see 'all his business', his bodily functions. In near public, he had to be 'cleaned up'. May watched all this too.

It was the war that broke Haron and his Worlds. Under the Japanese occupation of Singapore, the Worlds started to disappear. The Japanese censored *bangsawan*'s traditional subjects, Chacha Haron's cross-world love. They used the stories instead for propaganda, meting out punishment to 'resistors'. On the site of Great World, the Japanese built a prison camp, milking the gambling dens for revenue, while torturing Australian prisoners behind the scenes.

But when the British returned, under the Malayan Emergency, *bangsawan* remained censored. Everyone, it seems, was fearful of this wayward art. And when Malaya finally became independent, the cross-world love of *bangsawan* never came back. The cosmopolitan mix was put through a sieve of pure 'Malayan-ness', an attempt to get back to some never-existing pure form.

In his semi-transparent hut, Chacha Haron was still on the public stage. I watch him, as he replays in his head and in his broken fashion the performances that made him so famous on the stage of the Worlds. I understand what drove him mad.

9. The Ankle Bells

The camphorwood chest has become like a dressing-up box. Through the power of its stores and its stories, it has transformed my mother into a character I didn't know. And now, she becomes another. . .

My mother and I return her modelling albums to the chest. From a stash below – we're digging deeper, time-travelling – we take out the only jewellery. Two pieces from her childhood, both now very tarnished. As I rub them clean (feeling like Aladdin; what treasures will we find now?), my mother watches. She marvels at my persistence in removing the patina from her past. After much polishing, the two pieces turn out to be silver, of sorts.

There is a Chinese bracelet, so tiny that it could only have been worn by a baby. It tells me that, while they never had a lot of money, in Singapore, before the war, May and her family didn't live in complete indigence. Then there's an anklet, larger, which would have been worn by May as an older child. It has no decorative engraving, and it feels more primitive than the bracelet. Interspersed around its loop are tiny bells, looking like imitation nutmegs, which still sound a gentle jingling. Immediately I recognise it as an Indian dancing anklet. It's squashed out of shape, and one bell has broken off completely, as if from the uncertain movements of their young wearer.

Suddenly my mother remembers. As a refugee child in India, having fled the fall of Singapore, she used to sleepwalk. She must have been disturbed by the camp surroundings, not to mention the traumatic journey on the last boat out of Singapore. Were the bells to alert her parents, or to wake the child herself, if she walked at night?

Between the bracelet and the anklet: the war, and the fall of Singapore.

*

There has been much written about what Churchill called 'the worst disaster and the largest capitulation in history'. 'The honour of the British Empire and of the British Army is at stake', Churchill said on the eve of the fall. 'The whole reputation of our country and our race is involved.' There has been much written from the British point of view, that is: taking apart why Singapore fell to the Japanese, and the experience of white colonials under the Japanese occupation. There has been much, in other words, on what Churchill meant by 'our race'. There has been a good deal less presented from the non-white colonised perspective, and very little on Singapore Jewish experience.

Every year in the UK, I mark Holocaust Memorial Day. As I light candles and attend lectures, I'm conscious that so much is now known about the effect of war on Jews in Europe, yet so little is recorded and shared about the internment, killing and disappearance of Jews in Japanese-occupied Asia. Singapore's war was no Holocaust. But this is an episode that reshaped many communities in Singapore, especially the Jewish community, that determined the future of an island as an independent city-state, and that hastened the end of two empires, the British and the Japanese. It's a story that deserves to be told.

The story of the war also unites, and then splits apart, members of the Elias family.

*

When Japanese planes began bombing Singapore, at the end of 1941, Singaporeans tried to continue as normal. Even on the night of 7 December, when the American fleet in Pearl Harbor had been obliterated – thus clearing the way for the Japanese air offence on Singapore – dancing continued, uninterrupted, both in the colonial preserve of Raffles Hotel, and in the multi-ethnic hodgepodge of the New World. In just a few hours, as people watched Chacha Haron or sipped their Slings, the Japanese crushed American defence in Hawaii; invaded Hong Kong and the Philippines; landed troops in Thailand and north Malaya; and began the assault on Singapore. The Japanese effectively danced across the islands of the Pacific and the South China Sea, an easy-step waltz, with no opposing partner.

Raffles Place, the heart of colonial and commercial Singapore, where my parents would later meet for lunch or tea, was one of the first places to be bombed. Robinson's Department Store, where May would buy last-minute things for England, had its windows blown out. Subsequent raids hit shophouses, the distinctive Chinese-run terraced stores, where the owners lived above. They caught fire as if they were tinderboxes. Roads were gouged with craters and became unnavigable. Wrecked cars littered streets. Restaurants and other meeting places shut down. Those who ventured out could happen on unclaimed, sometimes unidentifiable, body parts. Fires were left to burn, and a black pall hung over the entire city. With a destroyed sewage system and unburied bodies, Singapore stank of shit and death.

The first death in the family was great-uncle Joseph, the elder brother of Jacob and Chacha Haron. Joseph couldn't resist going gambling during the worst bombardment. He ignored his sister Flora who pleaded with him to stay at home.

Flora's daughter and May's cousin Hannah Kichi, then twelve years old, was taken by her mother to a mortuary to see what was left of her uncle. Flora spat the betel nut from her mouth as they went inside the building. She led her daughter by the hand to study the body in pieces. 'This is what death is like', she said. 'Never be afraid. This will happen to you and it will happen to me.'

What was Flora preparing her daughter for? It's a harsh thing to say to a child. Was this a traumatised person speaking?

The British realised they could no longer defend the city once the water mains were destroyed. The fires couldn't be controlled, and the population was at risk of an epidemic. On

31 January 1942, with 30,000 defeated Allied troops having streamed into Singapore from fallen Malaya, British engineers were ordered to blow up the Causeway, in an attempt to slow the Japanese invasion. But the three-quarter-mile bridge between Singapore and Malaya, what Han Suyin called the 'umbilical cord of stone linking Singapore to Malaya' – the love road that Keith flew across in his Armstrong Siddeley – proved fatally indestructible. Within days the Japanese had managed to rebuild the Causeway enough to cross at low tide.

On 7 February – the day after May and her family managed to escape from Singapore – the Japanese occupied Pulau Ubin, the island to the northeast of the city. By 13 February, the occupying forces were pouring into the city itself. On 15 February, Chinese New Year's Day, British command surrendered. And on the next day, Churchill was broadcast on the radio: 'I speak to you all under the shadow of a far-reaching military defeat. It is a British and Imperial defeat. Singapore has fallen.'

*

In the British story, much is made about which compass point the British guns were directed towards, and to what extent mistaken assumptions about the Japanese point of entry were to blame for the defeat. But the biggest weakness in the British defence of Singapore was the British mythology built around 'Fortress Singapore', the ideal of Singapore as the 'Eastern bastion' of the British Empire. Behind this lay the myth of the invincibility of the empire itself, and behind this lay unadulterated British racism, particularly towards Asians. Up until the final hour, Churchill was urging Singapore command, General

Arthur Percival, not to surrender the island, even at the cost of British troops and the entire local Asian population. Those first six weeks of 1942 exposed the racially divisive foundation on which colonial rule had fragilely rested.

Churchill was right in one regard. The loss of Singapore meant that the British Empire would never be confidently restored. What Churchill called the worst disaster, the Asian residents of Singapore describe as 'the time the white man ran'. Even at the time, when Singapore was bombed on 31 January 1942, future Prime Minister Lee Kuan Yew, then receiving an imperial education at Raffles College, turned to fellow students and teachers and declared, 'That's the end of the British Empire.' After the war, Lee, along with David Marshall, was one of those who helped secure the empire's end.

Having been taught British history and received a similar education, most members of the Jewish community were no different from other non-European residents in initially keeping faith with the British. As Singapore's Jewish community historian Eze Nathan said of his own experience, singling out that most imperialist of British writers, 'Had we not been brought up on the Kipling ethos, the superiority of the unflurried, brave, innovative amateur over the unimaginative professional?. . . We held fast to our belief in the impregnability of our island.'

Yet when Nathan and Marshall volunteered to defend the island, they were at first rejected by the British, on race grounds. The colonial governor issued a directive saying Jews born in the Straits Settlements were 'Asiatic' and thus 'exempt' from military service. 'To our amazement, we were told that we were not needed. This seemed to us a greater blow than any we had yet suffered', Nathan remembers. In truth, the exclusion perpetuated long-held British distrust of Asians. Even before the war no Asians were allowed in government or other senior official positions. And since the enemy of Japan was an Asiatic nation, classifying Singapore's Jews as 'Asiatic' branded them, along with the majority of Singapore's population, as also inimical during the war, almost indistinguishably so from the Japanese.

Historians have compared the evacuation of Singapore in the last days before the city fell to Dunkirk. As in the famous and recently cinematised withdrawal of troops two years earlier from France, the much less familiar flight of mainly residents from Singapore in 1942 is reimagined as a myriad of last-minute miraculous escapes. But in both cases, British or American retrospect seeks to snatch victory from the jaws of what were, in fact, military defeats. When I dig down into the personal stories, I find that the evacuation from Singapore is much more disturbing, particularly concerning Singapore's non-white population, than the label 'Singapore's Dunkirk' suggests.

*

A catastrophe at the beginning of December 1942 stirred the population's first thoughts of evacuation. The Japanese sank the two great British battleships, *Repulse* and *Prince of Wales*, which Churchill had sent to defend Singapore. This event shocked the colony into recognising the likelihood of war reaching Singapore. People of all ethnicities gathered in the harbour to await evacuation instructions from the British. None were forthcoming. The Colonial Office had not only *not* planned for evacuation, it could be said it had a no-evacuation policy. Evacuation was to be limited and on a self-organised basis. The ruling was that there was to be no racial discrimination; and yet, over-whelmingly, those who got on the last boats out of the inferno were white and European. Jewish families, as with other 'Asiatic' groups, were literally left off the boat.

British divide-and-rule was in full operation. For where was Singapore's 'Asiatic' population to go? Australia, one of the main destinations for white colonial evacuees, had a whites-only immigration policy. And although Singapore's colonised residents as subjects of the British Empire could have been brought to Britain on the troop ships that were returning home empty, Britain was busily imposing restrictions on refugees from elsewhere. Jews from Europe seeking asylum from the Nazis were being either turned away by Britain, or classified as 'enemy aliens' and bundled into internment camps around the country.

Only in mid-January 1942, with Singapore flattened and the Japanese speeding down the Malay Peninsula, did Churchill issue evacuation instructions. Military and colonial servicemen were to stay at their posts; their wives and children were to be rescued. Boats of all kinds were requisitioned for this purpose – hence the comparison with Dunkirk. European women and children began leaving in large numbers in late January. Again, no provision was made for locals.

If a film were to be made of 'Singapore's Dunkirk' – and the drama I think could rival the European context, not least because women and children were involved, and the tragedy shines a spotlight on the British Empire's racism – here's how it might look:

Scene one. Panicky evacuees gather outside the tower block of the Cathay Building. Their number is boosted by wounded and defeated military personnel pouring into Singapore from Malaya. Sunburned soldiers in khaki jostle alongside Singaporean civilians in Western dress and different ethnic costumes. Would-be evacuees attempt to make their way to the docks, their numbers bringing traffic to a halt. Europeans try to commandeer cars, but it becomes impossible to move, except on foot and by trishaw or rickshaw.

Scene two. Black smoke thickens over the burning city. The godowns, the port warehouses, are on fire. The pungent smell of burning rubber makes it hard for the people to breathe. Now that defeat seems imminent, the governor has issued orders for all commodities to be destroyed, to prevent them falling into Japanese hands. Godown managers are setting light to their own goods, smashing bottles of Western alcohol, dispersing among their workers and residents other imported foods.

Coughing and with eyes watering, refugees trundle through the smoke to the docks. They lug belongings in carts or on their backs. They carry, hurry and shield their children amidst the creeping throng.

Scene three. People cram onto the docks. Even as they await or attempt to board the few boats, the desperate refugees are bombed and strafed with machine gunfire. Japanese planes fly viciously close and scatter those standing at the edges of the crowd. Neighbours who have been civil with each other for decades fight over fewer and fewer passages. They bribe and beg colonial officials, who are seated impassively behind desks improvised out of boxes. Families are split apart. There is weeping and screaming. The lucky depart.

Meanwhile, ships bringing supplies and reinforcements for the defence of Singapore leave the port empty. Those stranded on the docks gaze at their wake in disbelief.

There was little evacuation of non-white or local Singaporeans. There is no evidence of British-sponsored Chinese evacuations, unless the Chinese were working in the civil service and in very high ranks. These cases were few and without exception men. Contra the command, racial discrimination is precisely the policy practised.

In J. G. Farrell's *The Singapore Grip*, the Chinese Eurasian fictional character Vera Chiang doesn't make it onto the *Felix Roussel*. The *Felix Roussel* – a real ship – was the very boat that would take May and her family to safety, including my Chinese grandmother. In the novel, Vera's 'half-caste' status does her no favours in the eyes of the fictional officials. But in real life as in fiction, decisions to issue visas or exit permits were made based on some official's perception of identity, even on skin colour.

Thus, another scene.

Responding to the call of 'Next!', Singapore Iraqi Jew Ivor Nathan – historian Eze's dark-skinned brother – seats himself in front of the desk of the Australian immigration officer. Following application by their sister, who is lighter skinned, exit permits for the entire family have already been agreed. Ivor needs only to collect the permits. After studying Ivor's skin colour, pen hovering, the official refuses to sign the papers. He offers no explanation, but the family suspects outright racial prejudice. 'Dorothy and Ivor were speechless before this lack of compassion and unforgivable act of discrimination', Eze remembers.

Mother and sister find a captain to take them to Ceylon without permits. They survive the war.

Nathan is interned by the Japanese in Singapore for the duration of the war. He (just about) survives to remember.

Dark Ivor does not survive.

*

And if a film were to be made of this moment, it would have to have a strand that follows Hilda and Zaida Elias, the nieces of my great-grandfather Isaac. Aunt Hilda and Zaida are the other Elias sisters, from the affluent side of my mother's family.

12 February 1942, Japanese soldiers amass across the Causeway. In their respective, well-furnished apartments in Amber Mansions, Zaida, tall, slim, regal, and Hilda, rounder and jollier, stuff clothes into suitcases. The city resounds with rumours that Japanese soldiers are raping women in fallen Malaya. Zaida's husband, Jack, and Hilda's husband, Geoffrey, have persuaded the sisters to leave.

A sergeant in the Royal Army Medical Corps, Jack arrives in a jeep. He drops the sisters at the docks, where they board the *Mata Hari*. The ship flies the Rising Sun Flag – an attempt to dupe the Japanese into thinking it one of their own. It is packed with British evacuees. Seeing men amongst them, Hilda decides she must collect Geoffrey, who is a civilian. Pushing past the protesting captain, she returns to Amber Mansions. She throws some clothes at her surprised husband, and they make their way to the docks. They find the last launch ferrying passengers to the departing ships, but, in the pell-mell of smoke and boats, the launch can no longer locate the *Mata Hari*. The couple are turned away from three other departing ships. In despair, Hilda and Geoffrey head back to Singapore.

Then they spot the *Mata Hari*. Recognising Hilda, the captain allows the couple to board. The sisters – who thought they'd never see each other again – embrace.

All three of the ships that refused Hilda and Geoffrey boarding are bombed. Many of their passengers drown.

The next day as it crawls through the straits of Sumatra, the *Mata Hari* is also bombed, but the bombs fall just wide. The following dawn, they are blockaded by a Japanese destroyer. Japanese soldiers storm the ship. They herd the passengers off at bayonet point onto the island of Sumatra. That night on the pier at Muntok, Zaida, Hilda and Geoffrey lie on cobblestones and cement. The soldiers march between the sleepless evacuees, confiscating watches and jewellery.

At sunrise the prisoners are forced to march three miles inland. They are pushed into a building, which they recognise as a slaughterhouse. Zaida and Hilda are relieved to discover the slaughterhouse has showers, and they bathe their filthy, exhausted bodies. Some evacuees throw away luggage which now seems ridiculous. Women throw off high-heeled shoes and walk barefoot. At this point, the men are separated from the women. Hilda watches Geoffrey go.

Hilda and Zaida are interned in a prisoner-of-war camp on Sumatra, along with other, white, colonial women. Here they remain for the next three and a half years. Here, every morning at 6 a.m., they undergo 'Tenko' – Japanese 'roll call', during which they must stand in the burning sun, so like that flag, until they have been counted, sometimes several times over. Becoming progressively weaker with malnutrition and illness, more and more women collapse each morning. Some die from malaria or malnutrition. The little rice they are given crawls with weevils and worms. They receive no vegetables or fruit. Survivors learn to forage the jungle for greens. Those who eat everything live to tell this story.

Zaida helps to bury the dead. She carries bodies on make-shift stretchers away from the camp and digs their graves.

Zaida lived to tell this story. She left us a twenty-page account of her life, from which I take these details. Titled 'Auto-biography of a Woman Named "Zed"', the memoir was begun when she was ninety and completed four years later, just before she died.

Immediately on release, the sisters search for their husbands. Hilda learns that Geoffrey was imprisoned in a camp close to hers. She receives confirmation of his death. Zaida learns that Jack was captured by the Japanese and taken to build the Bridge over the River Kwai, part of the Thai-Burma Railway. She doesn't know if he has survived or not.

Hoping for news, Zaida decides to visit Jack's family in Aber-tillery – 'a coal-mining town in Wales', she writes. On her boat journey she discovers Jack's fate. For on board is the very doctor who cared for her husband as he died, and the very Army padre who buried Jack.

'The Padre handed me a sealed brass container with his name and date of death', Zaida writes. The part of her story in the film would end with this scene, I think: with Zaida greeting her mother-in-law with this gift – the seal of death of the Welsh soldier whom they both loved. And the mother places the seal in her storage chest, for another family to discover, and years later for some descendant to trace Jack Short's war stories.

Like Keith, Jack was not Jewish; like Keith, Jack was in the military; like Keith, Jack had Welsh roots. Like May and Keith, Zaida and Jack met at a dance; they had married just before the war. After Jack's death, Zaida will become a successful businesswoman. There are many parallels between Zaida and May. Even when she was a child, Jacob used to tell May she was 'just like Zaida'.

*

And what of the Jews who, unlike Zaida, Hilda and May, did not manage to leave the island, those who stayed who formed the majority of the community?

If, for the British, Singapore's Jews were Asiatic and prohibited from joining the defence, for the Japanese, Jews were definitely not Asiatic. There are repeated claims of Japanese admiration for the Jews, a lot by the Japanese themselves after the war, even up to the present day. But Japan adopted the antisemitism of its ally, Nazi Germany. The occupiers made Singapore's Jews identify themselves by wearing armbands with a red stripe and the word *Utai* ('Jew'). Jews had to register and acquire new identification documents. These they were instructed to carry at all times or risk arrest. Within a month of the occupation, the Japanese interned Jews in Changi Jail, including community historian Nathan. Those who failed to register or display their new identification risked being captured and killed.

Such was the fate of Uncle Zeke (Ezekiel) Elias, Zaida and Hilda's eldest brother – the father of Moshe the author – and also Ivor, the darker brother of Nathan, with whom Zeke disappeared. In the early days of the new regime, Zeke, Ivor and another Singapore Jew, Max Wooltz, were together stopped by the Japanese for an ID check. Charged with not having the right documents, they were arrested by the *kempeitai*. They were never seen again.

Hannah Kichi, who stayed in Singapore during the war, told me of 'curfews, internment and near starvation.' Beyond the story of Uncle Joseph, she chose to give me few other details of her experiences. Did that moment of witnessing his body in pieces traumatise her into not telling, perhaps even not remembering? There are silences in the war stories left out of the camphorwood chest.

Decades later as he was growing up without a father, Moshe went to a medium – not Badriah. 'I see a lot of wood', she said. 'I see your father, among trees. There are other men running; there is shooting.'

Before he became a writer, Moshe was a naval architect in Singapore. Then, in the 1960s, Lee Kuan Yew's 'Great Reclamation' project started building along the East Coast, reclaiming land from the sea. Early on in the development, a skeleton was found. Digging by machine was halted, and excavation continued by hand, with men working gingerly with changkols, Malay hoes. More skeletons turned up. Tens, then hundreds, then thousands of remains were unearthed.

With these bones came an answer for those whose loved ones had disappeared under the Japanese. They had been murdered and their bodies fed to the sea. The remains were interred. A war memorial erected over them was opened by Lee in 1967. Its four towers are supposed to symbolise the unity and shared war experience of Singapore's four main races – Malay,

Chinese, Indian and Eurasian. Zeke Elias, along with other Singapore Jews, lies unacknowledged, somewhere between these towers.

Given the disappearance of generations from history, is it surprising that Singapore Jews have continued to put their trust in mystical clairvoyants, to foretell the future and to try to fill gaps in the past? Lives have been eliminated, tenses skipped generations. The work of reconstructing what happened has to be an act of imagination, at once crazy and necessary.

*

An old French postcward (late '40s?) I acquired via eBay.

And so to my mother, and for me therefore the most dramatic of scenes.

May was just over three years old. She remembers nothing of the time. Hence my wanting to put first the scenes I do know. But we know the name of the boat that saved her, and we know that she left with her parents and sisters Sally and June. Her second sister, Mimi, remained with her Chinese foster-mother in Singapore, where she survived the war uninterned, because she was not identified as Jewish, because she was kept safely hidden.

I've studied the *Felix Roussel*'s records from the War Office at the National Archives in Kew, just a cycle ride from my parents' south London home. I've listened to or read testimonies from Jewish refugees who were on the same ship. And even if my mother doesn't remember, I need to get May and her family onto that boat. I need to see them escape the falling, burning city, just forty-eight hours before the Japanese cross into Singapore.

May stands on the dock with her parents, holding her sister Sally's hand. Her mother holds the baby. Her father rubs his hands repeatedly and touches his uncustomary beard. The white of her parents' shirts – Jacob's kurta, Esther's samfu – is pristine. This despite a walk and a wait that, in the mind of a three-year-old, could have taken days or weeks.

A ship is in sight of the harbour. It looks like it's been made by a child, odd parts thrown together. For twenty years the *Felix Roussel* has been used by the Free French Navy to ferry civilians to the French colonies. Now she has been hastily refitted as a British troopship. Towering anti-aircraft guns have been fixed above cabin balconies.

From their place on the docks, the Eliases watch troops on the ship seep up from below and press against the railings of the upper decks. The Northumberland Fusiliers are anxious to land. It has been two weeks since they set sail from Bombay. One in their convoy of three, the *Empress of Asia*, was sunk en route. The men on the *Felix Roussel* do not want to be next.

As the ship noses towards the dock, a steadily increasing whine-buzz can be heard by everyone in this scene, as if a swarm of giant wasps was approaching. The Eliases look up. Japanese planes roll inwards, three waves each of nine planes, as choreographed as a line of chorus dancers. My family watches with the other refugees. They gape in disbelief as the troops are swallowed back below decks and gunners take up defence position. They see two gunners killed in post before the ship can even return a shot.

At this point the Eliases grab their children and scatter for shelter. They find somewhere they can still try to watch.

A massive explosion. The *Felix Roussel* has been hit. Smoke rises from between her two funnels. The fire licks skywards, and with it Jacob and Esther see their dreams of escape go up in flames. May's mouth is an 'O' of astonishment. She is thinking of the Chinese firecrackers she has seen with her mother. But as soon as she catches sight of the unfamiliar horror on her normally impassive mother's face, she begins to cry.

But as suddenly, the *Felix Roussel* is hit again. The second bomb plumps squarely onto the ship's water tank. Water spurts out and extinguishes the fire from the previous hit, without the crew having the opportunity to react. Some will think of this as sheer chance. Jacob will think of it as an act of God. Once the planes have dropped 200 bombs, the skies go quiet again. The *Felix Roussel* lands, and the troops disgorge. They are the last convoy to reach Singapore.

But as soon as the refugees unfold themselves from their hiding places, and May and her family begin to press through the crowd towards the gangplank, the Japanese bombers return. The ship is hit three more times, with each attack stalling the process of boarding. One bomb puts out an engine entirely. But the damage is sufficiently repaired, and the *Felix Roussel* considered seaworthy – or at least worth desperate refugees' last chance of escape.

When the skies finally clear, the refugees resume boarding. That night, 6 February 1942, the Merchant Navy takes onto the *Felix Roussel* just over 1000 women and children, plus some military personnel from the sunken battleships *Repulse* and *Prince of Wales*. Without a tug or any help from the port unmooring, Captain Albert Snowling manoeuvres her out to sea.

On board is space for just over 400. The Eliases sleep in stairways. Or they sleep on deck in life jackets, and below deck every time the sirens sound. They live on Ovaltine and cereal. Or cream crackers and steamed rice cakes. Or *buah kana*, dried fruit Esther has stuffed in a pillowcase, along with some jewellery sewn into seams.

With one engine knocked out, the journey takes twice as long. Eighteen nights. Nine times the Japanese planes return to sink the ship. Nine times they fail. To Jacob and Esther, each familiar with long boat journeys, it feels that the ship zigzags all the way to Bombay. At one point, a plane gets close enough for Sally to claim that she can make out the pilot's face.

On board is a huddle of Jewish women. They hide children under their skirts. They pray constantly, whispering and in more hopeful moments singing the Hebrew liturgy. Already thirteen, Sally wanders from her sisters and parents to join the group. She recites the bits she knows, mumbling the other parts. The ancient prayers. The Shema she knows by heart, since her father has her say it every night: 'Shema, Yisrael. . .'. 'Hear, O Israel. . .'. The *Aleynu*. The *Hashkiveinu*. The Menorah psalm. When the *Felix Roussel* docks in Bombay, Captain Snowling thanks the women as they disembark. He says that only their praying ensured his ship's safe arrival.

For the fifty-year commemoration on Singapore TV, Sally re-enacted her experience. 'I cried and I prayed to God to reach Bombay', she said to the camera, crying again, wringing her hands. For Sally, the scene was still alive. There was no past tense.

*

Once May had reached India, where she turns four, she starts to register her surroundings again. People and places come into focus. She remembers a compound, and within it a small 'dwelling'. Cotton mills. Rolls of cotton and rough calico. The smell of fresh-cut fabric. Lots of people, sewing, selling: a sort of outdoor factory. An area named Byculla. A street called Ripon Road, on which their compound – or is it a hostel? – is located. Wrought-iron gates: to keep people out, or in? Old colonial buildings. Sally still looks after her. They play with a new sister in a crate. May's best friend is a Muslim girl.

In her letters to Keith sixteen years later, May anticipates that, when she revisits Bombay on her voyage to join him, she will remember her time there during the war. But while she can remember patchy details with me now as I push her, in the 1960s she is too caught up with looking forward to that new journey to recapture the refugee child she once was.

The War in Asia as in Europe creates gaps in Jewish memory.

*

5 September 1945. British warships return to Singapore. The three miles from Empire Dock to the Cathay Building are lined with flag-waving, cheering crowds. The Union Jack is restored to government buildings and at Sime Road camp. The old rule is back, but under a new name: the British Military Administration (BMA), led by Lord Louis Mountbatten, Supreme Allied Commander of Southeast Asia.

Documents in the camphorwood chest also recast May. 'Asiatic' no more, her 'nationality' is now given as 'Jew', an identity that post war carries a heavy weight. She is also a 'British Subject of Singapore', but in brackets after her Jewish 'nationality', as if the authorities were aware that the days of British identity in the colony are numbered.

Neither the resumption of British rule in the city, nor May's arrival with her family at the end of March 1946, amounts to a triumphal return. Finding it almost as hard to get a passage back as it had been to leave, May and her family are home, but, as they had been in Bombay, homeless. Over the next five years they pass through a string of refugee camps and temporary shelters. The family are placed in Sime Road, the camp that had been British Command Headquarters. This main transit camp for liberated prisoners of war and returning refugees which is now May's home had also been the final internment site for Singapore's Jews, a spooky connection. May acquires her first toy. It makes for a poignant picture. A girl of seven, among the wooden huts with rattan roofs haunted by the ghosts of prisoners. She squats in muddy puddles, delighted to be making tea out of the dirty rain with a cracked tea-set.

By July, the BMA are able to settle these 'remaining destitute campers', and May's family moves to York Hill Home, a brick house shared with Chinese, Malays and Indians. Each family occupies a single room. May's parents now have five children: Sally, May, June; and Hannah and Sunny, born in India. From boxes of donated clothes brought to the house, May falls in love with a cream-coloured dress with a strawberry appliquéd on its pocket. By the end of 1946, the family is rehoused again, in a colonial bungalow in Short Street, not far from where they lived before the war.

Reading about this period, I'm startled to learn that some conditions were worse under the British after the war than they had been under the Japanese during the war. The weekly rice ration actually fell from what it had been during the occupation, going from 3 *kati* in December 1945 (a *kati* was a Malay measurement equal to about 1 ½ lbs), to 1½ *kati* by May 1947. As a result, the black market thrived, and the BMA was soon satirically glossed as the 'Black Market Administration'. On returning to Singapore, prisoners of war liberated from the Thai-Burma railway were shocked at what the civilian population was still suffering under the British.

My mother remembers a lot about this deprivation.

'Sometimes all we had to eat was boiled rice. Sometimes a small piece of dried fish; sometimes vegetables. One day my sister Sally went to a neighbour to ask for a little soya sauce, something to add taste to her plain white rice. Ma was furious. She told her to take it back immediately. We are not beggars, she insisted. Ma would always wait for us to finish our food first, then if we were still hungry she'd give us food off her own plate.'

In my own childhood, my mother re-enacted this ritual. She sneaked food from her plate onto my own and my brother's plates. She was insistent, at home, and, most embarrassingly, in restaurants. My brother and I scolded her and shuffled the food right back. 'MUM. I've got my own food', we said, defensively, proprietorially. We never went short.

Now I realise that, in giving me her food, my mother had been giving me the gift of life itself.

*

Jacob finds it difficult to get any work and, despite Esther's insistence about not needing handouts, the family become dependent on the Jewish Welfare Board. The Jewish community was much depleted after the war, most of the wealthy having emigrated, to Israel, the UK, Australia, the US. As my grandfather tries to re-establish himself, he takes May to meetings with Indian business friends. May performs the Hindi songs she learned in India. The traders are entranced by this pretty, racially and culturally mixed girl, who knows their music and language. They slip her ten or twenty dollars, which already she knows is a lot of money. She refuses to take it, but they insist. As soon as she gets home, she gives the notes to her parents.

Was the singing a way to get money? I ask my mother. 'I don't know', she sighs. 'We were very poor.'

I'd thought that the Indian anklet with the squashed bells must have been used by my mother as a child for Indian dancing. But my mother is insistent: she performed *no dancing for money*, although she did dance at home for the entertainment of friends and family. It's clear to me nevertheless that every cent counted.

*

Things start to pick up for May's family, also for the Jews and the city, when a former prisoner of war, an intense, up-and-coming politician and lawyer, returns to Singapore and is one of those shocked at what he finds. David Marshall was just as important in May's early life as he was to her teens and twenties. Marshall begins challenging the colonial government first on its failures to resolve the housing shortage for refugees. Under Marshall's vision, the authorities knock down the shared old colonial house and the family are put across the street. Here, on Cheng Yan Place, the Eliases have their own flat, although the kitchen and bathroom remain communal. Schoolgirl May has to wait late into the evenings for all the families to finish cooking and eating before she can do her homework, sitting on the bare kitchen floor.

For her eleventh birthday, she asks her mother, who by then had acquired an old Singer sewing machine, to make her first long dress, with an extravagantly frilled collar, and to buy her some matching high-heeled shoes, also her first pair. When they are moved again, it is to the flats on Short Street that will remain May's home until she leaves Singapore.

My mother and I return to Singapore to retrace these steps of her childhood. We stop at the 'original cake shop', which she was afraid to walk past as a child because the cakes were both too tantalising and unaffordable.

A retired lawyer who took over the business from his mother, Mr Wee has just finished the morning's baking. The shop claims to make 'the best pineapple tarts in Singapore'. Mr Wee gives us a tart to share, fresh from the oven. The pastry melts in my mouth, the pineapple centre is unsweet – precisely a little tart – and the combination is heavenly. We buy several jars of tarts, and Mr Wee says to my mother: 'Oh, yes. I know you. You're one of the Elias clan. I remember, all the sisters, the one brother: June, Sunny . . .'. We tell Mr Wee his pineapple tarts are the best in the world.

Food occupies many of my mother's memories of these post-war years – not surprisingly, I now realise, given the decade of hunger. There was the Chinese man who set up on Bencoolen Street, from whom the children bought *roti pranchis*, French bread, which they took back home and smeared with coconut jam (*siri kaya*), or just margarine that melted while the bread was still hot. Margarine was a treat. They couldn't afford butter. There were once again Malay cakes such as *kueh lapis*. *Mee* came from the *mee tok-tok* man, so called because he announced his arrival with a shout of '*Mee!*', and then hit a small wooden board with a bamboo stick to make the 'tok-tok' reply. As soon as they heard that sound, Sally and May ran down the spiral stairs. Their favourite noodles were from the Indian hawker, who called out '*Mee goreng rebus!*', 'Indian' *mee*: Chinese noodles with Indian curried sauce. The family drank tea made with condensed milk, in glasses that were sturdy enough to withstand the heat.

On Friday evening before Shabbat, May walked with Esther from Short Street down Albert Street to Tekka Pesa, the covered market, to buy bruised fruit and vegetables and help her carry it home. Unbruised was beyond their budget, and May watched her mother count cents from her handbag. She started going again with her mother to Chinese wayang, which played outdoors on Albert Street alongside the cinema. And then there were family outings to Changi beach, where they ate a huge curry made by Esther, or to the Botanic Gardens to feed the monkeys with nuts, which they ended up eating themselves.

My grandmother found it hard to cope with the poverty, not helped by having so many children. When one of the children played up, she arranged them all in a line and thwacked each of them around the legs with a rotan, a rattan cane, the oldest the hardest, but not exonerating any of them, whoever was to blame. 'Ah, sorry Ma! Sorry Ma!', they cried. As the eldest of her parents' children, May learns to carry responsibility for her family on her slight body.

*

May's report cards show she starts school late in 1949. The schools had to be re-established after the war, and the resumption of full registration awaited the return of European teachers.

There were too many children to attend a full day, so they went for five hours, either in the morning or the afternoon. As there was no Jewish school in Singapore and because its language was English, May went to St. Anthony's Convent. Her teachers were nuns and the religious knowledge she acquired here was exclusively Roman Catholic. The school building was round the back of St. Joseph's Church on Middle Road, and whether Jew, Buddhist, Taoist, Muslim, Protestant, or occasionally Catholic, the children were bustled into the huge church every morning for Catholic prayer sessions.

Playing Mary in the scene of the annunciation, as chosen by the Mother Superior, St. Anthony's Convent

Playing Judith in preparation for her beheading of Holofernes, enemy of the Jews, Menorah Club

The report cards give May 100% in English. I'm sceptical, especially as an ('there's no such thing as a wrong or right answer') English professor, but clearly May was already an anglophile ('the English one'). The only history she is taught is English history; the only literature English. The English teacher Mrs Sheares writes that May is her 'best student'. Under this inspiring Eurasian teacher's direction at first, but then soon pursuing her own passions, May reads all the English classics: Shakespeare, Dickens, the Brontës, Kipling and, later, Graham Greene; large, hardcover World Books she gets sent directly from England. She stacks the books admiringly on the bookshelf in her own room her parents have now allowed her. Meanwhile her siblings are bundled together variously around remaining bedrooms and the verandas. It was my mother who got me into literature and writing. For decades now, though, I've been the one to give my mother books to read, which she hoards in stacks and forgets to give back.

The family becomes larger again and, despite improvements in living conditions, the children still can't get enough of the right things to eat. Jacob starts putting pressure on May to leave school and go out to work. He comes into her room one day, pulling her away from a book. He sits on the bed and looks at her squarely. He is firm. There is no sense that she won't fulfil her filial role.

'You are the oldest', he says. 'Old enough now. We need your support. I can no longer work.'

At fifteen and a half, half-way through the academic year, unable even to sit her exams, May finishes school. She has no qualifications. It is a huge sacrifice.

She takes a secretarial course, works for the British Army, then for Firestone Tyres in Geylang, on the east coast of Singapore. At the end of each week she gives every cent to her parents. When she is eighteen, she comes back to the city and starts at Alcan Aluminium, around the corner from Raffles Place.

As a way to escape the grind of the day initially, and then as a means to bring in more money, May goes to modelling school, and at evenings and weekends she begins to model clothes in fashion shows. Then she starts to show for designers, and to appear in magazines and newspapers. And it is at this point that she acquires her single pair of designer shoes: the ones made of English-field dark green suede, with a solid brass full circle for a heel.

The ankle bells are now fully banished, if not yet tarnished as when I found them.

*

I take the anklets back to the camphorwood chest and replace them. My mother and I prepare to move down another layer, a deeper stratum of family memory. As she pushes aside papers and photograph albums, I know what we are looking for.

The smell hits me again.

Camphoraceous: the wood even has its own adjective, a word so drawn out, softly syllabled and harmoniously voweled, that I can almost taste camphor when I say it. As I discover while my mother and I have been travelling through her archive thus far, the main source for modern camphor is the mountains and valleys and nearby islands of my grandmother's southern China. There the bark and leaves of the evergreen *Laurus Camphora* are boiled to create an oil that is the key ingredient for inhalants, balms and insect repellent.

But camphor is listed not only in Chinese medical classics, it appears also in Arabic and Sanskrit Ayurvedic texts, going back almost two thousand years. It was treasured in ancient India, Egypt and Babylon. I find that there is a Chinese camphor, an Arabic camphor – even a Jewish camphor. As we retrace my grandparents' journeys and those of my great-grandparents, I know I will need to visit and discover such places and cultures, especially China, India and Babylon, or Iraq. It's perfect that the camphorwood chest now holds the archive of lovers who travelled across Asia. For centuries, camphor was used to preserve documents from decay, cloths from insect infestation, and keepsakes from the general disintegration of time. It was even applied to the process of embalming bodies, especially those of ancient kings, so much were its scent and preservative power revered.

Our chest is hand-carved and antique. We can't know exactly how old it is, or who owned it, and what were its stories before my mother came upon it in an antique shop in Singapore. But chests exactly like ours were used by travellers in the trade of opium, tea, silks, and also spice: the spice trade that was the profession for generations of my grandfather's family. Camphorwood boxes dotted the Spice Route, that certain but invisible ancient sea road. Camphor joined the China of my grandmother, the Iraq of my great-grandfather, the India of my grandfather, and the Singapore of my mother's own childhood. What I smell in camphor, then, is the scent of people across the East brought together from different worlds.

We are looking for my grandparents, Jacob and Esther. We are looking for a handbag.

FINDING THE ENTWINED TREES

10. Jacob and Esther

Retrieving my grandmother's handbag from the camphorwood chest feels like an exercise in excavation, even exhumation. The brown leather is brittle, less like leather and more like cardboard, as if the living hide it once was is transforming into mineral, becoming earth. Before it was rehomed to the chest, two decades in Singapore's heat and damp, at the back of a cupboard in Uncle Sunny's house, had caused the handbag to grow an external skin of mould and partially to rot its stained inner lining. But inside this state of decomposition a haul of papers is still to be found, carefully preserved, just as they were when Esther died.

There is a single photograph.

My mother and I make a beeline for it. It's the first photograph we have of my grandparents and the first of my mother. My mother is amazed that her parents look completely unlike how she remembers them. Taking the image from her, I'm startled too. They are not like this in my memory, or indeed in later photographs. And yet this photograph – the sole photograph in the handbag, the first photograph – tells me a good deal about the relationship of Jacob and Esther.

In the image Esther, or, as she then was, Koh-wei, is wearing a crisp white tunic, and from the edge of black that can be seen below her hips it's not hard to surmise that she's also wearing wide-legged black trousers. She's dressed in the samfu, the traditional suit of a Chinese servant. Her hair is pulled back tightly, hard away from her face, as if ready for work.

Jacob wears a high-collared white shirt, hanging long over his trousers – a kurta, an Indian smock – of a kind more Eastern than he ever wore again, and in a style still to be found particularly among Arabic and North Indian Muslim men. It's also the only photograph we have that shows my grandfather with a beard, though my mother insists she doesn't see one here. My grandparents also look more different from each other than they will ever look again. In later photographs, as in their relationship, she came closer to his world mainly by wearing Western, or colonial, dresses, and he to hers, in his sarongs, sandals and T-shirts.

In the first photograph, Jacob looks like a Middle Eastern merchant. Koh-wei looks like his Chinese servant.

But the layout of the photograph tells a different story: that they are a couple. Koh-wei is placed equally with Jacob, at his right side on a level with him. He was a small man – at 5' 6", the same as me. But she was an even smaller woman, so the levelling in the picture has been arranged. The children are spaced evenly between them: May sitting on his lap; June, the baby, on Koh-wei's; and Sally standing between the couple. Sally is the yoking child, though I have to remind myself looking at this photograph that Sally was actually the child of his first wife who had died and not Koh-wei's child, unlike these others. Nevertheless, the photograph presents these children as their children.

Why is this the only photograph Esther carried in her handbag? And why is the photograph so choreographed?

In the old days when people were about to migrate, they would often sit for a formal family portrait to leave with family members who stayed behind, to capture a moment of transition. So perhaps the first question is not 'why', but when. When was this photograph taken?

Sitting on Jacob's lap, May looks to be about three years old. June, her sister, held by Koh-wei, seems to be between six and eight months. June was born in March 1941, so this photograph must have been taken some time in the autumn of 1941, just a couple of months before the bombing of Singapore started in December. Knowing what's about to happen, in their faces I tell myself I can see anxiety, fear and weariness; a sense, perhaps, that their world is going to be ripped apart by war. No one is smiling in the photograph, unusual for a studio photograph this late in the twentieth century. Everyone, except perhaps the startled baby, looks exhausted, and everyone looks directly into the camera. They are rabbits caught in the headlights of history's juggernaut, as much as of the flash used for the exposure. Despite being a studio portrait, the photograph has the air of an official or identity photograph, in which, in our passports explicitly now, we are instructed not to smile.

The photograph is tiny, just two inches by three. Evidently stored for a long time, it has almost come apart, and only a worn strip of Sellotape across most of the width of its backing is holding the photographic paper together. It must have been repeatedly pulled out of a small wallet and replaced, refolded along the same line. The photograph is also the only photograph to have made the journey with the family all the way to India, and to have made it all the way back. It survived – like the family – evacuation, repatriation, refugee camps, multiple rehomings, finally making its way to Esther's handbag, where it remained the only photograph, in among all the official documents, and which she was carrying around still when she died.

Here is how I divine The Only Photograph.

Given that my mother's family would have needed something to get them on that ship, the *Felix Roussel*; given that no Jewish men or Chinese women were being helped to emigrate, let alone together; given that evacuation plans were racist and confused about whether official documentation was required; given that this image must have been taken within weeks of the war, perhaps with the Japanese air raids already having started; and given that this is a studio portrait exhibiting a family: given all these contingencies and exigencies, might not this photograph itself have worked, I reason, talisman-like, actually to keep the family together?

Wouldn't this photograph, pulled out and shown in a hasty, possibly panicked moment to an official, who was faced with piles of other documentation in front of him, have been some kind of validation, in other words, of Jacob and Koh-wei: of their relationship, and of the children between them, as a family?

More than anything else we find in the handbag or elsewhere in the camphorwood chest, this photograph announces: this, here, is a family. In spite of the fact that she is Chinese and in his service, that he is an 'Asiatic Jew' and her employer, we are husband and wife. And these, as if to prove we are married, are the children between us.

*

My mother and I ease out the remaining contents of my grandmother's handbag – a pile of folded, faded papers.

At first glance, they appear nothing out of the ordinary, made up as they are of the medical, marital and other legal and religious documents that constitute the official story of almost all lives.

But as we unfold and open the papers out, we discover that there exist several copies – sometimes as many as fifteen identical replicas of the same document – within the concealed pockets of what is, after all, this smallish, modest bag. All of these documents and their replicas Esther carried in her handbag, everywhere she went, until the day she died.

The multiple replication suggests an extreme anxiety: about identity and belonging. My mother comments that her father was similar in this regard – not as extreme for sure, but also anxious about his legal records. Like me, it seems my grandparents were apprehensive about legacy. And while Esther's handbag indicates that their shared quest was largely preoccupied with legal recognition of their match, for them, also, this legacy centred on Jewish belonging.

*

The oldest handbag paper is a petition for legal recognition of my grandmother's name. The change is from her Chinese name to a Jewish name. In 1957 my grandfather states:

> I, Jacob Isaac Elias, residing at No. 20A, Short Street, Singapore, do solemnly and sincerely declare that I was married to Madam Sim Jua in Bombay on the 17th day of July, 1942. After the marriage she has been known and called as Esther Elias. The purpose of my making this declaration is to have her name in her Identity Card to read as Esther Elias (nee Sim Kua).

'Elias' is the Jewish name of her Jewish husband, Jacob. 'Esther' is the biblically important Jewish woman's first name she was given to go with it. It is an unequivocally Jewish name.

Yet even in a document that seeks confirmation of her Jewish identity, there's uncertainty around her prior, Chinese name. The first mention gives it as 'Sim Jua', the second, as 'Sim Kua'. The uncertainty is compounded by the rickety typography, which has the capital 'K' hovering indecisively between lines. 'J' or 'K'? Jua or Kua? Actually, we've always written my grandmother's Chinese name as neither of these but rather as 'Koh-wei Sim'. This document reminds us that her last name was 'Sim', her first name Koh-wei – or Kua, or Jua. It reminds us of her Chineseness, since the Chinese put their family name first.

My mother and I shuffle onto the next document. We find that seven months later my grandparents are making an application to register the now legally named Esther Elias as a British subject. Since Singapore was still a colony, its residents were subjects of the British Empire. Jacob and Esther are seeking to secure her identity further. At the same time, they apply for a 'Certificate of Registration of Citizenship of Singapore' for Esther. They are hedging their bets, making sure that Esther's belonging – British subject, citizen of Singapore – is not in doubt. Esther's Singapore citizenship comes thanks to David Marshall, whose Citizenship Act of 1957 secured Singapore as a legal home for the 200,000 alien-born Chinese.

Numbered among these Chinese aliens without legal belonging was my China-, not Singapore-, Chinese-, not Jewish-, born grandmother.

*

But my grandmother's application for citizenship is made not on the basis of her residency in Singapore. Instead Koh-wei/

Esther becomes a citizen through Jacob Elias, based on the declaration of their marriage, which they say took place in Bombay, in July 1942.

I think very hard about this declared marriage, about its timing, location and motivation. If the declaration is true, it would mean that, four months after their arrival in Bombay, in a time of war – having only just escaped Singapore before it fell – my refugee grandparents arranged a wedding.

By that point Jacob and Esther had already been together for at least three years, given that May, their eldest child, was born in 1938. I go along with it. The fact of their being in India during the war could well have prompted them to want to obtain public legitimacy for an existing private bond. And perhaps they married in Bombay because they already had anxiety especially about Koh-wei's status. After all, she was a not yet legal subject or citizen of anywhere, whether by residency or marriage. She was also a lone Chinese woman among a group of Singapore Jews in a refugee camp in India whose own status was precarious.

The declaration of marriage makes me think harder about the war. It makes me wonder how my grandparents even managed to get to Bombay in the first place.

For given the prioritisation among refugees at the time, neither Jacob nor Esther was really entitled to have been on that boat. While other Jewish men in Singapore were interned, how did Jacob, both as a Singapore local and an 'Asiatic Jew', manage to board the *Felix Roussel,* which was otherwise transporting mainly European women and children? I can find no comparable story of a Singapore Jewish family that managed to stay together during the war.

'It's true', my mother says when I share my wonder. 'I had never thought about it' – the exceptionality of the war story, the fact that both her parents escaped, that the family were not split up. 'It's a miracle', she says, now echoing the thoughts I attribute to Jacob in my imagining of the scene as he stands on Singapore's docks and witnesses the extinguishing of the fire on the *Felix Roussel*. I realise that what we find in the camphor-wood chest – and what I write – is revealing some family stories, but I'm not sure how much they were already there, and how much my mother and I are creating them together.

And if Jacob's evacuation is a puzzle, I struggle even to wrap my head around the fact that Esther, especially as an uneducated and unmarried Chinese woman, managed to get to India, when so few Chinese were evacuated and only those working for the British. Koh-wei must have been completely alone: first on a mainly European refugee boat from Singapore, with a few Jews carried as extras on board; then in Bombay, in a refugee camp run for 250 or so Asian Jews by the Jewish Relief Association.

In photographs from India Koh-wei certainly appears exceptional: a Chinese woman, first in her samfu and sarong, standing in a dusty refugee camp, surrounded by her own children, alongside a young Indian girl, who is holding the new baby, Hannah, born like Sunny in Bombay. What must it have felt like to be so out of place? Yet in some of the later photographs from this time, Koh-wei surprises me and my mother by looking confident, even comfortable, in front of the ornate colonial Indian architecture and the piles of rubble in the camp. Increasingly in these images, she wears the Western-style dresses my mother says she always wore. Koh-wei becomes more like her mother, Esther. After the war, Esther wouldn't be seen in trousers at all but rather always and only what my mother calls 'proper dresses', as if the Chinese costumes needed to be left behind. Following the boat photograph, in later photographs Koh-wei has already grown her hair and is now allowing it to fall loose. She clips it back only at the sides, making it flare out femininely to her shoulders, in 1940s Western fashion.

If we can see a narrative in a handful of still images – and there's so little from my mother's life when the family were war refugees, so little that could be carried and kept – the photographs suggest that, in India, Chinese Koh-wei underwent a process of transformation. She was already becoming less Chinese, more cosmopolitan. More Jewish.

*

When I went to Bombay a few years ago to try to retrace my grandparents' steps, I studied all the Jewish marriage certificates, the ketubot, emanating from two synagogues. I looked especially at those from Byculla, the synagogue Jacob and Esther were most likely to have frequented, right next to the camp, the one for poorer Jews. Jews were even in a war, even among refugees, very good at keeping records, and the certificates I saw showed that marriages continued to take place during this period. But while I spent many hours, fans whirring, in the wood-panelled office of the synagogue, kept topped up by the archivist with layers of documents as well as with delicious masala tea, I could find no evidence at all, no records, nothing, showing that Jacob and Esther had ever got married here.

I acknowledge there's a small chance they might have had a civil wedding. Colonial authorities in the East, particularly with the uncertainty about whether to classify Jews as Europeans or Asiatics, didn't record Jewish marriages until after the war, so there's no way of ascertaining this. But my grandmother's later handbag documents – in which Esther and Jacob write in more detail that theirs was a marriage 'by Jewish custom' – and the timing of their declaration of this marriage fifteen years later, lead me firmly to believe that any marriage would have been Jewish, and therefore that they were not in fact legally married in 1942, or even by 1957. If they'd been married at either date – if there was a ketubah or a civil marriage certificate from this earlier moment – I've no doubt the document would be in the handbag. The declaration of marriage in 1957 is, I'm left to believe, motivated by the sense of needing to obtain her citizenship.

This makes that 1942 'marriage' retroactively wished for and untraceable. A counterfactual marriage, I think. So I strongly suspect that by 1942, even by 1957, the bond between Jacob and Esther was not yet legal.

Which made the basis for Koh-wei's evacuation from Singapore in 1942 even more tenuous, I realise, as it made the grounds of her claim for citizenship in 1957 unfounded.

My surmisals both are and are not revelations to my mother. Instinctively she knows these things about her parents. But the fact of their not being married yet was not important, her parents' connection was irrefutable, her mother was part of Singapore.

So why are they important to me? What am I doing shifting undisturbed ground, digging up buried handbags? Because of legacy. Because of legitimacy. Because I see Jacob and Esther struggling for belonging and acceptance in the Jewish community in ways that echo for me. Because I am looking for my own way in and to return.

*

Documents in archives, even legal ones, don't necessarily give the full truth. Statements of fact can conceal emotional truths. People who resort to getting the law to validate their own versions of their lives – their outright fabrications or what they wish to be true – are those who tend to lack control and authority. The powerless. Those at the margins of systems and communities. Those seeking legitimacy.

Strangers.

The picture of why May and her family might not have been considered 'good enough' starts to acquire perspective, in ways not spoken by the community or by the family, or – I think, due to all kinds of loyalties she holds – by my mother, not even to me. My grandparents' love crossed the divides of religion and ethnicity. But there was also a difference of class between them that was as vast and that emphasised the other differences.

Their bond had started as a contract of employment. Jacob hired 'Madam Sim Kua/Jua' to look after his first wife and his children by her, Sally and Mimi, when the first wife became sick and paralysed. After a period of living with their aunt Flora, Sally and Mimi returned home. Koh-wei began to clean and cook for Jacob and his children, and Flora taught her how to prepare the food they liked. Saffron cabbage. Fried fish. 'Jewish food', the family called it. Flora trained Koh-wei, effectively, in how to keep a Jewish household.

Koh-wei worked extremely hard, according to my mother's older cousin Hannah Kichi, who spent lots of time at the house and who was partly raised by her. Though Koh-wei was small, she was strong and determined – 'like an ox'.

'Madam Sim Kua/Jua' started out in practice, then, as an *ah-ma* – meaning 'nanny', sometimes 'maid'. But *ah-ma* is an intimate familial term, since *ma* means 'mother' in Chinese. *Ah-mas* raised the British Empire's children in white colonialist families. They were normally Indian. A Chinese *ah-ma* was called a *ma-jie*, which also, you can see, has 'mother' at its root. The joining of employee and 'mother' is what's fundamental in these terms. And this is the crossing that my grandmother made at this time, from Jacob's servant to his children's mother; then to become his partner, and eventually his wife and my grandmother.

As I situate her back into her historical context, I realise that Koh-wei was one of many women who came from mainland China, from its southeast provinces in the 1930s, to work as servants, mainly to colonial houses in Southeast Asia, including Singapore. These women sacrificed their own family life for that of their employers. Their hair was combed tightly into buns and they wore clean white tops and black trousers, as my mother and I now see that my grandmother does in the first photograph. In English, they were known as 'black-and-whites'. These Chinese women took a vow of celibacy. Their nun-like renunciation made them vital, but unthreatening, at the heart of colonial families. They were part of the family, yet kept at a distance.

From the outset, Jacob's motherless children and the children of his siblings – all re-mothered now by her – called Koh-wei *Auntie. Auntie* could be used for any older female, not necessarily related, who became an intimate and respected member of a family not based on biology. If all of these terms have degrees of outsider and insider to them, Koh-wei's first years with Jacob show how she closed the gap of her strangeness in stages. The children adored Auntie – she made them *jumpot-jumpot*, the local dish of Malay bananas fried in flour which was loved by all – and she adored them in turn as her own children. At five o'clock sharp every afternoon, she was waiting for Hannah to come home from school, as she later waited for May, as May later waited for me. I treasured those reunions with my mother before I was sent away to school. Mugs of tea and her home-made coconut tarts (her adaptation of Singapore's pineapple tarts). My day wasn't real until I had told her about its every detail. In return, of course, she would tell me stories.

In 1936 Jacob's first wife died. Once the lack of any actual mother made clear that she could no longer be a secondary mother, with a strong sense of propriety of her place as employee, Koh-wei left the family. She returned to the Chinese village in Singapore near Changi, where she had been living before she came to work for Jacob. Immediately Jacob went to fetch her back – in those days with few cars it was not an easy journey, several, probably uncomfortably bumpy, miles by trishaw. He surprised her by asking for her hand in marriage, making a proposal for her to return with him, not as his employee but as his wife. But she told him she wasn't sure, and she continued to hold out against his advances.

I imagine Jacob hadn't expected to be refused. Even now, Koh-wei's rejection of Jacob surprises me, especially given the vast differences in their social status, and the fact that she then had to go back to hard casual labour.

But perhaps this difference in their status was part of the reason for Koh-wei's refusal and led her to question Jacob's intentions. For in her mind, in my mind too, could you really go from servant to wife? Jane Eyre went from governess to wife, but the difference between Jane and Rochester was only that of wealth, and by the end of the novel even that difference has been levelled.

Koh-wei may have been poor, but she didn't want to be Jacob's common-law wife, or worse, mistress. And could she ever really cross the threshold from Chineseness into Jewishness? This must have been a much bigger question for her, absolute outsider as she was to Judaism. Latecomer myself, I'm sympathetic. To Koh-wei, Jacob, as a British subject and an Asiatic Jew, must have seemed from a different planet, and she had returned from this planet to the Chinese village in Singapore, which was home from home for her. So she didn't come to Jacob.

Jacob travelled back to her village. In the absence of any of her family or guardians in Singapore, he turned next to the towkay, the Chinese village leader, to intercede. It was this Chinese elder who persuaded Koh-wei to trust Jacob. 'Go with him', he told her. 'He'll look after you, in a way you hadn't thought possible.'

I find a storyteller's satisfaction that this liberal Chinese towkay, in his village, plays the same mediating role in my grandparents' story as the foresightful Arabic fortune-teller Badriah, in her village, played in bringing together my parents. Both dei ex machina figures, these seers imagine, approve, and thereby usher into being relationships that broke down the divisions of empire. They are the magicians in my story.

Of my grandmother with my grandfather, then, to paraphrase a famous line from *Jane Eyre*: Reader, she went with him.

*

But as Badriah didn't make the decision for May, the towkay doesn't wholly determine the outcome of my grandmother's romantic plot.

In 1933, the British colonial government in Singapore had passed an Aliens Ordinance, which introduced immigration restrictions on the island. Since the British, and the Indians by the fact of their homeland already being colonised, were British subjects, 'aliens' targeted illegal Chinese immigrants. My grandmother. During the 1930s, the colonial government was repatriating large numbers of immigrant Chinese. Koh-wei was in danger of being sent back to China.

But if Sim Koh-wei married Jacob, who was a British subject and therefore a legal resident of Singapore, she would obtain immediate protection from repatriation through him. This would be in addition to the fact that marrying Jacob would give

Koh-wei greater financial security. The Depression of the 1930s made casual labour scarce. Koh-wei was very exposed once she left Jacob.

The handbag's paperwork trail of my grandmother's anxieties is starting to make a good deal of sense to me and my mother as we spread the papers over the floor.

And yet although Koh-wei went to Jacob surely with this expectation that he fulfil his promise, we discover that my grandparents didn't marry at this point, no more in 1936 than they did in 1942.

Jacob and Esther were on opposite sides of a class chasm that overlay the race divide. Singapore was built on that colonial hierarchy of white masters and their Chinese or Indian domestic servants. I find that, in the 1930s and '40s, interracial marriage was much more taboo than in the '60s and risked community excommunication. For Jacob and Sim Koh-wei to have got married, in the 1930s, or in the '40s or '50s, seems to us, as it must have to them through these decades, impossible. They certainly couldn't have had a Jewish wedding. Marriage might give Koh-wei citizenship, but marriage to his Chinese servant risked Jacob's place in the Jewish community. It was an unresolvable dilemma.

Reader – Mum, because, as I say, I don't think my mother had given much thought to this previously – she went with him as his common-law wife.

Later when they were having arguments, Jacob teased Esther about the transformation of their relationship, from that of employment to partners, strangers to lovers. 'Don't sass me', he said. 'I picked you up with your Chinese garb and your pigtails and I made you the mistress of my house.' This was a clear jibe about the class and race differences between them.

I ask my mother if this was said in jest. She's not so sure. But I have reason to believe he could mock her origins and her migration into the family because of a deep intimacy, in full acknowledgement of all their differences. I'm sure she went with him because she also felt that.

*

I certainly felt it, even as a three-year-old. My mother had taken me back to her home, her parents' flat on Short Street. It was for a period of only a month. But the light and the heat, the scents and the sounds, the people and above all her parents, were so unlike anything I had encountered in my own little life, and so strongly outlined, that the visit is engraved in my memory as a much longer time, almost an endless present.

My grandparents sit side by side in the sitting room. He, in an ornately carved cane chair, with large-petalled flowers floating up the sides. Just as on our camphorwood chest. He wears a sarong and singlet. In contrast to their dazzling white, his skin is rich shiny coffee. His eyebrows are feathery eagle wings outstretched in flight. On his carved cane chair he sits, legs apart, a magus on his throne.

My grandmother perches next to him on a plastic kitchen chair, ready to make anyone who enters feel welcome. She will hand you the most delicious tea you've ever tasted, made with sweetened condensed milk, all the more nectar-like for being served in a glass with the spoon still in it. She wears a flowery housedress, hitched up above her knees to catch the cool of the fans and the breeze from the windows which are open on all sides. She smiles shyly, but says little.

A black-and-white television releases its tinny sound, but people are ignoring it. There is too much else going on in this room, with family and friend and neighbour visitors coming in and out, and my grandfather at the hub of these spokes of activity, with my grandmother at his side. I realise that the conversation and communion *is* the entertainment.

Sometimes, when I don't see my grandparents here in the main room, I toddle out to the veranda, and I find them there, sitting again companionably side by side, on a seat pressed against the open lookout. They always seem to be doing little when I happen on them, only talking quietly to each other or in an easy silence. I realise that they are two pieces of a puzzle. They fit together.

As soon as I appear, however, I become the star of their show. My grandfather immediately engages me: singing a song that plays on my name, calling me to him, showing me how much I'm loved.

He smells of the tobacco that I watch him continuously smoking. But also of spices, of cinnamon and cloves. Then there is the smell coming from the kitchenette, of my grandmother cooking saffron cabbage. It steams gently on the hob for a long time, and the sweet, buttery smell infuses the air and mixes with my grandfather's spices. Eating the cabbage merges with the heat of the sun, and the whole moment is bathed in those golden tastes and scents, which I'll absorb as love, which is as deep and long-lasting as the spices.

These are the infusions I'll remember when I find them, again and again, every time I open the camphorwood chest.

*

The handbag tells me that Jacob and Esther did marry, but long after the war and after the return to Singapore. There is a certified copy (in multiple copies) of an entry showing that Jacob and Esther were married, in the Singapore Marriage Registry office, in 1958. It takes place under the Singapore Civil Marriage Ordinance of 1940, which allowed couples to have their marriage recognised civilly and legally by the colonial authorities, outside religious settings. The easing of marriage regulations addressed mixed-faith couples who were otherwise prevented within their different religious contexts from getting married.

If my doubts about the claims to the Bombay wedding in 1942 are correct, this is the moment when Jacob and Esther became legally married, and when she, therefore, became a fully legal citizen of Singapore, through her marriage to him.

Extending protection to Esther as Jacob's legal wife, the civil marriage seems to have been an exercise in recording officially the relationship which has been as good as a marriage. They had been together for over twenty-two years. They had, in their heads, in the previous claims, tried to marry so many times before. In 1958 he was already sixty-six; she, on paper at least, fifty-one. Twenty-two years without legal recognition of their relationship. The fact that they're seeking this validation at all indicates that they still felt insecure, probably about her status as a Singapore citizen based on being his wife, but above all insecure about the legitimacy and public acceptability of their relationship.

And I remind myself that their daughters are approaching marriageable age. Jacob and Esther wouldn't have wanted them to be in any way disadvantaged.

*

In these later documents, more of Esther's Chinese identity and past emerge, as if the passage of time has eroded some of the earth heaped up to bury a former self. Their marriage is registered under her old (no longer legal) name, 'Sim Jua'. She states that her last name was 'Sim'; that she had been born in China; and she declares, under her parents' details, her 'origin unknown'. She gives her birth date as 1907.

My mother and I unfold another declaration, made in 1974, about her mother's birthplace and the status of her birth certificate. Esther Elias's entry reads, in someone's neat, capitalised handwriting:

I WAS BORN IN A PROVINCE (WHICH I AM UNABLE TO REMEMBER) IN CHINA IN THE YEAR 1907. THE PURPOSE OF THIS DECLARATION IS TO SHOW EVIDENCE OF MY BIRTHPLACE. DUE TO THE FACT THAT I HAVE NEVER BEEN ISSUED WITH A BIRTH CERTIFICATE AT THE TIME OF BIRTH OR ANY OTHER TIME ~~ELSEWHERE~~.

I read this document over and over. Could an exercise in declaring origins get more paradoxical than this? Here is Esther, providing 'evidence' of her birthplace, in order to obtain a birth certificate, by declaring that she is unable to remember the province of her birth in China. My mother is also bewildered by it. She thinks she knows the place in China her mother was from, so why would her mother say she can't remember this? Given that Esther is so sure of her birth year and that we know that she didn't leave China until she was in her late twenties, we find it surprising, incredible even, that she can have completely forgotten such a fundamental geographic fact as her birthplace. How can someone have forgotten everything documentable and nameable about where they were born?

Then again, my mother and I reason together, if Esther can't name the place of her birth, this might well have been because she was illiterate. The neat handwriting is not hers. She could never read writing in any language, and couldn't write therefore, as is shown on all of these documents that required her signature. In the space that was left for her to sign her name, there is always instead the impress of her small 'R.T.P' (her right thumb print). Pictures might stay in her mind. Words – and especially names in a language she no longer had a place or a reason to speak – could easily slip.

But then we wonder if Esther's not naming the place of her birth was rather a refusal to name: a deliberate withholding, an awareness that she was speaking to authorities who, in her mind, might still have the power to turn her back to that place that she had good reasons for wanting to escape. Refusing to name – or 'forgetting' – places of origin is not unusual in life stories where people fear repatriation to terrible conditions and brutal regimes. I tell my mother about the countless Chinese memoirs I have read of wars, revolutions and famine punctured with such holes. Esther, I suggest, is worried that if she reveals too much detail, remembers too much, she risks being sent all the way back to China, to that vital-to-forget place of her birth.

My mother thinks that the taciturnity, as she euphemistically calls it, in these documents that surrounds the place that her mother came from, also characterised Koh-wei in life. While she can't be sure, she believes that her mother never actually told her or her siblings the name of her birthplace – although Esther certainly described to her a city, a village, a river, in such perfect detail that she could now almost draw a map or reconstruct an architectural model based on her memories of her mother's stories. But Jacob did name Chinese places in association with Koh-wei, and my mother thinks she must have told him. On other occasions when Jacob wanted to tease Esther, he used to say she was a 'Chao-an', or a 'Swatow-ah': pejorative ways of saying she was from some little hole called Chao-an, or Swatow.

'So if these names are correct as her birthplace, and Nana refused to mention such names to anyone but Papa because she feared being sent home, because she needed to forget the past, did she entrust Jacob alone with her trauma?' I ask my mother. In other words, what I'm really asking is: was Jacob Koh-wei's repository, a locked safe for her secrets, as she later stored these papers, all carefully folded and concealed, in a handbag, as her handbag together with its memories is now preserved in our camphorwood chest?

Camphorwood chests are like trusty friends and honourable lovers. They store and keep hidden the most precious belongings of migrants, of people who moved across oceans and worlds.

*

The civil marriage record and later documents also state that 'Sim Jua' was 'previously married in China but lost her husband through death in 1935.'

'I told you about her first husband', my mother says.

Indeed she did, but it will take us going back to China before I can fit this piece between Jacob and Esther and see how it helps complete the puzzle of my grandparents' story.

Their dead first spouses made my grandparents alike. What they missed, and what they'd left behind, joined them. They grew around each other's losses. Their branches reached out to hold each other up, like the entwined trees they liked to rest against in the Singapore Botanic Gardens, when they were finally together and secure in their marriage.

*

After Esther's citizenship was granted, and after Jacob and Esther's civil marriage took place, there was another wedding. And finally, it was a Jewish one. While we don't find any ketubah or record from Bombay in her handbag, we do find a ketubah, a Jewish marriage certificate, for my grandparents. No surprise that this, Esther was also carrying around when she died.

The document shows my mother and me that the act of marriage was, finally for them, not simply about securing Esther's citizenship, nor even just a solidification of her emotional bond to Jacob. It shows us instead a Jewish ceremony, a cultural and religious blessing of their bond – a blessing that we realise they hadn't been able to get in 1942, in 1957, in 1958, or at any subsequent time until this point. The ketubah in Esther's handbag is dated 1965. The Jewish wedding took place when Jacob was almost seventy-four and Esther almost sixty. They had been living together some thirty years and had six adult children, who now had children of their own.

On this beautifully ornate document, Hebrew lettering on one side, English on the other, we see that some of the prescribed text on the certificate is crossed through (more telling crossings-out). We find that what's specified, what's deleted, are poignant. We note that the designations of 'bachelor' and 'virgin' are struck through. The space specifying dowry is completed, letting us know that she brought with her two hundred dollars, he another two hundred. What little money they had by now was equally shared. They were anyway by this point surviving only on their children's earnings – not only those of my mother but also her sisters then brother – and with help from the Jewish Welfare Board. That they had to write anything for these entries, that they put in these token figures, makes us deeply sad. The marriage certificate seems to be a document they have outgrown, in the sense that they should have been granted it a long time ago.

We find a photograph of Jacob and Esther from their wedding day, following the blessing in the synagogue and just at the start of the party. It's the counterpart to the first photograph, what we now see as the pre-war, boat photograph. In this they are smiling. They look relieved. And they are touching. The photograph captures Jacob and Esther in the moment of cutting the wedding cake, with Sally standing to their side.

Jacob appears intensely happy, the shine of his eyes speaking volumes. Esther, glancing off at something or someone away from the camera, wears her more reserved smile. In her hand she is holding the ketubah, rolled up and as yet un-xeroxed, that we have now in the handbag. He has somehow managed to tuck this same document simultaneously under his right arm. Jacob and Esther are entwined through this Jewish marriage certificate, which I'm holding now, and more intimately also through their hands, which come together in the act of just having pushed the knife through the wedding cake. They have become like those entwined trees they used to visit in the Singapore Botanic Gardens. I am now resting against their union.

Without doubt what Jacob and Esther were seeking here was religious approval for their relationship, in follow-up to the civil approval. Without doubt they had been made to wait a long time to find this validation of their relationship, of their very unorthodox – although finally, absolutely Orthodox – marriage. And they found this acceptance under good old Rabbi Shababo, remembered both for his quarter-century of faithful service to the Jewish community in Singapore but also for his liberal interpretation of Jewish law, interfaith work, and his embrace and encouragement of conversions, of particularly the Chinese in mixed marriages with Jews. Shababo, Egyptian, Romanian, traveller across empires. I greet him as fellow loving stranger. Family, ultimately. For it was Shababo who finally married Jacob and Esther, in the way their repeated declarations referring back to 1942 say that they were originally seeking. Thirty years after they began their relationship, they sealed their connection and won Jewish acceptance.

*

The handbag also holds a conversion certificate, signed by Rabbi Shababo, for my grandmother. For Esther, too, was converted to Judaism, and like May also by Rabbi Shababo.

The dates of Koh-Wei/Esther's conversion, so close to the wedding, just two days before, suggest that she converted in order to get married, and perhaps therefore that her conversion came about as a result of pressure from Jacob, or from the Jewish community more generally. And yet, as my mother emphasises, it was Esther herself who wanted to be converted, and a Jewish wedding to Jacob was further acceptance, a second-level confirmation, of her becoming Jewish.

For rather like my mother, my grandmother had in her identification and many of her practices been 'Jewish' by this point for a long time before the Jewish wedding and conversion. 'For years she wore a Magen David that my father bought her', my mother says. And indeed in other shots from the wedding I can see it more clearly. 'She had long been eating Jewish or "clean" food, decades before the rabbi prescribed it as a commitment of her conversion "contract", at least since the war.'

On the way back from India, my mother remembers that Jacob refused to eat any of the food that they were provided on the ship. 'He would say "foul" when he saw the food – Papa used this word a lot – and he would send Mama down to the ship's kitchens to prepare food.' My mother's cousin Hannah tells me that, from when she had arrived in his house, Koh-wei never cooked or consumed the food of her fellow Chinese-village neighbours (chicken's feet, pig's tails), but only and always what they thought of as 'Jewish food' (curry puffs, saffron cabbage and chicken curries), grinding fresh Indian and Middle Eastern spices on a flat stone board with a stone rolling pin. 'When Auntie came, no pork', Hannah nods approvingly.

I look back over the early photographs of Koh-wei, trying to fathom this transition from Chineseness to Jewishness. The photographs in India now look to me like Koh-wei becoming not simply Western but Jacob's Esther. And this transition seemed fulfilled by the end of her life since, when sick in hospital, one of her proudest moments was the prestigious Singapore Jewish surgeon – a Cohen no less, a name indicating descent from Jewish priests – telling Esther that she no longer looked Chinese but simply like a little old Jewish lady. She beamed with pleasure at belonging, even as she was dying. She had become what she wanted to be.

Esther's fulfilment in becoming Jewish suggests to me that Koh-wei wanted to get away strongly from being Chinese. Identifying as Jewish so fiercely explains why she was carrying around the conversion certificate from a religion that she hadn't been raised with.

And yet, again I'm struck by the duplicity or at least the duality on some of the documentation. My grandmother is named 'Mrs Koh Wei Esther Elias' on the conversion document. The doubling Chinese-Jewish hybrid tells me that, even though she had given up her name and apparently the Chinese identity that went with her name-change document, who Esther was before – Koh-wei: Madam Sim Jua/Sim Kua – had never been fully crossed through or forgotten.

*

My mother was in Singapore for her parents' wedding, in what was her first return visit since she had left home. Herself now married for three years, May writes a letter to Keith a few days before the event (I am back in my parents' letters): 'My parents – after 28 years of marriage at a Registry Office [this must have been what my mother believed; the timing would have made her own birth legitimate] – are having a Jewish ceremony this Sunday. This "wedding" takes place at home [in fact, as the photographs tell me, it was held in the synagogue; living abroad, my mother must have been left out of the planning], and it is to take place after all this time because my mother is being accepted into the Jewish faith.'

Yet while some of her facts are wrong, my mother's order of causality corresponds to my grandmother's emotional truth; not conversion because of wedding, but wedding as part of conversion. She goes on: 'I myself feel very much like an onlooker as far as the ceremony goes, but it means a lot to my parents – my mother especially, because she's spent the last six months receiving tuition (from the Rabbi).'

May feels like an onlooker also in Singapore. Although loving the chance to see her parents, she can't wait to return to England, and her letters show a love for Keith that is less compulsive and a longing for her translated life. She yearns to return to him, to all the things that seem to her so very English: to wake up to the sound of bells on Sunday mornings; for their walks on afternoons in the cool spring hills of their home on the Welsh borders; and for their warming tea by a roaring fire. 'I have grown to love England. I love its quiet clean way of life – I love its wholesome, good food, and I like your people.'

'Your people.' I note that her translation is not complete. May is still something of an 'onlooker' in England too, apparently. As with her own mother, an ocean has been crossed, and home is no longer the same place. Yet as with Esther/Koh-wei, the former life isn't completely erased but rather crossed through. Secreted away, archived. Waiting for someone to decipher it.

*

The Chinese have a saying that falling leaves return to their roots. But the falling leaf returning to its root is not the end of my grandmother's plot. Or my grandfather's. The tale of Jacob and Esther is not about 'returning' to an ideal home, but brings to my mind instead the Book of Ruth.

'Why do we read the Book of Ruth at Shavuot?', the Jewish festival of 'Weeks', our rabbi asks at one of my York community services. We all have different answers.

For me, the Book of Ruth is one of the most poignant Jewish and biblical stories about people who travelled, who crossed cultural divides, intermarry, and who make new homes among strangers. Like Koh-wei/Esther, Ruth goes from being a foreigner to a maidservant, to an *'amah'*, or 'handmaid' in the Hebrew, to a wife – to become mother and grandmother to Jews.

After her first husband dies, Ruth, 'the Moabitess' (a non-
'Israelite', or non-Jew, to translate the biblical into modern terminology), converts and marries the Jewish Boaz, and requests
to be buried in the land of her new loyalties, of her migrant
home (with the Jews). Her plea makes for what I find to be one
of the most beautiful passages in the Tanakh, the Hebrew bible:

> Whither thou goest, I will go; and where thou lodgest,
> I will lodge: thy people shall be my people, and thy God
> my God: Where thou diest, will I die, and there will I be
> buried. Why have I found grace in thine eyes, that thou
> shouldest take knowledge of me, seeing I am a stranger?

It could be Esther speaking to Jacob.

Ruth's is a story held dear by converts, since it celebrates
conversion, recognises her Jewish marriage, and the convert's
determined loyalty to Judaism, against more widely assumed
and well-known patriarchal views against intermarriage.
The book finishes by revealing Ruth's role as King David's
great-grandmother. So her story ends up being not only about
how foreign wives become exemplary Jews, but also about
their role in Jewish legacy. Ultimately, it lets us know, you can't
tell the difference between who's a future leader (or progenitor
of leaders) and who a stranger; who's native and gets to define
Jewishness, and who an incomer.

One Shabbat eve, Esther asked for her handbag. She was in
her seventies and had spent many months sickening in hospital; she had lost her beloved Jacob about ten years previously.
Esther didn't need to open the handbag. She just held it, reas-
sured. Having been unable to swallow food or liquids for days,

she took a few sips of the kiddush wine (wine blessed to bring in Shabbat). 'That's enough: now I can sleep.' May returned to her brother's house in Singapore. The call came. Sunny and May were held up on their way to hospital. They missed their mother's death by minutes.

The next morning, May found in the drawer of the small cabinet next to her hospital bed copies of two Jewish prayers. For May, the location was a portent. Since her mother had been in hospital – and who knows for how much longer before, given that my grandmother too was a hoarder of keepsakes – 'it was the first night she didn't have them under her pillow. I had forgotten to check them when she had been moved that afternoon in my absence. I put the prayer sheets into her handbag and hugged it to myself.'

The prayer sheets; the handbag. The absent mother; the missed parting. Did my mother blame herself for not checking the prayer sheets, as she blames herself for missing her mother's death? My mother, without a mother anymore, holds on to the handbag with its Jewish prayers. For the orphan, the handbag – the object her mother had always kept close – becomes the physical connection for May to her mother's living body.

I study the prayers now, before we refold them and replace them, along with all the other documents, back in the same handbag, and return the archive of Jacob and Esther to the camphorwood chest. One prayer is written in the shape of a menorah. I now recognise it to be the *Segulah* psalm. It is Psalm 67, which I've learned is recited by Sephardi Jews before a journey. King David is said to have arranged the psalm into a menorah and to have had it engraved on his shield. He made it a symbol of protection and light, for himself, and for all Jews thereafter.

11. GIRL MOSES

What we have of my grandmother's Chinese life are scraps, some consisting of details from the handbag. She was a migrant from China. She might have been from Chao-an, or Swatow. Her name was (or sounded like) Sim Kua, or Sim Jua, or Sim Koh-wei. She gave her birthdate as 1907. Other bits are from my mother's stories, passed on to her by her mother, about origins. A village with a courtyard. A foster-father, who is a fisherman or farmer. A husband dying suddenly of an illness. A child in a field. A child by a river.

Like the quilt which Sim Koh-wei/Esther Elias was making for as long as anyone can remember, there are only fragments.

The quilt remained unfinished, in sections and scraps, in the camphorwood chest. From time to time in my childhood, my mother took it out and I admired it. My mother spun her stories. Then she refolded and returned it.

Studying the quilt closely now, I see it's a patchwork of the family's sojourns across Asia, made up of scraps of material that are an index to their lives, their moment, their movement. I see squares of the faded Indian Madras-checks from Jacob's worn-out sarongs. There is the leftover material of the polka-dot dress that May wore to the synagogue. Here, the plain densely textured cottons used to make the kind of suit jackets and skirts she wore to work. Brown gingham, some tartan Scottish bagpipers, and a repeated cartoon dog – my mother identifies these as from their clothes as children. Pieces of the softest peach Chinese silk, including the ghost of a square I'll identify as coming from a Chinese childhood. There are richly coloured Malay wax-dyed batiks, and cuts of flowery patterns which Esther wore in her Western-style dresses.

I think of my mother's memory of my grandmother sewing the family clothes, first by hand, then on the old Singer. I think of my mother doing the same for me. Like my mother, Esther was resourceful. She never threw anything away, and she reused old clothes and scraps. I realise that the quilt is my grandmother's equivalent of what I'm trying to do here, piecing together the camphorwood chest contents into a story. Esther couldn't write. But with the quilt she created a pattern from fragments of a mixed-up family history.

Esther never finished her quilt, although she intended to do so when May got married. With increasing arthritis, she found it hard to sew. The quilt has this chapter too, since towards the edges the stitching is large, awkward, child-like. Leftover scraps, proof of her intention, are there in the chest, along with her ancient heavy sewing scissors. My mother lifts these out and puts her right-hand fingers and thumb where her mother's had worked for so many years previously. When my mother went back to Singapore for her parents' long-deferred wedding, Esther gave her what she had of the quilt, along with the left-over scraps and these scissors. She told her to complete the quilt for us: 'for the children.'

Over some forty years, my mother never got round to the commission. Only when I began this book did she pick up the literal pieces. She wanted to finish the quilt, for me, she said. She wanted to finish this parallel to the book. At first, she wanted to improve the quilt, to straighten out the wonky stitching. But I stopped her from doing that. 'The breaks and gaps and sudden stops are part of the charm', I said. So my mother simply added a backing to what her mother had managed to do, using a thick cotton that is the deepest of sea-blues.

I sleep with my mother's completion, my grandmother's beginnings, on my bed. They are the companion to my dreams.

*

Here is my dream, but it is also one of my mother's stories, her most fantastical.

Sim Koh-wei began life on water. She must have been days old when she was laid in a basket in the rushes at the edges of the blue waters of the Han Jiang, close to where this river meets the South China Sea. A fisherman, farmer, peasant found her, my mother says. As my mother has told me this story many,

many times over the years, there have been many, many variations in his occupation.

These multiple versions are understandable. Memories blur not only as they age and get passed down generations, but also as they travel. Family stories of migration are especially subject to unsettling. Facts lose solidity, stories float free of sure ground. Let me say that, in this most watery, fennish part of China, the most southeast you can go without disappearing into the South China Sea itself, life is anyway amphibious. Lotus roots and lotus flowers, crabs and bamboo shoots, all thrive here because they straddle land and water. Fish are raised with vegetables in pools at the edges of rice fields, in baskets like the one that Koh-wei was found in. I think her rescuer would have been a fisherman and a vegetable farmer together.

I'd like to haul Koh-wei's life onto dry land, to know exactly what happened before she left for Singapore, and why she left China. My mother tells me that Koh-wei was twice abandoned as a baby. She was abandoned by her birth parents, and then abandoned again by her foster-father.

One thing we know for sure: she had smallpox, most probably as a child. I remember the marks on her face, barely visible once she was old, as she already was when I knew her most, when she came to see us in south London just before she died. These marks still showed the illness. Perhaps merging in my child's mind with my mother's repeated telling of this story, these gentle scars always seemed to me like watermarks; as if they had been left by the water. Koh-wei's abandonment twice over in the river must have been at least in part a response to the smallpox. But we can't know for sure.

Even the date she states for her birth of 1907 is uncertain, since in giving their age the Chinese traditionally count time in the womb as one year, and a change in the lunar calendar as creating an additional year.

Here is the pattern I arrange from the fragments my mother gives, also scraps left over from the handbag.

At dawn, the fisherman-farmer poles his sampan several *li* along the river's mudflats, on his journey to work in a rich man's fields. The custom here at this time – it's 1907, or 1909, or thereabouts – is either to own the fields, or to work them. Without property, a poor-man fisherman-farmer is destined to grow another man's rice, lotus roots, cabbages and carp. As he pushes through the rushes, where the river shades into the rice fields, the fisherman-farmer hears a baby cry. Without doubt, it's a girl. Only girls are abandoned here. A kind man, an open-hearted man, he nevertheless allows himself a glimpse. Immediately he pulls back from the angry red marks on her skin. He recognises the rash of smallpox. He knows she's still contagious. He hurries to his work.

But then, in the evening as he punts home, something pulls him down the riverbank a second time. And here my imagination offers me different tributaries.

She is still crying. He's pulled back by compassion. The feverish baby hasn't been killed. She has been carefully wrapped in cloth, and her basket left visibly by the water. Someone wanted her to be found. The fine peach-coloured organdie that swaddles her tells him that this someone is rich and important. The child is special.

He thinks of the anguish of the mother who gave up her child. Mother and child might have had as much as a week together before separation. Smallpox marks come after a week, and smallpox is itself a disease of intimacy: caught by face-to-face contact, a kiss, or the inevitable gift at birth if the mother had it.

Or perhaps, the baby isn't crying at all. In that case he's won over by her silent resolve. She has been without food all day and is now in the sharpening evening air. She is already the girl who will become an ox.

Or perhaps, he reacts more simply as a fisherman-farmer. For once he's seen her in that basket woven of wicker rushes, just like the ones he uses to raise fish and vegetables, he knows she's destined to be his adopted daughter.

Whichever tributary is the right one for Koh-wei's beginnings, whichever thread I pick up to sew together the fragments into her story, we know he took her to his home in Chao-an, to grow her, this hot baby: to grow her – like fish, like vegetables, like children.

*

The fisherman-farmer, now foster-father, in his act of rescuing and adopting Koh-wei, begins the miraculous pattern of my grandmother's miraculous life. From her birth, there were still five – or three – more years before a revolution would bring to an end two millennia of the Celestial Kingdom of imperial rule in China, and the Son of Heaven, the emperor, would be forced to abdicate. These were still legendary times in China, and Chinese legends contain their share of abandoned, adopted and returning babies. (As also, of course, do some well-known Jewish stories, my mother reminds me.)

My grandmother's beginning is a fairy tale, and hard not for adult me to dismiss as fiction. But this was and still feels like a fairy-tale place, at least for those like me who go there knowing it first through family stories.

My parents and I take a tour of China. My grandmother's birthplace is our ultimate goal, the main reason for our journey and our final destination. Chao-an, now incorporated into the city of Chaozhou – in old Teochieu meaning 'the City of Tides' – was once a port on the South China Sea, a settlement with two thousand years of history. The city flourished in the most cosmopolitan of Chinese dynasties, the Tang. East formed a confluence with West in trade routes: first in the overland route of the Silk Road; and then in the ocean-going Spice Route, the route of Jacob's spice trade, which touched Koh-wei's Chaozhou.

Chaozhou seems to float. It sits, or rather moves, on the border of the two southeast provinces of Fujian and Guangdong. When we asked people in China about Koh-wei's hometown, they directed us to the province of Guangdong. But Koh-wei always insisted to anyone who asked that she was Hokkien Chinese from Fujian. And sure enough she spoke Hokkien, and not Cantonese. Speaking Cantonese would have meant she was from Guangdong. But Chaozhou is now just inside Guangdong, which the English called Canton. The borders in this area have repeatedly shifted.

Verging on the South China Sea, Fujian and Guangdong are home to the most ocean-going of Chinese groups: the Cantonese, the Hokkien, and the Hakka. And I learn that these are the provinces in China that have been most shaped by migration. Waves of foreigners have rolled in: Han Chinese, Vietnamese, Thai, Mon-Khmer, Miao, Taiwanese; later, Spanish, Portuguese,

British. In return, the Chinese from these provinces and their descendants were China's main emigrants. I find it a startling fact that most of the Chinese communities who live scattered across the world – which I've got to know in New York, in San Francisco, in Hong Kong, in London, in Manchester, in Leeds – come from just this tiny area in China. Like Koh-wei, most of the Hokkien Chinese who left Fujian went to Southeast Asia, including Singapore and the Malay Peninsula. They named this area Nanyang, meaning 'Southern Ocean'.

I think Koh-wei must have lived with her foster-father on the outskirts of Chao-an. As a fisherman-farmer, her foster-father wouldn't have been able to afford a house in the centre of the city. He would have rented a poorer tenant quarter, close to the river's edge. She told my mother about a courtyard, shared with other families. She must have had a foster-mother, but she spoke little about any maternal figure. My mother guesses that any foster-mother must have died when Koh-wei was young. But Koh-wei always spoke of her foster-father with a passion.

For sure she didn't go to school. Her new family would have been too poor, and anyway this was a place where the proverb was that it was more profitable to raise geese than girls. She never learned to read, Chinese or English. But it must have been here that she developed her love for the picture books my mother remembers from her own childhood that her mother would consume. These retold ancient Chinese legends. And it must have been here that Koh-wei was exposed to Chinese opera, the wayang she used to take May to as a child in Singapore. In Chao-an, the opera, staged in the streets, was the enjoyment of the poor, but the stories were about the rich.

From the city, Koh-wei would have learned much about her society and history, as we also learn in our return to it. Chaozhou is the most famous city in the world, we are told, for wood carving. When we visit the People's Hall in Beijing, we are startled to learn that it includes carving from my grandmother's city almost 1500 miles away. Chaozhou roofs are held together without a single nail, so intricate is the design. I imagine Koh-wei standing in her courtyard. I picture her taking everything in, her eyes wide above high cheekbones. She studies the carvings adorning the roofs. I see them in return. Fire-spouting dragons and fantastic phoenixes. People or gods riding out on clouds and waves. The figures could have stepped right out of our camphorwood chest. Migrants. Koh-wei is beautiful, as still and stately as a carving herself. Chaozhou stitches together ancient legends with the hopes of migration of everyday people like my grandmother.

After a few days in the area, my parents and I engage a guide, Wu Liang-yu, to help us uncover Koh-wei's Chao-an. Knowledgeable, friendly and eager to please us, Liang-yu tells us that the city was once surrounded by stone walls, although only parts are now visible.

Decades after she'd left China, Koh-wei could still describe the design. There was a narrow path on which she could walk the entire circuit of the walls above the city. Each wooden gate, with stairs ascending symmetrically on either side, was crowned by a tower. Black lacquer signs of auspicious characters and figures – still visible to us – guarded the city entrances. A long time ago, the city used to have seven gates, which were set almost equally on all the walls. But when Koh-wei was growing up, there were only four, and these were all on the east side, the side of the river.

From the city walls and her house at the edge of town, Koh-wei would have been able to walk to the grand Ming Dynasty mansions at the centre of the city, as we also do. With their heavy wooden doors and thick archways, protective corbel carvings and high-stepping thresholds, these were the houses of the civil servants and town governors. The encroachment of buildings on either side created from the streets a maze of narrow lanes, through which, in those days, no vehicle larger than rickshaws and palanquins could pass. The bare feet of the carriers running over the stones would have made a flat, pat-patting, sound. I imagine Koh-wei listening. To a child, these lanes of cobbled stones might have seemed themselves like walls laid flat.

The city walls and grand mansions had been built when maritime trading had been banned. In direct reversal of previous openness, the Chinese Empire had shut tight like a clam. China built her Ten Thousand Li wall, the Great Wall, designed to separate China, or the Celestial Realm, from the Barbarians to the north and the west.

But who were the Barbarians, I wonder – who the strangers here? And who were the Celestials? The Han Chinese, who made these distinctions, called the natives of Fujian and Guangdong 'Southern heathen' or 'barbarian'. Foreigners. Not properly Chinese, at least as far as the Chinese Empire defined itself. The Han wondered: where did people in these migrant provinces actually come from?

Chaozhou was physically cut off from the rest of China. And not only by the city walls and then the Han Jiang river to the south. The city was surrounded by Gold Mountain in the north, Penholder Mountain in the east, and Calabash Mountain in the west, mountains two thousand kilometres above sea level. Removed from ruling China on one side, the feeling was – still is to us – that Chaozhou is much closer to Nanyang, Southeast Asia across the ocean, Singapore, my mother's home. That stretch of water feels more crossable than the walls.

*

In the five hundred years since they have been built, Chaozhou's walls have been breached on a few famous occasions.

Once was when the city's inhabitants rose up against the emperor. They were crushed by the imperial army, and a hundred thousand citizens slaughtered, with only monks spared. The ashes of the dead were heaped up and merged with the overshadowing mountains. Alongside the trees used for carving, tea grew on these mountains of the dead. Fed by human ashes, the vegetation was so thick and the ledges of the mountains so precarious, that the people had to train monkeys – or so Liang-yu tells us – to pick the tea.

I laugh in disbelief. Then when we return home, I discover, in my local Chinese supermarket in Leeds, a brand of tea from the area, called 'Monkeypick Tea'. I decide I can't know what is legend, what is history.

In our return, we learn that Koh-wei's home is renowned for its tea: lapsang souchong, jasmine, green, oolong tea. *Gongfu cha*, or kungfu cha, translated as 'martial art tea', is its speciality. This plant decided whether families would migrate or not. A successful crop meant staying; a failed crop, departure. The flavour of the tea is smoky and strong. As I drink it back in Yorkshire, I think it tastes of ash, but then I wonder if I'm not just getting sucked into that story we were told of the mountains of the dead. An alternative name for the tea is Iron Bodhisattva, or Iron 'Buddha-to-Be' – a name that appeals to me as a Buddhist who never quite was. A very special tea ceremony developed, the rituals of *gongfu cha*, perhaps the very earliest tea ceremony, I learn. It involves throwing away the first cups, as if to quench parched spirits.

When Koh-wei first crossed over the river, she would have walked past one iron water buffalo. The second had been washed away in the yearly floods, the iron sunken with old skeletons of crocodiles. The town's main bridge, which had stood since the foundation of the city, had been swept out to the sea in the floodwaters.

In Koh-wei's day, everyone crossed the river by a span of wooden punts. The townspeople felt the water under their tread. *City of Tides.*

That one iron water buffalo is still there. My parents and I saw it, as I think we also saw real water buffalo grazing the river's banks. But I can't be sure. I have to admit that, in writing my grandmother's story in China, more than locating myself anywhere else on the family map, facts merge with the imagination. What I witnessed was already inundated with my grandmother's repressed memories, filtered through my mother's stories.

*

But what were Koh-wei's real origins? I mean who were her biological parents? Who, alongside where, was she from?

In her only mention of this in the handbag documents, Koh-wei declares her 'origins unknown'. But her fisherman-farmer foster-father told Koh-wei that she came from a wealthy, aristo-cratic family, and she told my mother this. As evidence, he gave her a square of peach-coloured organdie cloth, cut from her swaddling. And with this scrap, he gave my grandmother an adoptee's dream and the start of a quilt.

The story he told her was that she was a rich girl disguised as a poor girl. The swatch was a token not only of a biological mother's love, he said, but of her high status. Whether true or not – and why would she doubt her beloved father? – Koh-wei held on to that cloth and to her fairy-tale beginnings. The organdie swatch would eventually make its way to my grand-mother's own memory trunk in Singapore, where it would puz-zle my mother. Koh-wei would take it out, hold it, touching her most precious possession. The swatch must have been lost in the escape to India, but its ghost lives on in the Chinese pat-terns that resemble it which Koh-wei has sewn into her quilt as she also preserved her storybook past.

But what of identity, an official record? My grandmother said her name was Sim Koh-wei. At first I think that Sim must have been her adoptive father's name. But then I wonder about this, and also even if her personal name was Koh-wei. In the handbag documents from Singapore, we already detected the alternatives of 'Sim Jua' and 'Sim Kua', before, and predominant over, that of Sim Koh-wei. My grandmother didn't write and we have only English transliterations of Chinese characters. I point out to my mother that we can't even know her mother's real name. For my mother, a mother who was so familiar to her becomes mysterious in her Chinese origins.

*

Then I discover a detail that makes me question whether my grandmother's name even *was* a name.

There's only one transliterated letter difference between her declared Chinese name and the term in Hokkien for giving up girls. *Sim-pû-á* in Hokkien means 'little daughter-in-law', and it describes a custom common in southeast China, first encountered by Western missionaries at the end of the Qing Empire. Koh-wei's exact time and place.

A *sim-pû-á* could be a girl who was either given away as a baby to a rich family to become a servant, or was sold is better to a poor family to be fostered and become the wife of their son, hence offsetting the need for his family to find a dowry later. Girls were hardly ever truly adopted. Instead, they were abandoned. 'Adoption' meant being given up as a child bride. This practice was only abolished under the communists. Is Koh-wei's 'name' a clue to the history of the abandonment of girl children in China?

'Few societies in history have prescribed for women a more lowly status or treated them in a more routinely brutal manner than traditional Confucian China.' I am reading a book by Kay Ann Johnson, an American historian who devoted her life to the subject, and who herself adopted a Chinese baby. This is her opening sentence. She couldn't emphasize any more the misogyny of China in this period.

Even though in my grandmother's south, at least poorer Chinese women had relatively more freedom, since they could escape confinement by participating in field work, girls given up to be 'adopted' in childhood for marriage could still be used as family slaves. Their numbers increasing at times of economic difficulty, *sim-pû-á*s were part of a continuum of devaluing women, which at its most extreme included female infanticide.

Only one among many, I realise, my grandmother only just escaped that fate. But who decided she shouldn't be killed? This my mother doesn't know. She knows nothing before that moment of abandonment in the river.

And so, after we visit Chaozhou and get to know the area, and holding on metaphorically to that swatch of swaddling as tightly as my grandmother did the physical scrap, I conjure another set of images.

*

Down the road from where Koh-wei grew up, the wealthiest house in the area close to Chao-an. In the vast courtyard, lotus pools. Lush green leaves shade the surface from the sun. Out of the thick mud, white lotus flowers float above invisible stems. A vista of stone-ridged roofs, Chaozhou corners curling up, extending endlessly into the distance: less fixed stone, more waves of the sea.

Swallows swoop and glide, swoop and glide into the eaves, and sparrows gather up on the gutters to chatter.

This is the house of the local landlord, ruler of this part of the province. Hong Chen-ci is landowner, government official, trader, sheriff and warlord, all at once.

The first decade of the twentieth century marks an interval between China's grand acts of political transformation. The Qing, the last Chinese empire, is fragmenting. A strong leader has yet to appear who will unite the country into a modern nation. China is ruled by warlords, particularly here in these provinces. They hold sway with guanxi, the unbreakable bond of indebtedness, and inter-clan rivalry. Their rule brings even greater instability The people are being slaughtered and starved. The Celestial Realm is being broken into pieces, the ancient, massive, apparently unbreakable pot of the empire finally shattering. Newer, European empires are being pieced into the cracks. The warlords are the glue.

My parents and I visit Hong's house and learn its history. It is a vast compound – empty now – but I imagine what it might have been like in Koh-wei's day and how it might have connected to her story.

A village and a fortress more than just a house, one thousand people live inside. Within this walled-in compound (more walls), Hong keeps his own private army. They man the watchtowers. They guard the heavy wooden doors, which require several men to shift them. There are hundreds of rooms in the complex: thirty kitchens; fifty washrooms; one room just for sorting rice – the grain shelled with a large wooden pump. The workers have designated roles – plumbers, cooks, clerks. The house is so vast that the window cleaner is engaged in an endless cycle. As soon as he has finished, he begins again.

There are also locals from Chaozhou who come to work here on a daily or occasional basis. They include those who grow rice, lotus roots, cabbages and carp on the rich man's land, perhaps also a fisherman-farmer. The warlord is also a farmer, a wealthy landlord-farmer. With the increasing mechanisation of transport, he supplies food to the growing populations of the satellite islands near the southeast coast of China, Formosa (Taiwan) and Hong Kong. As part-return for their labour, some of his workers are allowed to tenant other property Hong owns in Chaozhou. Perhaps also, among them, a fisherman-farmer.

Hong makes most of his fortune from non-food trades. Old trades running between Siam, the Malay Peninsula, Singapore and further, to Europe, in tea and silk. And a trade in chinoiserie, to satisfy the fad taking over Europe at the start of the twentieth century: blackwood furniture, sometimes inlaid with jade, and Swatow cobalt-glazed porcelain.

And with the foreign imperial presence, a newer trade. Opium. Europeans, and particularly the British, hire Chinese merchants to help them operate via the guanxi that makes China otherwise mostly impenetrable to foreigners until the end of the Qing. Hong is one of these intermediaries, and it is opium especially that makes him wealthy. And I wonder if his name also is a common rather than a proper noun. For *Co-Hong*, or simply the *Hongs*, was the word the British use for their Chinese intermediary traders. Particularly in that precious, controversial and contested drug, opium, the Hongs, Co or Ci – also like the Asiatic Jews – were the cultural go-betweens: crucial links between British and Asian empires.

The merchant's position allows him to feed two loves. The first is for foreign things. Though he is walled off from his surroundings in his fort, he likes to think of himself as a cosmopolitan, and his house becomes a showcase of exotic imports. Under the Chaozhou roofs with upturned edges and Chaozhou wood carvings of his complex, he installs windows with stained glass imported from Italy. In the shrine room to his gods and ancestors, he insets the walls with turquoise and pink tiles from Spain, some of which are Islamic in their patterning. Alongside the burning incense and offerings of real fruit placed before the statues and paintings, the tiles offer their pictorial ripe peaches, apples and pears. When Hong eventually enters the shrine room as a portrait himself, the picture will show him and his principal wife correctly attired in late-Qing ornately embroidered and quilted silks. But the portrait will be taken with an imported European camera, one of the first ancestor photographs. We saw the portrait, and we saw the tiles.

Hong's other love is women. The warlord acquired several hundred concubines. Many of these women were kept inside their rooms day and night, and Hong accessed them as he wished and in secret. The house guide shows my parents and myself the maze of passageways. We gaze up at trap doors and broken ladders.

Was First Wife a jealous woman? The warlord's children competed in the hierarchy and for his fortune. First Wife was always looking for ways to depose, or dispose of, the children of the other wives. All of the warlord's progeny born into the household belonged to First Wife. Subsequent concubines were not allowed to raise their own children. When they married, daughters were always thought to have married out, that is outside of their father's family. Daughters were never really considered part of the clan. What Johnson calls, in an emphatic unholy chain, the 'patriarchal-patrilineal-patrilocal configuration' of Confucian, pre-Revolutionary China meant generations of males, their wives and children living under one roof. As was the case with Hong. When each of his sons got married, Hong sent out another celebratory wave of roofs to house the increase to his clan. Conversely, if a first wife put enough pressure on her husband, even a warlord might not be averse to letting a daughter go, particularly an ill child of a downtrodden concubine.

Did the merchant's loves ever combine? Foreign things plus women equals stranger-love? Koh-wei said the Chinese called her 'eagle eyes'. They didn't think she looked wholly Chinese. In her high-cheekboned face, her eyes were wide set, as well as being large. Another reason the Jewish surgeon told her that she looked Jewish. Jewish eyes.

I can't ever know if this wealthy trader-landowner was Koh-wei's real father. I only know that I've seen this house and heard its stories. And in memories that are not watertight, there is seepage between the knowable past and the imagination of those of us trying to put together the remaining scraps after the events.

Sim Koh-wei, whose name may be a practice rather than a name: at every stage of her Chinese life, she slips my grasp into watery uncertainty. My mother can't rescue her from this fate. She knows less about this period in her mother's life than I have tried to learn and reconstruct.

*

Our return to China constantly creates experiences that combine fantastic mythology with material histories. The Hong complex survives as a Qing palace. But during the Cultural Revolution, we learn, it was used as a prison. China transports us to long-distant imperial splendour, and to living-memory Communist brutality.

My parents and I seek to retrace Koh-wei's steps, in and around her home city. We have the best food we have anywhere in China. My mother, who has been wary of the dishes elsewhere in China especially since it feels as though pork can be smuggled into almost anything, is relieved to feel a sense of familiarity. 'It's Mama's food, her palate', she beams with delight. At last, something material of her mother that she can latch onto. She is a child again in her mother's kitchen in better times. In fact, the cuisine of mainly fish and vegetables, cooked very lightly on the hob, reminds me of what my mother makes now for herself and my father.

We ask Liang-yu to direct us to the best restaurant. It is both a fishmonger's and a restaurant that resembles a palace. As we enter, we pass a twenty-foot display of jewel-coloured fish on ice. Then the day's catch swimming around the tanks and still very much alive: our prey if we select our meal from here. There are also baskets of crabs, shrimp, eels, slugs and snails – animals of decreasing edibility; for my mother as a Jew; for me, then at my most Buddhist, as a vegan. Ascetically throughout China, I stick to tofu and steamed vegetables. The Chinese name these vegetarian dishes 'Buddha meals'. I'm painfully thin and I refuse to eat more than twice a day. My father eats absolutely everything.

My mother orders *mee fan,* a Hokkien dish of fried thin noodles, vegetables and fish, served with a pungent sauce. Refugee child that she still is at heart, she over-orders, as usual. At one point she is completely hidden by three huge bowls of different rice dishes and three huge bowls of different noodle dishes which have been placed before her.

The service is also excessive. The waitresses wait, literally, one positioned by the side of each table. Like herons scrutinising a pond, they stand transfixed, watching, trying to predict our every need. Our waitress is a girl of no more than twenty, short and sturdy. As soon as we put down our forks, she re-piles our plates, so that we become scared to finish and eat more and more slowly.

'Look', my mother says to me, her eyes sparkling with mischief as she notices the girl's attention. 'She's fallen in love with you. Why don't you take her home and teach her English?'

She's joking. I'm as likely at this point to begin a relationship as I am to eat a steak, and in my Buddhist heart I associate the two. Set on my monkish path, I am trying to discipline my body to give up all pleasures and attachments, to have nobody and no body. But I wonder if my mother is thinking of her mother waiting on her father, even of herself and my father.

We look for the house that could have been my grandmother's. We ask about her surname, and the people tell us that 'Sim' is common here. The Chinese abroad have a surprisingly limited range of surnames, since migrants often came from the same village, and village equalled clan or family.

As we walk the streets, we see people sewing. We learn that, in addition to carving, tea, porcelain, opera and the food, Chaozhou is famous for embroidery. And suddenly, my mother remembers. Her mother had said that in winter the women used to make quilted jackets. And sure enough we come across women making quilted gifts for girls' marriages. My grandmother's quilt, I realise, as much as it is made up of bits and pieces of her subsequent life, begins here: in her clan, in her village.

In her village, as the apparent only Westerners, we raise a lot of curiosity. Young people accost us in the streets to practise their English. The older ones simply stare or wave and smile. Four town elders invite us into their old Ming-style house. They seat us on a hard blackwood bench and insist on making us the local 'monkey-pick' tea. They warm the teapot several times. Then they pour the cups to overflowing, emptying them before refilling them. I tell my mother they are practising *gongfu cha* I have read about, the ancient tea ceremony with the special monkey-pick tea. My mother is moved I have learned so much about her mother's culture. Our hosts instruct us to drink the tea quickly. The taste is smoky and ash-bitter.

The elders talk to my mother about their memories of the old days. I'm shocked to hear my mother speaking Hokkien, a language that's similar enough to our old hosts' Teochew that they can understand each other. Even my mother hadn't realised she knew Hokkien so well until this moment. I wonder if May's fluency in her mother's tongue is simply the product of childhood shopping at Tekka Pasa with Koh-wei, or from when Koh-wei's friends Ah-Kim and Ah-Yee ('aunties') used to come round. Or is the language part of another forgotten memory: a time when May's Chinese mother used to speak in her native tongue to her daughter, my mother? Now that we are in China, in this Ming mansion with four Chaozhou residents only a little older than Koh-wei would have been, I see evidence for the first time that my mother really is half Chinese.

Given that my grandmother had for so long – fifty years? – mostly sought to leave behind her Chinese past, our experience of return, particularly for my mother, is both unsettling and moving. My mother laughs with surprise and pleasure that she can converse with the locals, that so much is familiar in a place that is yet strange to her. Her face flushes with excitement. She leans forward, her knees together, trying to decipher every single word. Because of Koh-wei's assimilation in Singapore's Jewish community, my mother has never thought of herself as Chinese. Yet the photograph I take of my mother with the four elders in their courtyard allows me to see, in the way that photographs sometimes can, what I've not really been able to see in life. It suggests that my mother belongs here, in China. The photograph captures my mother steadying – reassuring and at the same time bonding with – the elderly blind woman. They link arms. My mother beams and leans into this old Chinese lady, a woman who could have been her mother.

When my mother tells Koh-wei's story of her childhood and emigration, over and again, the people in Fujian nod. They recognise the plot, the journey. They say to my mother: welcome home. They don't say that throughout China. Just here, in my grandmother's home city.

'I am proud to be Chinese', my mother says after our visit to Chaozhou. 'I hadn't expected Mama's home to be so beautiful, to have such a rich history, for the people to be famous for so many things. It makes me realise my mother had an amazing life before she became my mother.'

If my writing this book is enabling this insight, the camphorwood chest keeps giving me the same gift in relation to my own mother's life, as well as to those of her ancestors.

*

Koh-wei was also welcomed, to the home of her foster-father. She had been lost and given up, but then she was found and adopted, and she proved a gift to her foster-father. She brought value as his child, and she worked out her value as a woman.

In these ways her story doesn't fit the usual Chinese foundling story. My grandmother always said that she loved her foster-father dearly. He must have loved her in return. After he had lost his wife, particularly if they didn't have any children of their own, he would have come to rely on her. She would have had to cook for him, to tend house and to look after his clothes. It was here, in her girlhood, that she learned to make hard domestic work her principal mode of love.

As he got older she would also have become the backbone of his business. She went to the new city, Swatow, to trade in the market. About half of what they farmed went to the landowner for rent, and the rest supplied their own food. But they had some surplus, and with that they earned money enough for other items needed to eke out a life – a few clothes, cups and bowls, a wok, a steaming pot. I imagine her as a young girl in Swatow, sitting before open sacks of rice, piles of thin purple aubergines and yard-long beans.

With her eagle eyes, she watched the world around her carefully.

*

The first morning of our stay in the port of Shantou, modern-day transliteration of Swatow, we are told that Swatow translates as 'head of the mountain'. I later find out that it doesn't. But our source, who declares much else on the area with authority, is a woman whose mother had also emigrated, from Swatow, in her mother's case in the early 1950s. Our informant herself was born in Thailand. We sit at breakfast together in the one big international hotel in Shantou, renowned for its revolving top-floor restaurant. 'Revolving' is an aspiration. A circle mechanism cut out in the middle of the floor turns the diners around slowly until we can almost see the sea, then it halts creakily and we are turned back the other way. As she and my mother swap migration-and-return stories, we dodge the static plants that would otherwise trail in our plates.

By the time of the Thai woman's mother's day, even of Koh-wei's, Swatow was displacing Chaozhou as the chief trading port. Literally. The new city was stealing ground from the old. In the annual floods, the Han Jiang picked up more and more silt washed down from the mountains and dropped it outside Chaozhou's gates. The City of Tides was becoming landlocked. The flooding created a new peninsula. Today a major trading port between China, Hong Kong and the rest of the world, Shantou is only one metre above sea level.

I try to imagine what Koh-wei's eagle eyes could have seen.

Down by the seafront, sampans buzz around large fishing junks, offloading the catch and rushing to get it to market. Men grapple and toss the fish: giant grouper, silver sea bream, red mullet, flatfish, eels. Close to the shore, women paddle and scoop sea slugs, sea cucumbers, crabs, lobster and shrimp. They retrace nets stretching across the shoreline, exposed wooden frames like the skeleton of some giant sea-monster.

Alongside their catch in the market, I picture her setting up her own wares, vegetables laid out in wicker baskets. Mid-morning, she gathers unsold things and walks back to the port. I go with her. In the lull of the hot part of the day, men play Mah Jong, sitting at tables in singlets in the shade of banyans. She notes when they get excited by the gambling, listening to the *clack-clacking* of the bone-and-bamboo tiles.

To reach Swatow from Chaozhou, Koh-wei would have had to take a steamboat downriver. This was the only route before the road was built, which would not happen until the 1940s, after she had left. By boat, the journey would have taken her five hours, and, as the main thoroughfare from the growing port inland to the rest of China, the river then would have been very busy.

I go back with her on this journey. Koh-wei sees changes. Fishing villages are becoming workshops manufacturing goods for world export. By the time of our own visit, the area is a Chinese 'Special Economic Zone', designated for attracting foreign investment and trade. Koh-wei witnesses early signs of the key role of foreigners in this international modernisation. The British, but also the French and the Americans, seemed to be taking over the rivers and coastline. Their gunboats – huge clanking, puffing, metal affairs, quite different from the smoothly gliding Chinese junks – would change China's relations with the world profoundly.

Trying to navigate our way around modern Shantou with the only map we can find (in Mandarin), we come upon a vestige of the British presence. In run-down old Chongshan Park, on an island in the middle of the river estuary, a part is labelled 'English Corner'.

That part of the park is completely empty apart from the sign. It's hard not to see this as symbolic. The British were here but, apart from us, are long gone now.

*

Swatow was Britain's product. In the late eighteenth century, Scottish Presbyterians established a church in the then village and sought to convert locals to Christianity. I learn it was they who bestowed the name Swatow and this was their attempt at the local pronunciation. They didn't have much success in converting the Chinese to Christianity. But the colonial entrepreneurs, who followed the missionaries, did persuade the Chinese, with a heavy hand, into trade. The East India Company, the principal European agency in China and the British Empire's chief vehicle for trade, had been established in neighbouring Guangdong since 1715. It was the East India Company that turned Swatow into an international trading port and that enabled the British Empire to bring the Chinese Empire to its knees, with a drug, opium.

The East India Company gets a bad rap throughout our tour in China. This isn't surprising. Its name crops up in popular memory and history books at almost every moment of British colonial exploitation in Asia. In China, opium was the cause of profound suffering but it was also the trade currency. The East India Company had a virtual monopoly on the drug. Opium was the Company's principal import into China, the only means to balance its essential export: the tea for which Britain had developed an unquenchable thirst.

The British used opium to solder parts of the empire across Asia into relations of dependency. Knowing full well the narcotic and addictive nature of the drug, the East India Company rerouted opium from India, where it was grown, to China, especially through the coastal provinces of Guandgong and Fujian. The drug was exported also to the Straits colonies, where it was used by the Chinese 'coolies' working for the British Empire, many of them from Fujian, to numb the pain of labour. Historians estimate that, by the mid-nineteenth century, a full third of the Chinese in Singapore, almost all emigrants from these southeast provinces of my grandmother's home, were addicted to opium.

So into these provinces came opium and Christianity, sometimes in unwholesome coupledom, and out went tea and coolies. *Coolie.* I discover that even this insult was traded all over the British Empire. You find it in British literature and history about Asia, the Caribbean, even the Americas. The word comes from the name of a Gujarat tribe in India, 'Kolis'. It then makes its way into Hindi, where it means 'transient labourer', finally entering the Chinese language via the British Empire as *k'ui-li,* which means 'hard strength'. Chinese slaves. Something echoes into Koh-wei's personal story here. *Strong like an ox*: what the cousins said of Koh-wei when she first worked in domestic service for Jacob. I realise that my grandmother was also traded across empires. 'My poor Mama', my mother sighs. 'She worked so hard.'

Seeking to stop the seepage of this 'foreign mud' of the 'foreign devils', the Qing Empire outlawed the opium trade. But the British bypassed the ban with the help of intermediaries – the Hongs, the same kind of Hong who lorded over what I imagine could have been Koh-wei's original home. The Chinese in self-defence sank twenty thousand chests of British opium, and the British went to war, setting off the Opium Wars. British victory ensured legalisation of the opium trade, protection of missionary work, and the creation of 'concession' or protected trade zones for Europeans, of which Hong Kong was one. Swatow also became one of those zones, a trade port in a chain that would connect, dot-to-dot, the eastern seas of the British Empire, from Shanghai to Singapore. This would become part of the Elias family's spice route, a line cast between Jacob and Koh-wei.

In Swatow, the British built godowns, big warehouses for their goods on the waterfront. They modelled part of the city in colonial style, erecting their three-story mansions around a circle in the centre. My parents and I come upon it in modern-day Shantou. It's another uncanny moment, now for us all, the familiar made strange as the streets radiate off the roundabout Piccadilly Circus style.

The foreign presence stimulated internal migration from villages to cities and emigration from the coast. At the same time, it stoked Chinese nationalism. Chinese martial-arts secret societies mounted protests against the evil knot of Christianity, Western colonialism and opium. Piles of opium were set alight in the streets. In Swatow, missionaries were attacked and some imprisoned, their books burned, their churches looted. Foreign businesses and British department stores were smashed, imported goods boycotted, and foreign-built railways ripped up. In reprisal, the British military found and decapitated the reputed ringleaders, and displayed their heads on poles. The Chinese we meet won't let us forget especially this. The barbarity reminds me of what the Japanese will do to the Chinese in Singapore, where the Chinese tell similar stories.

By the early 1930s, officially at least, all foreigners had been expelled from China.

*

Although Britain had wound down its imperial presence in China by the 1930s and had returned the majority of concession zones, including Shantou, China was having to contend with a new empire. Japan acquired territory as the Europeans lost it. By 1938, the Japanese were in southeast China, bombing Shantou and Guangdong, the latter where they made their headquarters, close to Koh-wei. Koh-wei would have witnessed some of this too: the atrocities of Japanese invasion and occupation, killings and rape, forced labour and forced prostitution, on top of the civil war between communists and nationalists. And I think she can't have failed to remember these scenes when, just a few years later in February 1942, the Japanese bombed and invaded her new home of Singapore.

'It's true', my mother says. 'She fled her home twice. She took two boat journeys. Now I see how brave she was. She left everything she'd known to go to my father.'

We are sitting in a small open-fronted café in a street seemingly devoted to fixing bikes. A man in the shop next door squats down and does something with wheels. My mother sees past me, into the distance of her mother's life. She speaks with genuine wonder. She seems innocent of how much her own plot repeated that of her mother's. I am revealing her mother's life as she's never seen it. But I am also seeing anew my mother's courage and drive. It's not explicitly Jewish, but this also, I think, is legacy.

In Fujian under the Japanese in the late 1930s, people starved. Walking skeletons looked for food down by the docks. War and unrest had come on top of a series of natural disasters – floods, drought, failed harvests. My mother and I have peered at photographs in dark Chinese heritage museums across the world – Singapore, New York, San Francisco – devoted to the history of this area and the ancestors compelled to leave. There was an exodus – another parallel with the Jews – not just for work, but for life. Only the fortunate got away.

My grandmother was among them. She packed her few belongings into a wooden chest. This was the chest, I'm sure, that May remembers from her early years in her parents' house, from which Koh-wei would take out a scrap of organdie to study, her most precious keepsake. Neither the trunk nor its contents would survive the fall of Singapore.

*

Koh-wei must have married quite young, betrothed even as a child if she was a bride daughter-in-law, since, as she says in the Marriage Registry Book, her first husband died in 1935, when she would have been twenty-six (or twenty-four). She would have had little choice in husband. If her foster-father was still alive, he would have arranged the match. If her foster-father was already dead – and he drops away from her account at this point – her impoverishment would have compelled her into marriage to survive.

Her husband probably couldn't afford a dowry. More than likely he was some kind of agricultural worker. And I realise that 'Sim' might have been his name rather than her father's. The work she must have done before she came to Singapore, I think, is farm, because she talked to my mother about how the women would leave the field just before they went into labour, and how they would return to work straightaway, their newborns strapped to their backs.

Her husband was poor if his wife had to engage in such hard work: *K'ui-li,* I think. They had one child, a girl. The name Poh-kim has carried over oceans of loss and forgetting to lodge in my mother's memory. Koh-wei gave birth and went back to the fields, Poh-kim on her back. She was so intent on working the land that she rarely saw her daughter's face.

These scenes from my grandmother's life could be from *The Good Earth,* the 1931 novel by Pearl S. Buck which my mother insists I'm exposed to. She loves the melodrama, the story of loss, struggle and survival, but also because it evokes what could have been her mother's Chinese life. A poor, rural Chinese couple work the earth, exploited by rich landowners. They suffer drought, famine, migration. The mother kills a baby girl at birth, to give the family a better chance of survival.

Koh-wei absolutely didn't kill her daughter, but she did abandon her, repeating her own history on her child. One day her husband was found collapsed in the fields. He never recovered.

If the year was 1935 as my grandmother recorded in the handbag documents, China was in a state of further collapse. The Japanese invasion had devastated cities and drawn resources from the countryside. Civil war between nationalists and communists was ripping the country apart. In Fujian, a rebellion rejecting both communists and nationalists had to be quashed. In 1935, Mao began his Long March, from Fujian to the northern provinces. Koh-wei would have had few options to find work. With a child, no husband and no father anymore, she and her daughter were in danger of starvation. She decided to get out.

Through Shantou, half a million people from the southeast provinces emigrated, many to Southeast Asia. Women made up a significant proportion. In the Straits Settlements, the Aliens Ordinance of 1933 limited male but not, initially, female immigration. And so, from the years 1933 to 1938, some 200,000 Chinese women aged eighteen to forty left this southeast coast and made their way to Nanyang.

The unlucky among the migrant women were shipped against their will and forced into prostitution by triads, the organised crime gangs that operated particularly in Southeast Asia. The more fortunate majority left to work, as *am-mahs* and *ma-jies,* in the households of the Far Eastern colonies. These domestic roles overseas provided a new way for Chinese families to get rid of unwanted daughters. (Or for women who had not married, or who had lost their husbands, to survive, I think.)

And no longer a burden on their families when abroad, they could become a key source of support, with remittances sent to family who remained at home. The women who came from these provinces, unlike many other pre-Revolutionary Chinese women, hadn't been subject to foot-binding. They could work. *K'ui-li.*

My mother tells me that Koh-wei's remaining family – in-laws? she's not sure exactly who – wouldn't let her take the child. A man's family, even when he was dead, controlled her children. In any case, we reason, she couldn't have worked with a child in tow. She wouldn't have fit the nun-like image of the *am-mah* or *ma-jie.*

I believe that Koh-wei had every intention of returning to Poh-kim. I see in her the story of many migrants. Like most of them, she was leaving in order to earn and send money home. Like them, she planned to stay only until she had built up sufficient reserves. And I'm sure that expecting to return to Poh-kim in China gave Koh-wei reason to hesitate to stay with Jacob as his wife in Singapore. It makes sense to me now that she didn't want to leave the Chinese village in Singapore because she didn't want to leave her child permanently.

But Koh-wei never went back to China, and once with Jacob most of her Chineseness would start to ebb away. In Singapore she kept in touch with Poh-kim via letters, first via a community letter-writer in Chinatown, then with the help of her eldest stepdaughter, when Sally was competent enough to replace the professional scribe. By this stage, when she was becoming part of the Elias family, it was getting too late for Koh-wei to return home.

Koh-wei tried to keep Poh-kim's existence completely hidden from May. Was she ashamed, or was she protecting May from her previous, Chinese life – the time when she was another daughter's mother, a daughter who would have no idea of what being Jewish was? But when the family came back from India, my mother remembers her mother opening a letter from China. 'It told her that Poh-kim had died. It was the first time I saw her cry,' my mother says '– and the first time I realised she had another daughter.'

Poh-kim was simultaneously born and died in May's consciousness. This Chinese sister would have been about ten years older than my mother: sixteen, already becoming a young woman.

*

The lost Chinese daughter plays a much bigger role in the family story than featured in my mother's accounts by the camphorwood chest when I was growing up. I think that, without needing to support the Chinese daughter, Koh-wei might never have left China. Yet without Poh-kim's death, she might not have stayed in Singapore. She might not, eventually, have married Jacob. I see the abandoned Chinese girl as the dark shadow of May's own girlhood; indeed, as the condition of my mother's existence.

This lost Chinese girl is Koh-wei herself, of course. But the abandonment is repeated because of the impossible choices Koh-wei faced around her own motherhood. Steered by fatal historical events, she left her own daughter to look after another woman's daughters. The lost girl might have made her even more open to look after a stranger's daughters, and also, I realise, to take as her own this stranger's family when they lost their mother.

I also think it must have made it additionally hard for my grandmother to let my mother go from Singapore, her remaining and now eldest daughter, to go for love and with a stranger. I remember May describing how her mother 'weeps in her heart' as she watched her daughter pack her things into the camphorwood chest ready for her journey to England. No wonder my grandmother held on tight to that roll of thread as it unspooled with May's ship departing from the docks of Singapore.

And who is this lost Chinese girl to me?

Before I began this book, I was a serious Buddhist. For its purity, I was drawn to Chan Buddhism: Chinese Buddhism; the original Zen. I studied Dharma and became part of a Tibetan Buddhist Sangha in the Yorkshire Wolds, some twenty miles or so from where my synagogue is now. I went on regular retreats and to many Buddhist festivals around the world. I read Chinese Chan poetry and studied mandalas. I did a Buddhist pilgrimage to the birthplace and key locations in the life of the Buddha, in Nepal and North India. In China, I visited as many remaining Buddhist sites as I could. I saw Buddhas in Chinese caves. I walked round and round Wild Goose Pagoda in Xian and saw the first Buddhist sutras to be carried to China. They were written in blood on wood and animal skin. The power of these ancient documents, of a life path handed down, is not dissimilar from the Torah I now read from in the synagogue.

On many occasions back then before I began this journey as an adult with my mother through the camphorwood chest, I stayed in my beautiful local Buddhist community. My task was to care for the gompa, the temple. I thought then that I had found my perfect moment, my purpose, when I made the 'one-hundred-water-bowl offering' before the statues of the Buddhas in the temple. This involved filling, very slowly, and all to exactly the same height just below the rim, rows and rows of a hundred brass bowls with sweet-smelling saffron water. The meditative absorption and calmness silenced my busy mind and stopped all wanting. Here, I thought then, was my belonging. If I'd stayed here, I would have reversed my grandmother's becoming Jewish. Koh-wei must have been Buddhist before she left China, though she never left any sign of this. My return would then have been to a kind of Buddhist DNA.

But Buddhism proved to be about not belonging. What was eventually troubling in Buddhism for me was precisely the reason I was at first drawn to it: detachment, the willed failure to feel connection or, therefore, its loss or absence. I just couldn't get myself to renounce anything *enough* – the world, family, this intense, all-absorbing love for my mother. Not all beings were my mother. That felt like a lie. *My* mother is unique, irreplaceable, I knew, and I know I will feel her loss as unique and almost unbearable. As she felt the loss of her own mother. As Koh-wei surely must have felt the loss of Poh-kim.

A few nights after our return from China, a dream woke me up. My mother was showing me something, some relic of my grandmother – not of hers, but of *her*. It was a locket containing her hair. My dream self thought, as my conscious self would have done at the time, how sentimental, how sentimentalising, and then switched off and became distanced. And suddenly the dream pans out, and I'm the one holding the locket, and it's my mother who is dead, and the locket still contains my grandmother's hair, but I see one of my mother's own hairs in it.

I stopped being a Buddhist. I began to get more interested in the sticky, conflicted attachments of Judaism, the willed refusal to forget or disconnect. I became aware of what my ancestors had kept alive, passed down, and practised. Breaking the silence, I began to speak with them.

I can trace no relatives in China. The camphor wood chest is Chinese-made with Chinese scenes depicted on it. But there is nothing in it, nothing at all, except the Chinese silks ghosting my grandmother's quilt, that tells me about the Chinese side of the family. Poh-kim, my mother's sister and my Chinese aunt, embodies a lost Chinese legacy.

12. Shema

Say, darling, say, when I'm far a-way, Some-times you may think of me, dear;
Bright sunny days will soon fade a-way, Re-mem-ber what I say, and be true, dear.

The first memory of my grandfather, and my first time in my mother's home, the flat on Short Street in Singapore. I am three years old.

I wake to a mysterious clinking sound and leave my mother sleeping. We are sharing a big bed. I know I'm not in my own room at home. I move in the direction of the sound. It's still dark and the space is unfamiliar. Doors to rooms are open, or there are no doors. It is steamy hot.

I find where the noise is coming from. The small brown man I met for the first time yesterday, the one so unlike my father but who seemed to know me already, has lined up a series of glasses on the kitchen counter. He is tapping his spoon against each one in turn, making a kind of music. Absorbed, he cocks his silvery head, listening to the irregular notes and rhythms. He is humming, a strange, sad intonation. I watch and listen for a while until he sees me. He turns towards me fully. His face shines on me as brightly as I feel the sun does here. Sitting me on his knee, he starts singing now, in a language I don't yet understand, to a tune that I know is quite other from what I've ever heard before.

And thus my mother discovered us, her father and myself, when she rose some hours later, wondering where on earth I could have toddled off, so early on my first morning in Singapore. This was my first intimate encounter with Jacob and with a new, strange, sad music.

Later I will hear this music in synagogues, and I will think of this moment as like a call to prayer.

Shema, Yisrael. Hear, O, Israel. Listen.

*

Say, darling, say, when I'm far away,
Sometimes you may think of me, dear.
The bright sunny days will soon fade away.
Remember what I say and be true, dear.

If my grandmother's life is submerged in a watery silence, my grandfather emanates as pure voice. He resonates. He chants and enchants.

He is an outpouring of words literally, in the object from the camphorwood chest that most brings him back to life. This is a cassette tape of his voice, recorded when he was eighty years old, three years before he died. Audiocassette technology had just been introduced, so the fact that I can listen to my grandfather's voice, half a century later, is because of an accident of material histories coinciding with the whims of someone in the family to record him, my cousin Annie-girl, Sally's daughter.

Annie-girl's making of the tape also coincided with my first visit to Singapore, and I'm caught on the recording too, singing the English nursery rhymes I was growing up with.

'Baaa-Baaa-Black Sheeppp!' My child's voice rings out, with confidence and determination and a refusal to be drowned out by the voice of my elder brother.

My grandfather must have been listening to me then, as I listen to him now.

In the early magnetic tape, I can hear the sounds of Singapore as I remember them. Shouts come from the yard on the ground floor, including the hawkers' calls, repeated in Hokkien and Malay, through the veranda and the open windows. Neighbours' radios and televisions hum gently. Traffic honks and revs. The voices on the tape rebound off the concrete floor, making the flat sound much larger than the four rooms it actually was. I can visualise the scene. My grandfather sits in his cane chair wearing his sarong, the sarong which my mother gave me and that I now wear – one that did not end up as scraps sewn into my grandmother's quilt.

On the tape Jacob mostly sings, with a deep projection remarkable for an old and small man. The heartrending tone, the resonance, as well as the accent and pronunciation, recall my grandfather so fully to life that my mother can't bear to listen to this tape. The recording is the ghost of her father. He is there and yet – voice only – not there. She gives me the tape, but not before I make a second recording, of her accompanying her father's songs, singing alongside him.

Even when we can't see a beloved, we know them exactly by their voice. 'Who's there?' we say. 'Me', comes the reply, and somehow we know exactly who the 'me' is. And what of the recorded voice of a loved one who has died? Voice is so imbued with a person's presence that the earliest audio recordings summoned the bereaved. They turned to the new electric voice to tune into their dead and break through the cold wall of silence.

'Say darling, say, when I'm far away. . . Remember what I say', my grandfather sings. This song, 'The Spanish Cavalier', is about a soldier who is about to go to war, a war from which he knows he may not return. The singer imagines that, if he does not return, the audience's memory of his song will keep his words alive, his presence in their memory.

The American writer Gertrude Stein, who like Jacob loved 'The Spanish Cavalier', had an idea, not fulfilled, to write her biography based on the songs she loved. But if such a biography existed, it would be not a chronicle of a life but rather the capturing of a person's soul. The songs someone sang and left, especially in their own voice, take the listener inward. The songs are clues to the times, but the singer's performance expresses their feelings.

Unlike other bits of the family archive (photographs, letters, objects), music needs only to be carried in our bodies, in our heads, hearts and voices. Portability is especially important for families on the move, migrants and refugees, such as Jacob's line.

*

There goes, there she goes, there goes my boat today.

Who knows where my boat goes today?

'Na Jaane Kidhar Aaj Meri Nao Chali Re?' ('Who knows where my boat goes today?'), a Hindi song, from the Bollywood film *Jhoola* ('Swing'), 1941.

The three most poignant letters in the camphorwood chest are all from my grandfather, written close together after the tape was made: the year that he died. These letters so capture my grandfather's voice that, again, my mother can hardly bear to read them. Nevertheless, she knows that they're important, that I want to see them or rather to hear my grandfather. So we sit again by the camphorwood chest. Holding the letters between us, we decipher Jacob's increasingly spidery scrawl.

The first is a flimsy aerogram written to my mother in England; the last May would have of her father's words. Within six weeks she would receive a telegram saying that he was sick. Over the two days it took her to fly to Singapore, Jacob fell into a coma and didn't regain consciousness.

Dearest May

Thank you for the money you sent us. Today I am 83 years old with four illnesses. I am living on complan and taking treatment from an English doctor. You may not recognise me as I am become a 'drumstick' (!). As you know, my eye sights are failing and in a few months I will be totally blind. My days are numbered. I am only praying to see you before anything happens. A daggar perces my heart. Abdalek May, try to come early. Awaiting your arrival soon.

Your most loving Pa.

The second is a short note that Jacob has written to a neighbour, asking to borrow money to buy medicines. It is inscribed on the back of a page torn from a day-to-a-page diary. By that date on the diary, Jacob will be dead.

Finally, in an envelope addressed to 'The Director, Borneo Sumatra Trading Company, Holland', returned, hence, as 'UNDELIVERABLE':

In the year 1926, I became the sole broker for the Borneo Sumatra Trading Company in Singapore. When Mr F. J. Witt left Singapore for South Africa in 1937, he entrusted me to look after his properties for 9 years. As such, I hope that you will be kind enough to give me a helping hand in my present stricken health condition. I am now a total 'shipwreck' suffering from an incurable heart disease. I am 84 and my eye sights are fading.

For me, this last is the most unbearable letter of the three. Why? Because a voice was speaking but no one heard. The letter was undeliverable. Like the note to the neighbour, the letter was never read (could not be read) by its intended recipient, because of that desperately general, unrooted address.

And yet it's precisely because it was never received and read that I can read and hear it now. It not reaching its addressee means that it comes to me, to whom it has much more personal, familial power. In these letters, I hear Jacob at the end of his life: sickening, and so impoverished as to be fully dependent on migrated children, on neighbours, even on long-departed employers.

So how did his boat get here?

My mother has few answers on this, so I use the letters, and particularly the last one, along with Jacob's songs, to reconstruct his sad, downward journey.

*

Founded in 1894 and known in Dutch as Borsumij, the Borneo Sumatra Trading Company was a merchant house whose head offices were indeed in Holland. Jacob got that right. As its name suggests, the Company, based in The Hague, had run trade routes from Borneo and Sumatra, also Java, and the Moluccas, formerly the Spice Islands, which together constituted the Dutch East Indies. In Jacob's day, the Company connected the Dutch colony with colonies of the British, namely Malaya and Singapore, and also extended to India, Africa and the Americas.

The Borneo Sumatra Trading Company was a successor of the very first colonial company, the Dutch East India Company. But by the beginning of the nineteenth century, the Dutch had ceded influence, treaties and ports to the British East India Company, which I find is back again in my story, now in Jacob's plot. These organisations and their rivalries created the colonial Singapore my grandfather lived and worked in. Sir Stamford Raffles, who founded the colony, was sent to Singapore as an agent of the British East India Company. In 1819, he established Singapore as a trading post, and it was trade that attracted Jacob and his family to the island.

One of the earliest and most lucrative of trades was in spices: Jacob's family business. It had been spices that had motivated European explorers to venture east in the first place. Under British rule, Singapore became a centre of the spice trade. Spices were Jacob's principal ware as 'sole broker', and they resonated in his Company's name, for while Borneo was an island, it was also the name of a kind of camphor from that island.

By the time Jacob began his brokerage in the early twentieth century, the Company's head office in The Hague subcontracted trade and gave advances to merchants via brokers like my grandfather in the colonies. A system of tender meant that merchants, who were mainly Chinese, Indian and Arab immigrants, and brokers, who were also not white, were always in debt to the Company. My grandfather asking for money from his boss is nothing new. This system was so exploitative that even a European inspector judged that the Borneo Sumatra Trading Company 'in Borneo's heart of darkness was terrorising the region', transforming native merchants and brokers into colonial 'puppets'. It breaks my heart that Jacob, my beloved grandfather, ended up being one of these colonial 'puppets'.

Mr F. J. Witt, the ex-boss Jacob mentions, was a leading figure in Dutch colonial life. He presided as manager of the Singapore branch of the Borneo Sumatra Trading Company. Under Witt's lead, the Company acquired its own named building: the Borsumij (Dutch name) Building, 41 Robinson Road. The *Malayan Saturday Post* marked the inauguration. One photograph taken outside the building shows European Company men, dressed in white suits, being delivered to the new doors by Chinese rickshaw pullers, dressed in black. From inside the building, two further photographs. One of the 'company's staff' – all white Europeans. Another of the local 'mercantile community', Chinese and Indian men predominating.

I can't find Jacob in any of these official Company images. And then I realise his absence itself is telling. Or rather, it asks me a question. For which 'side' would Jacob Elias have been on? Company staff or mercantile community? White European colonialists or Chinese and Indian traders? As a broker Jacob was between the Company and the merchants. He was also between whites and 'Asiatics'. As an 'Asiatic Jew' he was neither European, nor yet fully 'Asiatic'. I discover that for this reason, because of their in-between-ness, brokerage was a common profession for Iraqi Jews in Singapore such as Jacob.

In most of the family photographs of Jacob in the chest, my grandfather is dressed in white, usually in a suit, rarely without his trilby, and later, as he got older, also with his bamboo cane. He was natty, stylish, a man not only loved but also after my own heart. Like his boss Mr Witt, he enjoyed a day at the racecourse, the most popular colonial recreation ground.

In the earliest photograph we have of my grandfather, from around the 1910s, Jacob wears a bow tie and white jacket, his short-back-and-sides slicked back in a fashionable, Rudolph Valentino style. The Italian famous for playing a sheik was something of an icon for Jacob, one of the several actors he modelled himself on. The man on the right of the photograph has something heavier and less animated about his face.

My mother takes the photograph from me. 'This must be Papa's eldest brother, Ezekiel. He lost a leg and died young. The man in the middle is their cousin.'

Of this older man, I note that the chain crossing his chest, presumably attached to a pocket-watch tucked into his jacket, and his hair parted towards the middle, give him a more Edwardian look. His collar is Nehru or Indian style. The young men, Jacob and Ezekiel, are definitely dressed in a more modern and Western fashion.

In this photograph, Jacob couldn't be more different from how he is in the First Photograph, where Jacob appears, with his beard and kurta, every bit the Middle Eastern, almost nineteenth-century, merchant. Looking to flee 'Fortress Singapore' in 1941, Jacob is undeniably 'Asiatic'. Here, working for the Company in the secure British protectorate thirty years before, he is the young – Europeanised – man about Singapore's colonial town. The only trace of the East in this photograph is in the cousin's Raja-style jacket; although identifying with Valentino who identified as *The Sheikh* draws Jacob back interestingly into murky East-meets-West waters.

How, then, from my bearded, Arabic-looking grandfather do I reverse time to find this clean-cut, Europeanised young man?

*

WITH ENGLAND'S CROWN TODAY
WE HAIL OUR QUEEN AND PRAY
GOD SAVE THE QUEEN
MAY HE DEFEND OUR QUEEN
AND EVER GIVE US CAUSE
TO SING WITH HEART AND JOY,
GOD SAVE THE QUEEN!

The song Jacob sings on the tape with most gusto, belts out and almost shouts, is the British national anthem. I think he must have sung this at school. My mother told me that Jacob attended Raffles Institution, the very school I discover that Raffles set up to teach local languages to 'officers' of the East India Company and English to 'the sons of the higher order of natives and others'. Raffles said he intended it to be 'the means of civilising and bettering the conditions of millions.'

Raffles Institution shared the British public-school rituals to which, I remember with both contempt and rage, I couldn't – and didn't want to – make my confused, awkward self conform. Children were organised into 'houses' with 'housemasters'. The best-behaved were elected as 'prefects' and 'house captains' (my brother got to be head boy). All of us were subjected to the outdoorsy, fair-play teamship values of 'games' (cricket, rugby, lacrosse). I hated and failed at the lot.

And, like me, Jacob was expelled from school. 'He kissed a girl when he was about ten years old. At least that's what he told me', my mother laughs. 'He said that, after that, because of what he did, all the girls were put in a separate building. He claimed that it was his misdemeanour that led to the founding of Raffles Girls School and a separate Raffles Institution for boys.'

Actually, I find out that Jacob wasn't even *born* when Raffles Girls School was established. Was Jacob's boast or exaggeration an attempt to disguise not belonging? I can relate here. When people ask me what I was expelled for, I also usually pass not disclosing off as boasting. 'You'd be bored', I say. 'How long have you got? Many, many things. The list is too long.' Did Jacob also feel in between, in his case among Raffles's 'others'?

To continue receiving the English-language education necessary to advance in colonial Singapore, Jacob, like most Jewish children in colonial Asia (and like May after him), then attended a Christian school. The Anglo-Chinese Boys School was founded by American Methodist missionaries, and it must have been here that Jacob learned the rousing American protestant hymn, 'Stand up, Stand up for Jesus, ye soldiers of the cross'. Except I note that, when Jacob sings it, he changes the words: 'STAND UP, STAND UP FOR JESUS. . . HE'S ONLY TWELVE YEARS OLD.'

Then I realise he also changes the words in the national anthem on the tape, in the additional verse. Mind you, he's singing it at a time when few people in Britain even knew their own anthem had additional verses. I myself didn't know of it, until I listen to my grandfather's tape. But when I try to discover which verse this is, Jacob's version appears nowhere, at least not exactly like this. The first couplet seems to have been wholly of Jacob's own making, though it proves apt for his not quite British identity as a British subject of the colonies: he is 'with' England's crown, not quite of it. Then he drops any reference to 'laws' and exchanges 'joy' for 'voice' (it should be 'To sing with heart and voice').

I make up my own words for songs when my memory loses words, or because I never heard correctly in the first place. In my head my own versions get repeated and cemented and they come to displace the 'official' lyrics. But I think the mishearings say something about the improviser; about the scripts we've got going on in our own heads.

I realise that changing the script is what Jacob does in almost all his songs. In 'The Spanish Cavalier', where the lines are supposed to read, 'The blessing of my country and you, dear', what my grandfather actually sings is, 'you're the blessing of my heart and true dear.'

No country, but too much heart. The country of the heart. Appropriate in someone who would never have a fixed home and who lived in his feelings.

*

The roads are of my own country   galiyan hein apne desh ki
But even they are a stranger to me phir bhi hein jaise ajnabi
Who will I call as my own?   kis ko kahey
                               koi apna yehan.
I have no destination or companion   Saathi na koi manzil
I have no tribe

'Saathi na koi manzil' ('I have no destination or companion'), Hindi song made famous by Muslim singer Mohammed Rafi, from the Bollywood film *Bombai Ka Babu* ('The Gentleman from Bombay'), 1960.

From Uncle Moshe, I discover that the Company broker's family ran a trading company of their own. Jacob's father and uncle managed their own spice-trading business, called the Elias Brothers. It turns out that their office was close to the original offices of the Borneo Sumatra Trading Company, just around the corner from Change Alley.

A cross between a Western stock exchange and an Arabic bazaar, the area was the equivalent of Wall Street, the City of London and the Paris Bourse. I picture Jacob here. He makes his way past awning-covered stalls and shop fronts of the commissioning agents, exporters and importers, which line Change Alley and Market Street. He studies the exchange rates chalked up on blackboards for all goods passing through this hub of global trade. He meets his fellow brokers, stops, chats. They continue their work, inspecting samples before they make deals. Through magnifying glasses, they peer at the precious jewels and metals harvested from across Asia. Pearls from the South China Sea, silver from Kelantan, Malaya, gold from Kalimantan, Borneo, rubies from Burma. They stroke and hold to the sun cottons from India and the swirling wax-dyed Batik patterns from Java. Their fingers sift through opened sacks of tapioca and sago flour. They assess raw materials of the new industries of empire: rubber, tin, and copra, or dried coconut.

I see Jacob strolling through the spice row. He sniffs the spices, sometimes testing them on his tongue. Pepper, cardamom, cinnamon, ginger, nutmeg, cloves: the spices I imagined I could still inhale from his body when we visited Singapore. Spices so identified with their provenance they were known by geographical name: Singapore and Muntok white pepper; the untranslatables of 'Palembang', 'Jelotang', 'Banta', and 'Sarawak'; and 'Borneo', camphor itself. Jacob examines their colour, their freshness. He argues about rates and agrees contracts.

My mother and I carry forward the spice man's gestures. We can't resist a good haggle, and not only in markets. May will go back and forth repeatedly between carpet shops showing each business the others' quotes, saying magnanimously she wants to give them all the opportunity to lay her carpets for her, until she has the price and the company that satisfy her. She is drawn to the theatre of bargaining, and like her I feel a sense of triumph if I get a good deal. Keith, like many British in this scenario, is visibly embarrassed. He would rather pay over the value than negotiate.

The fulfilment of Raffles's dream of making Singapore an East-West emporium left the welfare of its inhabitants vulnerable when Depression hit in the 1930s. Within a few months, the Company was letting part of the main office it had moved to with such fanfare in the previous decade. Witt himself left the Company in July 1936, and left Singapore altogether soon after.

The Company was dissolved completely just after the war. The collapse was devastating for Jacob.

By the time May was born, just before the war, Jacob was calling himself a 'general broker'. On foot, no telephone, no office, he arranged deals between a variety of independent merchants. Even this income was not enough. As he tells Mr Witt in the pleading letter, he 'looked after the properties' for the Company, probably of abandoned houses of former employees and their un-let or un-sold warehouses.

He ended up as a caretaker, a Company man in this regard only.

'Poor Papa', my mother says. 'He did quite well as a young man, but especially after the war, he could never get his business going again. That's why he needed me to go out to work.'

I am struck by her selflessness, but I also see how my grandfather fell prey to colonial exploitation and was, like those houses and godowns, abandoned as colonial trade began to wind down.

*

Abdalek: 'Darling' (Arabic).

The national anthem and 'The Spanish Cavalier' are the only two songs on the tape that are in English. The rest are in at least three different Asian languages, which I have to get friends to translate, or identify by trying out different transcriptions and Googling song lyrics.

Jacob was a polyglot. The languages of the Company were Dutch and English. With Arabic and Indian merchants Jacob spoke their languages. With European Jews, also traders, Yiddish. Although his familiarity with the Torah meant Jacob could read Hebrew, unlike me Jacob couldn't speak it. In Arabic, however, Jacob was fluent.

In Jacob's multilingual singing, I hear a soundscape to the culturally kaleidoscopic worlds he brokered in his in-between-ness. English, as a colonial company man. Malay, as a resident of cosmopolitan Singapore. Hindustani, the language he most sings on the tape, expressed nostalgia for his family past in India. Hebrew was an inherited religious script. Arabic was something else, a tongue that escaped simple ascription. Jacob used Arabic for swearing and for the sweetest terms of endearment.

Ma fullah backah, 'for goodness' sake': a verbal explosion of pent-up frustration that my mother still uses, when she is pushed past limits (driving; or with my father). And the opposite of this outburst: *abdalek*, 'darling' in Arabic.

'Here again? What are you doing, *abdalek*?' I am by your camphorwood chest, Mum. I am telling stories. I go back to my childhood memory.

Abdalek. Abdalek May – from Jacob's letter to my mother ('Abdalek May, try to come early'). Pronounced *ab-dal-aq*, with a very soft final consonant, the vowels – Arabic, as also in Hebrew – barely heard, swallowed. The Arabic word not only sounds beautiful, it expresses the nearest, dearest relation possible. '*Abdalek*', my mother still sometimes calls me, and so gently it's like a touch. *Abdalek* – darling, sweetheart, my love.

'Abdalek May'. As we read his letter to her, kneeling by the camphorwood chest, I hear the same cadences of sadness in my mother's voice as in my grandfather's on the tape. A bittersweet love; joy always tinged with longing. *Abdalek.* This single word has the power to unknot for May a sack of memories out of which spill stories of Jacob, as sweet and redolent as the spices he would bring home.

'When I was working, I used to give him an allowance to buy his clothes. We would go to the tailor together. I was in my first job and things were becoming increasingly difficult for him. By my third job I was earning very good money, so he didn't go out to work at all. When I gave him the money on my pay day, the first thing he would do was go out to the local fruit stall. He would buy me a bag of plums – always plums, they were expensive – and hand them to me, saying, "for you *abdalek*." He didn't hold onto money. He immediately spent it on me, gave it back.'

My mother speaks softly and incessantly, as if she has been taken over by the memory. Her face is suddenly exhausted. Her irises, once deep brown, are filmed over with the faded blue of cholesterol and cataracts. These are now the eyes of my grandfather, I realise. She has his eyes. *Eye sights.*

This giving back – spontaneously, sentimentally and at points almost irrationally – is what everyone most remembers about Jacob. From his grown-up children to the stranger, Jacob treated all as *abdalek*. In strolls from one end of Singapore to the other, he would find what he called 'down-and-outs', bring them back to the flat and say to his wife, 'Esther, give them some food.'

'If he saw a beggar and had just one dollar in his pocket, he would give his last dollar', my mother sighs. She always tells me that I have this same unbounded generosity, but I know this isn't true. It's her love that projects her father's generosity onto me. I give possessions away and then regret it, or give a gift to a friend and then want one for myself.

In contrast, although in later years he had fewer clothes and, as his letters indicate, became largely dependent on the charity of others, Jacob was ready to give the shirt from his back – literally. His children would reason with him: 'Why are you giving away your clothes? What are *you* going to wear?'

One rainy day, Jacob saw a man wearing his shirt collar up, hugging himself, obviously cold. Hurrying to his room he brought out two coats of his own: 'Which shall I give him?' he asked his family. Again they tried to stop him: 'Why are you giving him your coat? You have only these two.' Jacob's response was always the same: 'He needs more than I.' Handing one of the coats to the man, Jacob discovered four dollars in its pocket. 'You take two, I'll take two', he insisted to this new *abdalek*. He would return to his exasperated family: 'We are poor but there are always people much poorer. At least we have a roof.'

Jacob's *chesed* – one of my favourite Hebrew terms that I've learned, which brings together spontaneous kindness and overflowing love and which I think best describes Jacob's way of being – was legendary in Singapore. On the day of his funeral, after the family had returned from the cemetery, a beggar came to the flat to ask for a meal. This had never happened. It was always Jacob who used to find the needy in the street and bring them back. But this time the family gave the beggar a meal, uncomplaining, convinced that, in this act of treating the stranger as *abdalek*, Jacob had invited the outsider in, an invisible presence.

*

The LORD spoke to you out of the fire; you heard the sound of words but perceived no shape – nothing but a voice.

In services and teaching at my synagogue and in reading the Tanakh, I'm grasping that Judaism is above all a religion of voice and word without appearance. This comes as a relief to me, since I struggle to believe in God, which was one reason why I turned to Buddhism. There are Jews, including many I've met at services, who don't believe in God, but who are drawn in by the words alone. In Judaism, God is precisely the force that can't be seen, but in the Torah a voice is always speaking to the Jews. It resounds from a bush. It calls a prophet out of sleep. To a migrant patriarch in what is now Iraq, it makes a promise of a journey, a new home, children: a legacy. If the voice is silent, it's normally because it's considering giving up on the Jews, who were not listening.

What's passed down in Judaism, I'm learning, is faith in the continuity of language, of sound and word, despite all the displacements of individual bodies, generations, countries, centuries, in spite of all the gaps. Even as you are saying the words, the prayers say you should take them to heart. You should recite them at home and when you are on the road; when you lie down and when you rise up. You 'shanatam l'benecham': you memorialise them in your children. It's the words, voices, stories that are passed down in families. On the second tape I made of my mother singing to her father's voice, she remembered all the words to his songs.

Given that I'm the only one left who even knows that I'm meant to say prayers for dead Jewish ancestors, who am I to *stop* the recital? If I don't listen and learn the words, there would just be silence.

*

And so I force myself to volunteer to lead a prayer for the first time in a service. I have agreed to sit on the steering committee of my synagogue in York, and here I'm being expected, and expect myself, to play a more active, a more vocal role. It's a step along from reading the Torah in my mother's synagogue in London, since this is *my* space and I'm independent of her, and increasingly I'm imagining the time when she won't be here at all. And also, since the prayer I'm reciting is the most important prayer in Judaism. The Shema.

The closest Judaism has to a creed, the Shema is all about listening, about hearing a voice. 'Hear, O Israel, the Lord is our God, the Lord is one', it begins. The Shema is the first prayer every Jewish child is supposed to learn; the last thing a Jew says also before sleep; and the last thing before death. It's the one prayer that Jacob taught May, as he must himself have been taught it, and before him, his ancestors. The Shema is the one prayer May still recites daily. Though her bones are growing dangerously brittle and her skin becoming tissue-thin, her voice is unwavering.

When she married out, my mother omitted to teach me the Shema, probably because she thought her children too much assimilated into the Army, non-religious world of their British father. And so I stagger through the claggy mud of the Hebrew. I re-shape my tongue to roll off the soft *shushing* and *rrrring* sounds. I feel deep down into my throat, trying to draw forth the gutturals. 'Shema, Yisrael. Adonai eloheinu; Adonai eCHad.' 'Hear, O Israel, the Lord is our God, the Lord is one.'

But who is calling me to hear? I know I can listen to the voice of my grandfather. Jacob is the source of May's and thus my own Jewishness.

I learn the Hebrew prayers so well, my mother is amazed. 'You know all the liturgy', she says. We are visiting a Reform synagogue, which my mother is joining, in addition to her Orthodox synagogue, because the Reform unlike the Orthodox allow burial of non-Jewish spouses, together with their Jewish members, in a Jewish cemetery. My parents want to be together in death. In a Reform synagogue, my mother and I can also sit together. It's the first time this has happened, so my mother has not heard me say the prayers before. 'You know it better than me', she whispers too loudly. I don't feel pride, but I do feel a sense of fulfilment. I have picked up that baton and I am carrying it forward, running with it now. I feel the transmission is well under way.

*

Do I look like him?

In the first photograph of Jacob, with his too large ears and lopsided smile, his heavy eyebrows and dark pools for eyes – eye sights much older and sadder than his years – there's something impish and deeply unguarded about his face. He's not what you'd call handsome, but his oversize features draw you in. When I've shown this photograph, I've been asked if I'm aware that I look just like him. I'm still not sure of it.

With my grandfather I always felt already home. His inclination to turn out rather than in; his naïve desire to intervene and remedy; his sentimentalism; his wayward but still deeply held spirituality; his childish and bodily sense of humour: all these resonate strongly in me. The sarong fits, body and soul, you might say. The good notes as well as the bad, my mother says I echo Jacob's voice. 'You have a heart of gold and you are the only one who makes me laugh.' My mother can't see my flaws, but I did identify with my grandfather.

The Short Street flat became a kind of theatre around Jacob. What he really wanted is to have been not in trade but on the stage, an entertainer like his older brother Haron, the professional performer-singer at the Worlds. His jokes and stories challenged orthodoxy, a questioning that began when he was a boy but continued in what could have been a rule-bound adulthood. As a young man, my mother tells me, Jacob and his brothers ran their father ragged.

Many of the scenes my mother recalls of her father's youth have slapstick's physical upending. An Indian woman is sitting under a tree. Boy Jacob comes up to her. From behind his back he takes something, a Jack-in-the-box. He snaps it open in front of her face. It gives her such a shock that she dies on the spot. Or so Jacob said; for in the telling there was continued mugging, and he would say in the case of this story that he prayed God to forgive him for murdering this woman, overdoing his mea culpa to win another laugh.

Another story. As a boy he was fascinated with Nonya (Malay-born Chinese) women and whether they wore underwear under their *sarong kebaya*. As a bet with his brothers, he approached a wealthy Nonya woman riding on a rickshaw and threw marbles under the feet of the rickshaw puller. The rickshaw-wallah went flying, the rickshaw upended and with it the Nonya passenger. The punchline (boom, boom!) – Nonya women didn't wear underwear!

I like to think that Jacob's humour and his holiness derived from the same source. He read the Bible obsessively – the Torah but also the New Testament, the latter profane to Jews – and he would question Judaism. Now I see his practice as his own version of Talmudism, the debates and many opinions that

I so love in my Jewish community. He would ask his Jewish friends to consider whether Jesus really could have been the Messiah. They were all still waiting for the Jewish Messiah to arrive after all, and what good had ever happened to them? Yet on other occasions, Jacob would invite Christian preachers to the flat and challenge them to prove that Jesus really had been the Messiah. He would then take great delight in refuting each of their points in turn.

Jacob's Jewish practice was more felt than ritual, more familiar than high temple. He didn't light Shabbat candles, didn't ask the family to do this or, at home, mark the festivals. This was why May was raised not, initially, to observe Shabbat. He was definitely less observant than Esther. But when Jacob did go to the Maghain Aboth, he would bring back a small stem of leaves from the myrtle tree that grew outside the synagogue and give it to May: 'Here's some yas for you, *abdalek*.' He used the Arabic for myrtle. 'God gives you nothing that you can't bear.' This was Jacob's creed, what he sought to live by.

There's no *yas* in England, but as my mother and I go through Jacob's songs and stories, I decide to light Shabbat candles on Friday nights and recite the blessings for my ancestors, *l'dor va dor*, from generation to generation. For in Jacob's embrace of all that life offers and rejection of nothing, as an opportunity to survive but also to suffer (*and* to lament that suffering very loudly and to joke about it), I find not only myself. I think I'm also finding Judaism.

*

This bazaar which is life has been swept away by our yearning.

By far the most moving song on the tape that Jacob sings is a ghazal, a poetical and musical form originating in the Persian-Arabic world, but this one rendered by my grandfather in Urdu, the language of Muslims of North India (now also Pakistan). *Ghazal* is an Arabic word meaning both 'talking to women' and 'the painful wail of a wounded deer'.

Much of the music that my grandfather sang – and that moves me – is about passion crossing prohibited divides. It could be that music is Jacob's true language, his lingua franca, because, connecting with others' words, in song we escape our own singularity. Such is the case with Jacob's ghazal.

> My beloved; may God's blessings be upon you.
> We've separated, and yet maybe fate will bring us together.
> I have perished in love for you and shown you steadfastness.
> You've rent the longings of the lover with the dagger of
>   depression.
> This bazaar which is life has been swept away by our
>   yearning.

The ghazal's words bring back his own words, in his letter to my mother: 'A daggar perces my heart.' 'Our yearning' recalls 'the indescribable yearning' May had expressed to Keith in her letters. The words of my grandfather and mother speak to my own yearning for love and belonging. In a voice with a strength and clarity that belie his eighty years, Jacob belts out the song, all cadences intact.

Is there an unconscious auditory family memory in the recitation of songs? This ghazal is the single song on the tape that Jacob brings with him from the world of his ancestors before

Singapore. 'Eastern' music, strange to Western ears with its off-tones and irregular rhythms, its extremes of feeling and yet delicate detail, compels me into absolute attention. Its effect is always double – turning happiness into sadness, connection into loneliness, and vice versa. The Kaddish, the prayer for dead Jewish ancestors and expression of darkest grief, is a song of blinding praise. This sad undertow, the dominance of the minor keys, is what most pulls me into synagogues. It echoes that first song I heard from my grandfather in the flat in Singapore when I was three. The liturgy, the singing, especially of Sephardi or Mizrahi Jews, feels familiar to me: known. *Hear, O Israel.*

The last line of this ghazal strikes home as particularly apt for Jacob. Life as a bazaar, swept away by yearning.

*

Our Beloved Papa from us is gone
A loving voice is still
May our Papa be remembered.

Just before he died, Jacob came round briefly from his coma. For two hours, he was lucid, laughing and talking with the family. May had already set off from Europe to see him. By the time she arrived, he had fallen back into a coma. But as she approached his bedside in the hospital, he regained a wordless consciousness. Pulling her hand towards him slowly, he kissed her fingers, one by one. It was his last act, and if I repeat the cliché that it was worth more than a thousand words, then blame the fact that it's my grandfather's (and mother's) sentimentalism speaking through me.

The verse on Jacob's gravestone announces the silence but memorialises his voice.

*

After we'd returned her father's letters to the camphorwood chest and I'd removed the tape, my mother tells me she had a dream about her father. She is sitting with him in a kopitiam, an old coffee shop with marble tables. She is rubbing his hand, telling him how much she loves him. Has our going through this story brought him back to life for her? Or have I made her lose him a second time? I am no substitute for my grandfather.

I switch to the second tape I made, of my mother singing over the top of her father's recording. The sounds of Singapore are filtered through those in my parents' south London home: birdsong, a train passing by. Father and daughter, both now and forever in their eighties, duet across death's wall of silence and a divide of half a century.

*

As my mother and I have journeyed into her parents' pasts, I learn that camphor was vital for oceanic migration. It connected empires and traders. Hard, resistant and enduring, the camphor tree became a staple of shipbuilding in the Far and Middle East: the worlds of my grandmother and grandfather. Above all, camphor was transformed into containers, boxes. On long voyages, camphorwood chests protected migrants' tangible memories from rot, termites and moths, as ours did for my mother when she came to England. Camphorwood chests secured whatever wanted passing down to the next generation. And now to me.

The perfume of camphor was transportive enough that some in the past felt it had divine qualities. In the extraordinarily beautiful, Shir Hashirim, the Song of Songs, the holiest book in the Tanakh, the Hebrew Bible, the beloved is compared to camphor and, the suggestion is, drawn to his lover by that same scent that lies between her breasts.

> A bundle of myrrh is my welbeloved unto me
> He shall lie all night betwixt my breasts.
> My beloved is unto me, as a cluster of camphire
> From the vineyards of En-gedi.

'Is it really about God?' my mother asks, when I share this with her. That question has been the subject of much debate. Is it a love song, or a prayer; about the relationship between real lovers, or an analogy for the love between God and the Jews?

'Why choose?' our rabbi says in York, when we read it at Passover. 'What is God, if not love? What, in the truest sense, love, if not God?' Jacob, my grandpa, would have agreed.

Shema. I listen carefully. I'm learning the songs.

RETURNING

13. The House at the Crossroads

> ———►◆◄———
>
> ## FATHER AND SON.
>
> ### TROUBLE IN A JEWISH FAMILY.
>
> Joseph Isaac Elias appeared before Mr Thunder, the acting fourth magistrate, yesterday afternoon, on the prosecution of his father, Isaac Ezekiel Elias to show cause why he should not be bound over to keep the peace for trespass in his (his father's) house.
>
> Accused wept throughout the proceedings.
>
> Complainant said that on Thursday he saw his son in the house and ordered him to leave. The son threatened to hire a Malay to strike him. He had frequently warned his son not to return to the house, and a magistrate had also warned him. One day he drew a knife against comp'ainant. He had been convicted previously at the Police Court.
>
> In reply to the defendant, complainant admitted chasing him out of the house with a stick.

Source: *Singapore Free Press and Mercantile Advertiser*

The camphorwood chest doesn't hold everything. In every family story, there are details that don't get passed down and don't make it into the archive of memories. And that's when we poke around in other archives for clues. Although even public records may not be more trustworthy than family stories. But if we find the missing pieces, we can be startled how a pattern has repeated across generations, even of what has been repressed or forgotten.

There are parts of Jacob's story that are a mystery to me. Why he never worked for the family business, the Elias brothers. Above all, why he married out. More to the point, why he had not just one but, successively, two Chinese wives. Koh-wei was his second Chinese wife. His first Chinese 'wife' (she was probably his common-law wife) died. Koh-wei had been hired to look after her. And it was when she died that Jacob made Koh-wei his second Chinese-Jewish wife, his Esther.

And yet despite this, how Jacob kept his Jewishness alive; how he passed it on to my grandmother, so that she should become so observant; also to my mother, yet in the form that it comes to me now, not as a solution but as a conundrum.

In relation to her father's choice of loves, my mother can't answer these questions, at least to my satisfaction. 'He must have just liked Chinese women', she shrugs. But loving strangers was so much part of Jacob's ethos, the lodestar that guided his life course, as it has guided hers. As I want to steer my Jewishness too, focused on others, *tikkun olam*, repairing the world. Loving strangers so much as to challenge the boundaries of the self. Giving away the shirt from your back.

So where, I ask myself, does this loving strangeness come from? To answer this question, to root my own Jewishness, I need to keep travelling backwards.

*

If Jacob had worked in the family business, the Elias Brothers on Change Alley, which became a successful shipping and property business, he wouldn't have become a broker for a European colonial company. And if this had been the case, he wouldn't have ended up a caretaker, then living on welfare and having to write begging letters to his ex-firm and family.

And if he had taken his place in the family business, with the business handed down over generations, I would have been writing a very different story. It would have been more like that of the Sassoons, I think. The Sassoons: the most famous Baghdadi Jewish family, the 'Rothschilds of the East', whom I must acknowledge here and bring into my family story. For the Sassoons have a parallel history to the Eliases of migration – Iraq, India, China, Southeast Asia – but with a very different relationship to Jewishness *and* to strangers. The Sassoons dominate not just the history of Baghdadi Jews and Baghdadi Jewish family businesses. They dominate the Baghdadi Jewish family history business, too. There continue to be many substantial and clear-cut histories of the Sassoon family, published even as I'm writing, including by the Sassoons themselves. The Sassoons so keep crossing my path, on my travels, in my reading and cropping up in my family's lives, that I can't avoid them.

If Jacob's life had been more like a Sassoon, Jacob might have 'married in'. Or to put this into an already familiar context, he would have been more like Edward Maier, the wealthy Jew who rejected May and whose family also had a successful trading business. Maier was also meant to, and eventually did, marry into a Jewish lineage, one considered suitable 'enough' by his family, having been made to drop May on these grounds. Like Maier and the Sassoons, Jacob would have married Jewish, and most likely married Baghdadi Jewish, again of what was considered suitable lineage. And he would have passed on, through his Baghdadi Jewish wife, a much less – I struggle to find the right word: unmodified? unqualified? unadulterated? – Jewish identity and Judaism. Certainly, his Jewishness wouldn't have been mixed. It would have been much less interrogated and interrogating. And this would have been passed on to me. This story would have been easier to trace as a result. But then I wouldn't have had reason to write this book, not having to answer the existential questions I began with – Who am I? What is Judaism to me? Can it give me belonging? And of course, I wouldn't have been here, wouldn't have been me.

I had thought, when I first heard of them, that the 'Elias Brothers' must have referred to the three Baghdadi Jewish Elias brothers who came to Singapore from Iraq via India: namely, in order of age, Isaac – my great-grandfather – Moses and Saul. I had thought that, as the eldest, Isaac set up the business, that my great-grandfather must have pulled the strings. But I discover that the Elias Brothers was very much concentrated in the hands of the second brother, Moses, not Isaac. There was evidently for a time a partnership involving Saul. But Saul soon shifted his trade to Rangoon in Burma, where his children were born, and from whom a whole family line is probably descended that we know nothing about. By 1935, Moses was so much the lead in the Elias Brothers that he was passing the business wholly over to his son, Ezekiel (Moshe's father, Zeke, killed in the war), with no mention of other family lines or split or shared inheritances.

I know that the Crash in 1929 affected the Elias Brothers, and that this was the year that Isaac died. I also know that, even before the Crash and his father's death, the family business had bypassed Jacob, which suggests that Isaac was cut out of the Elias Brothers.

It's a lost legacy in the family business. Why?

*

On a quest for the Elias Brothers, it's easy to find out a lot about Moses Ezekiel Elias. Dubbed Singapore's 'Copra King', Moses traded in the lucrative coconut grown in Southeast Asia and used in so many household goods at the time, from cooking fats to carpets, from toiletries to cleaning products. He also dealt in spices, including in some of the products shifted by the Borneo Sumatra Trading Company. Moses worked with the Sassoon family, most likely subcontracting from them, representing them in court, on one occasion to recoup debts owing for 'one case of mustard oil and one bag of coriander seed'.

More than a trader, however, and like many generations of Sassoons, Moses was a property investor in the British Empire's concessions zones and colonial trade cities – in Moses's case, in Singapore. Buying into the British Empire helped Moses Elias ride out the Crash and subsequent downturns in trade. Like many Sassoons also, Moses could afford to be a philanthropist. His regular gifts to charity were announced in the press, where he is often pictured with his wife: the Eliases, 'well-known members of the Jewish community'.

On one of my visits to Singapore, I visit Moses's two daughters, Zaida and Hilda, the sisters who were prisoners of war in the Sumatra camps. In their elegant apartment on Orchard Road where they now live together having stayed very close to each other since their war experiences, we chat and sip tea from china cups perched in saucers. Still beautiful, Zaida has difficulty moving. Younger and more agile, Hilda looks after her. Zaida directs Hilda to dig out from a long black sideboard a studio photograph of their parents. The image shows Moses as plump and walrus-moustached, in Edwardian evening dress with a flower in his buttonhole. He looks every bit the empire gent and, I can't help thinking, self-satisfied. His wife, Rachel, seems more uncertain. Their dress and the hand-coloured production suggest the image was taken in the early 1900s, after their arrival in Singapore. The image announces: here we are, we've made it. Immigrants, but fully assimilated.

When I return to the UK and share this other photograph with my mother, trying to prompt memories of her grandfather, she remembers that, as a child, she saw a picture of Isaac 'just like this' hanging on the wall of her Aunt Flora's house. Flora's daughter Lily burned it when she in turn lost her daughter and couldn't stand around the home likenesses of anyone who had died. This burning of the image, the only remnant of the

physical appearance of my great-grandfather, is another missing inheritance.

Like his brother, Isaac is also substantially in the newspapers, but not where I expect to find him, in the business pages.
He's in the Singapore general news. In police news no less.
He appears in court cases – not like Moses to seek repayment
of unpaid debts from those charged, but rather with his sons,
themselves subject to many different criminal charges, sometimes also pressing charges against each other. From the mid-
1900s over the next fifteen or so years, my side of the Eliases
leave a legal trail involving alleged homebrewing, disturbances
of the peace, trespass and 'swindling'. As I plough my way
through this slurry of material, I feel like I'm reading a lurid
tabloid.

I must admit that, at first, I'm intrigued – excited even. A
cluster of criminal records in the family? Bad Jews? A bunch of
rebels? Of these stories my mother has told me nothing, and it
seems that her father also kept shtum.

On a weekend visit to my parents in London, I bring print-
outs of the reports. Over mugs of tea in their kitchen, my
mother and I go through them one by one. 'Are you sure this is
my family?' she says. She laughs nervously, embarrassed. But
she can't deny that the names and the residences correspond.
She shuffles the papers away from her towards me. 'Don't put
this in the book', she says. She is pleading with me, also warning me. 'Why do you want to tell these stories?'

It's a good question. Why indeed do I want to tell these stories?

In part because of the thrill of uncovering a good story, the
detective work, I can't deny that. But also, I realise, I feel drawn

to these ancestors, because of their waywardness. I identify with them. They've also gone off the path, questioned family and conformity. They've struggled with issues of legacy. They haven't inherited a parental mantle easily. They haven't been obviously good Jews. And they are drawn to other worlds, other cultures.

The more I uncover, the more I learn to read between the lines of the newspaper reports. They tell me a good deal about the world the Eliases were up against: how they were treated in early twentieth-century, white-ruled, colonialist Singapore. The audience of the *Straits Times*, where most of the reports appear, was overwhelmingly colonial and white, British and definitely not Jewish. And the reports hone in repeatedly on the Eliases' Jewishness.

'A Jewish case'. 'An Unsavoury Case'. 'A kind of a happy family'. 'Trouble in a Jewish Family'. The headlines are estranging and snide. The content is pure soap opera melodrama. Father charged with cheating. Father himself charging sons with trespass. Both father and sons together being charged with 'assaulting the modesty of a woman'. Son threatens to stab father. But this is soap opera flavoured with Biblical epic. Sons banished on the 'Eve of Passover'. Wayward, prodigal son abandons family. Son returns seeking forgiveness from his father. Brother turns against brother. Isaac and the Elias Brothers is a story of sibling rivalry that could come from the Torah.

At the same time, the following scenes involving my family could be drawn from Dickens's more antisemitic portraits: 'a disturbance among some of the children of Israel'; 'three of the daughters of the tribe clung to [the white colonial policeman] and made life intolerable for the moment'; 'wrongful confine-

ment, insulting the modesty of a woman'; 'Jew conspired to
cheat'; 'the youth said he had no occupation'; 'Singapore Jew
Charged with Selling Illegal Intoxicants'. Even the names of
other characters are Dickensian, roles or attributes serving
as cartoonish nomenclatures: Judge 'Firmstone', Sergeant
'Payne', Fourth Magistrate 'Mr. Thunder'.

And so I convince my mother. I have to do something to
write back at these reports. Enough burying. This *is* our family,
but what is the story – *our* story? Those who have told the story
thus far – the journalists, the police, the magistrates, the judges
– are British, colonial, white, non-Jewish. There's no Asian Jewish voice at all. What would it mean for *me* to try to tell the other
side of the story: use the newspaper 'facts' to reach for the more
important emotional truth of our family, and particularly of my
great-grandfather, Isaac?

From this point on in my narrative, I'm dealing with ancestors whom no one alive knew, and about whom my mother has
almost no stories. Her storytelling has almost run out. Perhaps,
like his burned portrait, these vanishing traces are an invitation to enter the cave of repressed memories; for me as Isaac's
scion to use what sources I have to try to imagine his world. My
mother gives me her provisional licence, though she withholds
her verdict. She acknowledges that this story is now fully my
story.

*

Isaac Elias had been in almost every position in the foreigners'
ceremonial room, in this palace of theirs. He had stood everywhere, except with the white men with their curly white locks

and their long black robes, so oddly like the dishdashas worn by the men of his past in Baghdad. He had sat in the box on the stage, conscious of the policeman behind. He had sat on the bench next to one of the Britishers. Now he was sitting on the bench again, waiting for his turn to be called. He had been in the witness box before, too.

Isaac felt acid in his mouth and his stomach tightened. Even when he himself had called the policemen to help him control one of his sons – Joseph, always his rebellious second son – Isaac had never wanted it to end on this foreign public stage he didn't trust. In any case, they'd have troubles again, because settling was impossible.

Today Isaac was supposed to testify against a neighbour who had been making them arak, or as they called it, 'basri'. The English taxed everything, including alcohol, so making your own arak was illegal, Joseph had explained to his father.

They had made their own *basri* in Iraq, the recipe brought from Baghdad, from Basra, spiced in the way that English drink was not. Isaac admitted to himself that since his *abdalek* Sarah had died he had come to need his drink. He decided to answer the man in the wig who was asking the questions: *basri*. . . arak was his medicine. It made what he called his 'stomach-ache', by which he meant the pain in his heart, go away.

He acknowledged that drink – maybe the gambling also – was behind several of the events that had landed him previously in this room, including that time when two women friends of Joseph charged both himself and Joseph with imprisoning them, though the women had come voluntarily to his house and had attacked each other and then blamed himself and his son. Such domestic dramas meant that his fourth son Jacob was already a – what did he call it? he used an English word as if there was no equivalent in Jewish Arabic – a 'teetotaller'. Jacob wouldn't touch alcohol, and Isaac knew that already he was a spiritual man, so different from his other sons.

Sons. Not too many, but disrespectful of his authority. And Sarah not here to share the load, offer consolation, help keep them in check. Every day Isaac wondered if his decisions were to blame. Did the two-times leaving Baghdad, first for those years in Bombay, then again onto Singapore, kill her? Even when he had drunk enough to forget Iraq, he could never put Sarah out of his mind. If he hadn't appreciated her worth when she was alive, she now lived with him as an ageless ghost.

Before too long, he thought, his sons were going to have to strike out in this new city-country. Ezekiel was scrimping from hawking, also trying to tutor, in what Isaac never could under-stand. Haron was a performer, and while Isaac couldn't keep up with his guises, at least Haron supported himself. Jacob had got a minor broker position. Rachel and Flora, his *abdalek* daugh-ters, he just needed to find each a husband.

Joseph, though, had no work. Which is why Isaac had given Joseph an ultimatum that time at Passover: here's a set of clothes, leave the house, go and find a job, don't return until you've done so. The memory of his son returning with no clothes, no job, and a knife drawn, threatening to strike his own father, overwhelms Isaac. What had happened to 'honour your mother and father'? What of tradition?

Yet in Joseph he also sees some of his own rebelliousness. The spirit that enabled him to leave behind his family roots and make a life in two unvisited countries. His mind travelled to Moses and Saul. The three brothers had left Baghdad together, with a plan to create a spice empire, from Bombay to Singapore and back to Baghdad. Isaac was bewildered how everything had come to be in Moses's control.

When they first arrived, the brothers had shared the house at the crossroads, in the *mahallah*, the Jewish quarter, which Saul had left first, claiming it was haunted. At night he bumped into their ancestors, with their robes and beards, and he was done with ghosts, he said, with the old ways. He spoke about wanting to start afresh and left for Burma. Then Moses had gone, saying he needed air, a view, the sea. He had bought a mansion on the coast. Moses appeared always on the right side, the white side, of the court room.

So only Isaac was left in the crossroads house, the house in the *mahallah*. Although Isaac also knows that life in the *mahallah* defies the very idea of two sides only.

*

My mother doesn't want me to include these stories because the newspaper reports don't make her family look good. But while I don't know what my great-grandfather thought, and the above scenario is completely my imagining built up from the facts of the newspaper reports, the details of swindling and homebrewing hold a kind of truth, I think. And this is important to me. It's a story of assimilated Jews versus non-assimilated Jews. Or British Jews versus Asian Jews. Jews who belonged, if you want, versus mixed or mixed-up Jews. I see myself in the second category. Half-caste. Outcast. A quarter this, a quarter that.

My mother and I decide to take a trip to visit Singapore to recover this deep stratum of the Eliases' Singapore life. Hannah

Kichi, unique among my mother's cousins for never having left Singapore, is our guide in the *mahallah,* and our main informant. It's odd for my mother to be guided around her home city, although she's as interested as me in visiting old family sites she didn't know about.

The Elias brothers' house at the crossroads still exists. Hannah walks us to the corner of Mount Emily Road and Niven Road and identifies the ancestral home as an open-fronted, very colonial-looking building. The walls inside and out are a deep ochre colour. Like many of the houses in this old quarter of Singapore, and like most old parts of the city that remain, the building has been renovated, to a condition more pristine than I sense it ever attained in the past.

The house is now occupied by a Chinese family. Somewhat disconcertingly given the flavour of our heritage tour, the three of us agree, they're roasting a large suckling pig – head and all – on the terrace. When we explain to the residents the reason for our loitering outside their house, they seem on the verge of inviting us in. We cross the street quickly, and cousin Hannah points out the bad feng shui of this house at the crossroads: good energies going out, dissipated; bad energies coming in, family unprotected. She tells us that some in the Elias household (Saul?) were convinced that the house was already haunted when the brothers moved in. She recounts the escapade of a goat as a testament to this. Kept for its milk for the making of *laban manashaf,* the Arabic soft cheese, the goat was tied up outside the house by a thick rope. But its implacable bleating echoed for miles around Singapore, until one day it finally broke free and bolted down the city streets, never to be seen again. I can tell that Hannah believes the goat was onto something. Her eyes are wide and she is not laughing.

A tiny, twinkling lady ten years older than my mother, Hannah speaks in an uninterrupted stream, moving backwards and forwards between the generations.

When the Elias brothers from Baghdad arrived in Singapore, she tells my mother and me, they lived first in the *mahallah*. I'm not unfamiliar with this word. In my mother's stories of her childhood, I sort of knew *mahallah* meant the Jewish area in Singapore, the poorer quarter. But I never knew exactly what the *mahallah* was, or what its associations are, and neither, fully, did my mother. We didn't know, that is, until I started working with writers and artists with a connection to the East – Muslims, Jews and others – on a project about memories of the Ottoman Empire. And it was at that point that I discovered how this word *mahallah*, its character – for the *mahallah* was built out of the imagination as much as stone – travelled from a mixed cultural past, to unsettle the racist divisions of the British Empire in Singapore.

You will not find the word *mahallah* anywhere in the British colonial press, administrative papers, or on any British maps. For the British had another way of imagining Singapore, and this was according to the Jackson Town Plan. Commissioned and implemented under Raffles, Jackson's map divided the city according to the British Empire's divisions between races: 'European Town' for Europeans; the 'Chinese Kampong', the Chinese village for the majority Chinese population of Singapore, where Koh-wei first settled; 'Kulia Kampong' for immigrant Indians, now Little India; 'Arab town' for Arabs; and 'Bugis' mostly for the indigenous Malays. Everyone boxed in their own space.

This segregated city, which the British invented in imperial India in Madras, Calcutta and Bombay, was imposed on Singapore. This geography gave concrete form to the British Empire's ideology of divide and rule. The idea was that cities, like the empire itself, would be easier to administer if subject 'races' were kept in separate places. Do not cross, do not mix.

The *mahallah* escaped these colonial divisions. The *mahallah* in Singapore was equivalent to the Jewish quarter, but I learn that the word is Arabic, meaning 'neighbourhood'. My mother knew about the Jewish quarter. She didn't know about this other association. In the Middle East and elsewhere, particularly under the Ottoman Empire, 'mahallah' described the smallest unit of the city, a sort of administrative district. The word is made up of two elements, 'stopping place' and 'to alight'. While it could be used by other ethnic and religious communities elsewhere, in Singapore the *mahallah* was the 'stopping place' that Baghdadi and other Arabic Jews alighted. And in so doing, I think that they overlaid their Middle Eastern past onto their new Jewish neighbourhoods, even when these were in another part of the world or a completely different empire, as was the case in Singapore ruled by the British. The *mahallah* was a porous neighbourhood.

In Singapore, the *mahallah* described a small area of six blocks to the southeast of Mount Emily, including Wilkie Road, Sophia Road, Princep Street, Short Street, and Middle Road, on which the David Elias building went up and the road that May used to walk to school. Short Street, her home and the street which the newspapers associate with the litigious Isaac, was the living, pumping heart of the *mahallah*. That first house of the Elias brothers in Singapore where the brothers all lived was on the very edge of the *mahallah:* a symbolic 'stopping place'. All streets were within walking distance of the Waterloo Street synagogue, our family synagogue, the first synagogue in Singapore, which continued to be used by poorer Jews. This fact was important because the *mahallah* was a religious and a cultural home for Middle Eastern Jews.

The *mahallah* was distinguished not only by being Jewish and working class but for importing the Arabic culture of its residents. Men tended to work as merchants, traders or hawkers, as my grandfather Jacob and some of his brothers did. They spoke Arabic in the streets and sometimes at home. They ate Baghdadi food, Arabic flatbread, or *roti tanur*, and the Shabbat meal was *hameem*, chicken cooked overnight. Music and singing were the main entertainment, and gambling was a favourite pastime, a foible beyond Uncle Joseph killed-while-gambling. *Mustik* or *basri* – a bit of spiced homebrew – fit right into this scene; a starter from home brought to ferment in this new abroad.

At the same time as it was distinctly Middle Eastern Jewish, the Singapore *mahallah* was renowned, as I already know from my mother's stories of growing up Jewish, for not being walled in from Singapore's other immigrant communities. The Baghdadi Jews were surrounded by Chinese, Indian and Eurasian families. Doors stayed open and children played across divisions in the colony. The only exceptions were the British and Europeans, who never appeared in the *mahallah* – except as police. So I understand deeply that the *mahallah* was in no way equivalent to the European Jewish ghetto. It was not exclusive like the ghetto; and Jews weren't compelled to live within it. Indeed, the better off moved out. But when Jews first arrived, they chose to live in it – and they chose whether or not to remain.

Where we live can be constrained by circumstances, or a reflection of ourselves. In turn, home can come to make us who we end up becoming. Home can decide our education, our jobs, our personal and family lives. We might move in order to change these things. Yet even once it's been left – perhaps especially when it's left – the home in family stories can leave a mark, even on subsequent generations. These 'sites of memory', as the novelist Toni Morrison calls such places, can continue to be occupied, revisited, long after the family have moved, even by those who never lived there; even after the places no longer exist. On some level, I felt like I already lived in the vibrant, noisy, above all happy, in-and-out-of-each-other's-houses *mahallah* of my mother's stories.

The house at the crossroads of the *mahallah* is a turning point in the plot of my great-grandparents' generation: between East and West, past and present, British Empire and Ottoman Iraq. On the one hand, here were the Elias brothers, recent immigrants from Iraq, in a new city, country, empire. On the other hand, here they were *again*, in an Arabic Jewish neighbourhood, pretty similar to the ones they must have left behind. The edge signalled aspiration, as if this poorer area associated with the past were really only a 'stopping place', and they were soon going to leave behind their ancient Iraqi past and move on and out into their European future.

Their story is also a turning point for me in my identification as a Jew. If I can become Jewish, how much is my Jewish identity assimilated to Britishness, Europeanness, whiteness; how much can my Jewishness be an escape from these? Whether because of love for my mother or childhood memories of Jacob and Esther's love, I desperately want my Jewishness to stay in the *mahallah,* for it not to disappear in white, British, Western culture – an unmarked identity.

*

A youthful-looking middle-aged man with small round glasses and a downward-turned moustache steps off an English P&O liner in Singapore harbour. His black lace-up boots and dark woollen suit worn topped by a boating hat would not look out of place at the Henley Regatta. But although he is British, he is also a *shaliach*, a Zionist emissary or messenger, and he has come 'on a pilgrimage', as he will later write in his *Journal of a Jewish Traveller*, to the Jewish communities in the Far East, India and Australasia. It is 1920; the Balfour Declaration promising Jews a homeland in Palestine has been in existence for three years. And Israel Cohen has journeyed east, in order to recruit funds and win support for the promised Jewish nation that he holds so dear.

Cohen breakfasts with Manesseh Meyer, who will be his main point of contact with the Jewish community of Singapore. Meyer is the father of Mrs Nissim, the elderly lady with whom May will take tea and keep minutes for at the wealthy synagogue of Chesed El. Cohen is deeply impressed by Meyer's ways, whose black 'skullcap' declares piety. (Cohen uses this anglicised and peculiarly un-Jewish term for a yarmulke.) Cohen notes that Meyer has his own private shohet, his ritual slaughterer, an Orthodox chef to oversee his kitchen, and a personal synagogue, Chesed El, which he has built only yards from his palatial colonial residence. The richest Jew in the Far East, Meyer will be the largest donor to Cohen's cause.

When he leaves Meyer's supervision, Cohen discovers another side to Singapore Jewry, one that he hadn't expected. He heads to the *mahallah,* and the British gentleman that he is deep down in his habits and outlook responds with visceral hostility. Even as he knows he has come east to embrace all diaspora Jews and persuade them to support his dream of returning as one Jewish nation to the Holy Land, Cohen has trouble squaring what he witnesses in the *mahallah* with this Zionist vision.

In my family synagogue, not Chesed El but Maghain Aboth, Cohen can't help noticing that the hazan, or cantor, goes about barefoot and wears a fez and white dishdasha, though, translating into English again, Cohen uses the term 'gaberdine' for this long Iraqi cloak. He is shocked to hear the hazan speaking Arabic, of all languages, in the teaching of the Talmud. He notes in his journal: 'Bagdad [sic] was still his spiritual home, for though he had spent fourteen years in this thriving British colony he could not yet speak a word of English.' The hazan confesses to Cohen that he can't find much use for texts sent directly from the Holy Land. He struggles even to read Hebrew. He's considering raising money by selling the texts in a lottery. He is clearly concerned about the poor among the children he teaches. Cohen wonders how else this religious teaching, which bears no resemblance to any of his own experiences of talmud torah, can shock him. As if on cue, into the class cheeps 'a brood of chickens and their vigilant mother, which strutted from an adjoining yard into the room, leaving many an impression behind.'

One British Zionist Jew's visit. Two synagogues: Chesed El and Maghain Aboth. Two sides of Singapore Jewry. The *mahallah* and the house on the hill.

It makes me think of the Jewish joke about always needing to have two synagogues. There's the one you go to, and the other you wouldn't be caught dead in. Except in this context, and maybe all contexts, it's not so funny.

What Meyer doesn't tell Cohen as they break bread together, waited on by a Chinese servant holding a pitcher of water and bowl for them to wash their hands before they perform the blessing, is that he built Chesed El in order that he wouldn't have to go to Maghain Aboth, the synagogue in the *mahallah*. And yet at the same time, he sometimes has to rickshaw in enough men from the *mahallah* to form the minyan, the quorum necessary for a service to take place in his personal synagogue. Cohen is introduced to, but he fails to analyse, the divide between Jews in Singapore: rich and poor; landowner merchants and peddler tenants; Jews who were recognised by the British, and Jews who were regarded by the British as Asiatics. Meyer – like various generations of Sassoons – was knighted by the British for his services to the British Empire and his support of Zionism, even while my great-grandfather Isaac was being brought to face the British courts.

Before he leaves Singapore, Cohen returns to Meyer's mansion. This secular head of Singapore's Jewish community has assembled for his distinguished British speaker what Cohen is led to believe is 'the whole of the adult Jewish population'. Before this audience Cohen speaks passionately about his cause, and they give generously in response. Afterwards, Cohen makes a follow-up round of visits to the merchant houses around Raffles Place and Change Alley, in a final attempt to win support.

Would Cohen have met Moses Elias at one of these occasions, at Meyer's house or later at the Elias Brothers offices near Change Alley? Moses was 'well known' for his philanthropy in the Jewish community, the newspapers tell me. Would he have given to Cohen's cause? Would Isaac have counted among Meyer's 250? Would Jacob? Who gets to count as Jewish?

Like Manesseh Meyer, Moses Elias had moved out of the *mahallah* by then. He bought a bungalow and invested in other real estate opposite Meyer's Sea View Hotel on Tanjong Katong, out towards Singapore's east coast. Moses's property, 'Beach House', according to a real estate notice from the time, had twenty large bedrooms, ten bathrooms, tennis courts, 'ample servants' quarters', 'electric light and fans throughout'. By the 1931 census, Jews owned more real estate in Singapore than any other group, and half of the available housing to rent was owned by Jews, many former *mahallah* residents themselves now landlords.

By investing in properties outside the *mahallah*, Moses was not just moving up the social ladder; he was moving away from his past. Isaac instead burrowed downward and inward into the heart of the *mahallah*, to Short Street. Where he remained, as did his children, as did theirs, until May came to England in 1960. From one of the poorest and largest families in the *mahallah* (the poor tended to have many children), May crossed the divide when she went up to Chesed El and became President of the Menorah Club. In her life, for a moment, she brought together these worlds too.

In the period following the end of the Second World War, almost all children of the *mahallah* left. They emigrated variously to the UK, to Israel, to the US and Australia. To get out of the *mahallah* was to identify with the world in which Englishness as culture and language would dominate, even after the end of the British Empire. To identify with Englishness was already, in the cultural and class senses that determined a Jewish family's kind of Jewishness, to leave the *mahallah*. For the *mahallah* was an idea, as much as it was a physical place.

Now I see that, in leaving Singapore, May really left behind the *mahallah* – and inextricably also something deeply Middle Eastern in the family past. At least she left it then. In making the real and metaphorical journeys alongside me in my writing of this book, particularly here in the *mahallah*, she has remembered, and returned to, that site of memory. She is deeply moved as we stand before the ancestral home in Singapore and find the other, less grand, more run-down places where her family lived. This is a lineage of rootlessness and displacement. And yet the fact that it was passed down connects us to these ancestors and gives us continuity.

Back on his boat and bound for India, Cohen notes in his journal one final revelation about some of the Jews of the Straits Settlements. It is what most confounds him and his idea of what constitutes a Jewish life. This was his discovery that there were 'Jews from Bagdad [sic], mostly poor pedlars, who consorted with Chinese and Malay women and lived debased lives.'

Let us allow Cohen to depart this narrative, his account, for me at least, 'leaving many an impression behind.'

*

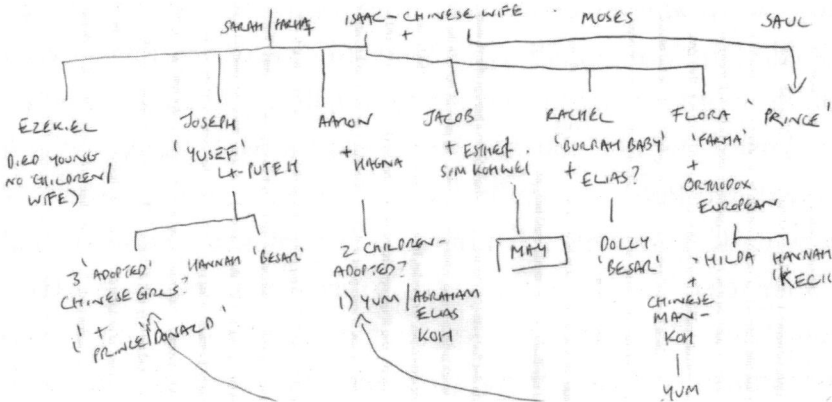

The further back we go, the more relationships become confusing. Growing up, May was not sure exactly who all her relations were, or how precisely they were related. We don't even discover certain people are related, or how, until this story required our going back, especially to the *mahallah*, speaking to informants, piecing together what we were told. And I now know that our affiliations can never be fixed finally, not only because of my grandmother's girl-baby abandonment but because, also on my grandfather's side, there are loose ends left hanging in the family plot.

I take out my notepad and sketch the relationships that we find out about in our return to the *mahallah*:

Isaac had six children. In order, Ezekiel, Joseph, Haron, Jacob (my grandfather), Rachel (or Burrah Baby) and Flora.

Ezekiel, who had lost a leg (but no one remembers how), died young before May could know him. He seems never to have married. Joseph, or as they called him using the Arabic, Yusef, also never married. May's generation found him a distant figure, unlike the next brother, Haron. Yusef used to spend all his time gambling; but he also kept many Jewish religious practices, for example kosher. Flora, his youngest sister, did all his cooking for him – making his food after preparing for her own family. Flora always had a wad of *paan*, betel nut, in her mouth.

Yusef was not married but he had a Malay lover, whom they called Puteh – meaning 'white' in Malay, though she was very dark. The name must have been relative to some colonial colour scale. Yusef and Puteh had a girl, whom they called Hannah Besar – 'Big Hannah', *besar* again being Malay. This was to distinguish her from another Hannah, Hannah Kecil, 'Hannah Small' (*kecil* also Malay). May's older cousin Hannah Kecil is the daughter of Flora. Yusef and Puteh also had three – apparently 'adopted' – Chinese girls. And this is the point on which my mother, as a younger witness and having left Singapore at twenty-two, finds the relationships especially confusing. Specifically, it was unclear how much children were adopted, and how much they were the family's 'own'.

'Adoption' in the family is not what it seemed to be. And it turns out to run parallel to my grandmother's story of adoption. Haron (Chacha Haron) had what Cousin Hannah calls a 'foreign mistress'. Hagna was a Belgian who had bright red hair and was Catholic. Haron refused to let her practise inside the house, but he did permit her to 'build an altar' just outside their home, Cousin Hannah tells us, 'with statues of Christ and the Virgin'. After Hagna died, Haron was heartbroken and he never married. But Chacha Haron had two children – whom my mother thought also adopted – a son and a daughter. Both of them were half Chinese, half Jewish, and Haron lived for them and his performances in *bangsawan*, until he ended up living out his days in the hut attached to the synagogue. Half Chinese and half Jewish. Were they really adopted? I ask.

But Hannah and my mother are moving on, both in the conversation and walking away from the house on the crossroads, as we now make our way out of the *mahallah*. I struggle to keep up with them in my pace and my notetaking, as I record the following on my notepad.

Rachel Isaac Elias, the eldest sister, they called 'Burrah Baby' (*burrah* meaning 'big' now in Hindi). Rachel died young, but not before having a child, Dolly Besar – 'big' Dolly. Rachel had married a first cousin, who even shared the same surname as her. This caused more of a stir among the younger generation than the adoptions did. In the camphorwood chest, we have a single photograph of Rachel, standing by a life-size porcelain dog. Everyone in my mother's family has Rachel's eyes, as large, dark and oval as Iraqi dates.

The youngest sister, Auntie Flora, married an Orthodox Jew and had two daughters – the second of whom is our informant Hannah Kecil. Then Hannah tells us that Haron's 'adopted' son, Yum, was actually the son of his niece Hilda, the eldest child of his sister Flora, and so the sister of our informant. At this point I have to invent new ways of diagramming a family tree to capture these circular, multiple relationships. I am no longer dealing with a tree at all. I draw horizontally across the page, curving my lines and adding arrows. A spider-web genealogy.

On Hannah goes, unspooling, narrating, marching. At fourteen years old, Hilda had an arranged marriage to a rich Dutch Jew. Among previous generations of most Baghdadi Jews, arranged marriages and marriages between near-children were common – as indeed was marrying relatives, cousins or distant uncles. But Hilda rebelled against the tradition. As soon as she got home from the wedding, she found the largest Persian rug

317

in the house – 'and rolled and rolled herself up inside it until there was no more rug left.' It was dark in there and the voices were muffled. She felt prodding and tugging but she turned herself into a dead weight and refused to come out.

'Whenever her husband appeared, she did the rug-rolling trick', her sister Hannah laughs. Not surprisingly Morris, the Dutch Jew, disappeared. But not before Hilda – somehow, miraculously, despite the rug – became pregnant and gave birth to Dolly Kecil, who was brought up by her grandmother, Tatchi Flora.

Left to her own devices, Hilda then fell in love with a Chinese man. In spite of her parents' fury and attempts to keep them apart, the product of this affair was Yum Koh. When Hilda went into labour pains and struggled with the birth, Chacha Haron raised his hands to the heavens: 'Farha' – they used Flora's Arabic name – he cried to his sister, 'if this child comes out alive, I will adopt this child.' The tragic but saintly Chacha Haron took up the child and named him Abraham, Abraham Elias Koh, but they called him by a Chinese name, Yum. Haron raised Yum as his own, ensuring the best for his education. 'Nobody could touch him', Hannah tells us. Haron and Flora, Hilda and Yum, they all moved to the same house in Geylang in Singapore, where Flora also kept twenty dogs.

As I try to keep track of the relationships, the marrying-ins so close the couples are family already, and the marrying-outs so distant it's to non-Jews, as I struggle to sketch onto the Elias ancestral tangle the apparently illegitimate children and the adoptions Hannah tells us about, I'm left to wonder: what's the connection between marrying out and adoption? Why are these repeated across generations and different parts of the family line, and why together? Again my mother has no explanations here, as she wasn't wholly sure who was adopted and who a blood relative.

Here's what I surmise. If marrying out risked weakening or even jettisoning Jewishness, adoption seemed to be a way to bring mixed Jewish children back, however tenuously, into the Jewish fold. In fact, the continuity of Jewish family lineages, especially in far-flung diasporas, seems to have required just the right balance between 'in' and 'out'. Intimacy, or endogamy, to use the anthropological term, but not too much, or you'll end up with incest. Outwardness or exogamy, but again, not so much as to lose that Jewish identity.

Marrying family and especially cousins was common practice among other Baghdadi Jewish families. For instance, the Sassoons. British historian Cecil Roth, who wrote a book about the Sassoons and who with his wife remained good friends with them, noted that, even while they were far-flung, the Sassoon tribe married frequently among themselves. I'm comforted to read that 'these marriages made for confusing family relationships' among the Sassoons also. Other Jewish families intra-married (that is, married their own family) to keep the family Jewish and keep the family name and business together, resulting in what seems to me a kind of double 'marrying-in'.

But there was another choice to being Jewish in the diaspora which the Eliases followed, if not clearly, at least discernibly to me. In our family, it seems that adoption and marrying out were the default practice, and that these worked in tandem. For adoption, as far as I can see, was the euphemism for how to avow a tie to the child that resulted from inter-ethnic affairs; affairs with non-Jewish women or men. To return the child as

Jewish, and to raise that child as Jewish, to give them a Jewish legacy. There were no 'half-castes', no outcasts.

Putting Jacob back into this context, I can see that this opposite practice – I want to say oppositional practice – to that common among conservative Jews elsewhere, of marrying within the family, followed even by fellow Baghdadis like the Sassoons, was deliberate. It's not just Jacob and Sim Koh-wei; Jacob's brothers, too, pursued intermarriage, even while they maintained their Jewish religion, culture, and never forgot where they came from.

*

My mother and I retreat with Hannah Kecil to a café. There, we make a whole new discovery. Hannah waits for us to sit down. Then she tells my mother another thing she never knew. After their grandfather Isaac lost his beloved wife, Sarah, also from Baghdad, when she was very young, he set up with a common-law wife. She was a Chinese woman, whether an immigrant like my grandmother or a Singaporean, Hannah doesn't know. It's unlikely that he married her. But he had a son by her, whom they called Prince, but whose given name was Donald. Prince who was so handsome and regal.

My mother's face turns from shock to recognition. She realises that this was the same Prince who had spent so much of her childhood at their flat, for whom Jacob always had time. She had thought Prince must just have been a very good friend of her father's. She had no idea that Prince was her father's half-brother, and therefore her uncle. She has found a new uncle, and she has found another side of the family that is Jewish but also Chinese.

But Hannah is not done. Prince also went to live with Aunty Flora and Haron, Hilda and Yum and 'the twenty dogs'; a kind of adoptee himself, I think. He then ended up marrying the 'adopted' Chinese daughter of Joseph, Jacob's brother, another son of Isaac's. He married, therefore, his cousin, who was, symmetrically like him, half Chinese and half Jewish. This is now more important to me than to my mother. For the magnet of energies at this point seems extraordinarily perfect: a marrying-out, that rebounds as a transformed marrying-in. And if this mixed-race couple kept alive their Jewishness, were the dynamics of their love – I ask myself – any *less* Jewish?

The family and immediate community among the Jews in Singapore certainly saw no contradictions between their love for strangers and their Jewishness. They all maintained the Jewish – the Baghdadi Jewish – traditions. This meant that they went to synagogue (the Waterloo Street one). They were all kosher. They had no problem reconciling Jewishness with intermarriage or common-law relationships to Chinese, Malay, or fire-headed Catholic Belgian lovers; with the gambling, the occasional drinking; or with cross-cultural intimate socialising. For all this was characteristic of the *mahallah*.

I think of Isaac, who came from Baghdad, and who I sense had problems fitting into Singapore's divisive colonial life. I think of how he had left Iraq to end up with a Chinese partner, who I hope brought him consolation after his beloved Sarah's early death. I think of the nature of this second couple's love: given that she was probably another nameless immigrant from China, did they connect because of their mutual displacement? What language did they speak, other than those of migration and transience? I think of how Jacob, and then May, continue this story. The pattern feels recurrent, chosen. And as I begin a relationship with a British woman, non-Jewish, but a writer like me, I wonder how far back the pattern goes, where it comes from, and what route it travels along the way.

14. HERITAGE HOTEL

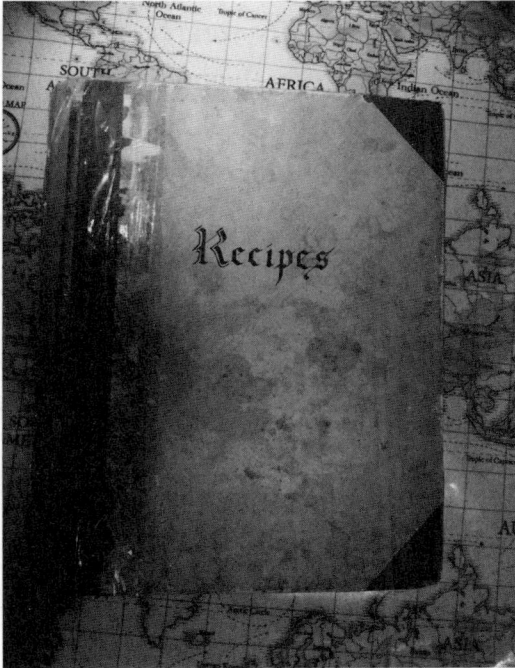

'You know the story of the Christmas cake I baked for your father that first year we were married? I put so much brandy in it, it was completely soggy. Inedible. We put it out for the birds and we watched as one little robin – Fred we called him – came back, day after day. He staggered about. We thought he was going to fall over. He was obviously drunk.'

My mother laughs. I know what's coming next. The story of the poached egg that ended up on the floor; of the chicken

cooked with a plastic bag inside because my mother didn't realise this was how the British back then used to pack the bird
with the giblets; of the Yorkshire Pudding that my mother at
first thought was a dessert.

I didn't know how to cook. That's the theme. We are sitting
at the kitchen table again. I have before me the recipe book
May kept when she first came to England because she *thought
she couldn't cook.* It's a weighty scrapbook, and when opened
takes up at least two places on the table which is covered with
a cloth that's an old-fashioned map of the world. I leaf through
the pages, layered with menus, recipes and tips that May had
clipped from British newspapers and women's magazines.

Many of the dishes strike me as outright weird. Most are
things we no longer eat, a few with names I've never even heard
of. 'Kentish Chicken Pudding', 'Blackcurrant Flummery',
'Melba Toast' – though I remember my mother making that
one, for dinner parties she used to throw for my father's Army
chums, in the 1960s and '70s. My brother and I munched the
leftovers, the skinny, curved toasted bread making for an exotic
breakfast, wherever we happened to be in the world.

Actually, May *could* cook, but not the foods Keith or British culture at the time wanted to eat. Now the food of Eastern
Jewry is all the rage, with TV chefs, restaurants and cookery
books hitching a ride on the Asian-Jewish-Levantine fusion
bandwagon. May could certainly cook *these* foods; indeed
she did for us as a young family. We liked these fusion, spicy,
exotic, healthier dishes best. There's a story of either me or
my brother – it has legendary status in our family – learning
to walk because my mother held out as the target prize one of
her pungent Indian-Jewish-Malaysian curries. But these dishes

were so much her family's food DNA, she didn't need to write the recipes down.

Scared of losing this culinary heritage, I prompt her for the recipes now. My mother is infuriatingly vague – 'just a little . . . but not too much.' So instead my aunts, who are also very good cooks, send me their more precise versions, which I subsequently paste into the blank pages at the back of my mother's recipe book. 'Chakla bakla – spicy fermented vegetable pickle: can be made from any raw vegetable to hand, including carrots, beans, cauliflower, choko (gourd), peppers. It will keep for a year.' 'Egg tikka curry with chickpeas and green beans'. Along with their carefully handwritten instructions, they send me packets of home-mixed garam masala. 'Store bought garam masalas are not aromatic or any good. Think about investing in a coffee grinder.' They are bossier, more confident in their cooking than my mother. Perhaps because most of them stayed in Singapore longer than she, perhaps because they remained together and so never had to take on another culture to the same degree.

Food is, for myself and my mother, our most sensuous route to memory. Once places like *mahallahs* disappear, food can be the only physical remnant of where a family lived or came from. For Proust's narrator of *Remembrance of Things Past*, it is famously the 'petites madeleines', the little French cakes, dipped in tea, that set him off on this seven-volume attempt to recover lost time. Their crumbly sweetness brings back, in instantaneous recall, an aunt sharing the same with him as a child, and along with their taste, all his childhood and subsequent history.

What flavours of memory are passed down through my mother? Eastern Jewish cooking is – like Eastern Jewry – complex, nuanced, seductive, and as colourful as a painter's palette. Above all, it's spicy. It's no exaggeration to say that the food would be nothing without the spices – the spices of my family trade – as Proust's madeleine wouldn't have prompted anything without the infusion of lime-flower tea.

When I return home, as I do much more often these days in order to retrieve things from the camphorwood chest and talk to my mother, I cook with her as I did in childhood, but these days much more *for* her. I take over her kitchen and roast a chicken I've brought down from Yorkshire (no giblets inside), a giant of a bird, as all food in Yorkshire is conspicuously larger than that down South. My mother has persuaded me to eat chicken to gain back some weight, as long ago, before I was Buddhist, I persuaded her to eat chicken to help her regain her strength to recover from cancer. Now I'm no longer vegetarian, I'm no longer ascetic. We have a glass of wine. I am dating. I am returning to the pleasures of the senses.

As I season the chicken skin (turmeric, garlic, salt, pepper, rosemary, lemon), my mother hovers by my side, curious, but also unable quite to cede control of her kitchen. We talk and eat, and we talk about the food. Recreating family recipes together, we're transported back to her Baghdadi Jewish ancestry, marinated in India, with Southeast Asian piquancy added in Singapore. I realise that the names, ingredients and methods of dishes that I grew up with are perfected in the course of my family's migration, as Baghdadi Jewish spice traders, across the Asian continent.

Hameem, a Hebrew word meaning 'hot', in Iraq was called *t'beet*, from the Arabic *tabayit*, meaning 'to stay overnight in a house'. This was the Sabbath food, the equivalent of Ashkenazi cholent, consisting of chicken stuffed with rice. The bird was put on a low coal fire on Friday night before Shabbat set in, and the fire allowed to die out, so that there would be no need for stoking or other human intervention, hence breaking the Sabbath. The meal slow-cooked and would be ready to eat for Saturday lunch. I remember this deliciously aromatic, tender dish as a child on visits to Singapore. The food was brought up from the kitchens of the Maghain Aboth synagogue, straight after the Shabbat service. With the still-thriving Baghdadi Jewish community in the '60s and '70s, we ate outside at a long table in the leafy courtyard of the synagogue. We finished off the meal with oranges cut into suckable quarters with the rind still on, a dissection that made the familiar fruit seem exotic and all the more delicious. I was satiated with the food and with the company, enfolded within a community and its schedule of repeating celebrations. As with Proust's madeleine, the food and its associations left an indelible memory.

My mother remembers the food from her own childhood. 'There were kubba, rice balls stuffed with minced meat, onions and spices. We called them "ball".' Having tried them, I find these dumplings a bit like matzo balls but lighter and – I have to insist, as opposed to what I found to be the bland Ashkenazi fodder during my years in New York – tasty. *Kubba* indeed means 'ball' in Arabic and is a staple for Jews from Arab lands and non-Jewish Arabs alike. Food refuses to adhere to strict national or religious boundaries. And the best food in our family turns out to be that which has travelled.

Onions, garlic and tomatoes form the basis of everything hereditary in my mother's cooking, and therefore in mine, as I learned to cook from her. Middle Eastern and Sephardi Jews have long been associated with onions and garlic. The conversos in Spain (Jews forced to convert to Christianity under the Inquisition) were thought to be detectable because they, or their homes, gave off the scent of frying onions and garlic. Fellow members of my triathlon club groan at the strong garlic scent my body seems to perspire at early morning training sessions. I hadn't realised that even my sweat remembers family history.

When it travels food, like music, picks up more specific elements and loses others. Dishes undergo unceasing revision based on their routes of transport. In India, the onion-garlic starter was combined with ginger (from *sringavera*, a Sanskrit term). Later, saffron was added, or mostly turmeric, so-called poor man's saffron, which my mother always pronounces as 'TUM-eric', a misnomer also handed down from her father, presumably, and now to me most of the time. One of my Elias cousins, Aviva, runs a kosher catering business in North London, called 'Saffron'. When we call to ask about her sense of the provenance of the family food, she happens to be cooking *hameem* that evening in the oven.

She and her father, Uncle Moshe, explain the translations, handing the phone back and forth to me and my mother. We get excited, remember, disagree, learn from each other. It's a very Elias conversation. I learn that *koftah*, an Indian word – a spiced meatball similar to *kubbah* without the rice covering – lost its surround in India, as the rice was more customarily cooked separately here. *Chetarni*, a slow-cooked dish of onions, tomatoes and spices, in which the onions are caramelised to make the flavours run deep, is an Arabisation of 'chutney'. *Aloo makala* (fried potatoes): *aloo* Hindi for 'potatoes', *makala*, Arabic meaning 'jumping', because the potato was so fried it threatened to jump off the plate. Even the names of the recipes spice and blend with each other.

The food picked up more flavour when a select group of the Baghdadis moved again, from India to Southeast Asia. The chilli became hotter, and some of it became *manis*, meaning 'sweet' in Malay. As we talk with Aviva and Moshe, I chart on the map-tablecloth the food's journey, noting the acquisition of flavours and names as the family migrated across the Asian continent. What was soured with tamarind in India was in Singapore and Malaya sweetened with *malacca* (sugar) or coconut. Arabic for 'stuffed', *mahasha* vegetables full of saffron rice and mincemeat evolved to use local produce, from peppers, aubergine, onions and tomatoes in India, then to cabbage in Singapore, possibly from the watery provinces of Guangdong.

So, when Esther (in name Koh-wei no longer) used to make cabbage *mahasha*, I realise that this was a kind of return home for her to China, but blended with the Elias family's Indian-Middle Eastern trade routes. *Sambusak*, the cheese puffs she made, turn out to be an Arab corruption of 'samosa'. These 'cheese pillows', as Linda Dangoor, a British cook of Baghdadi Jewish ancestry, has delightfully described them, are a Baghdadi Jewish Indian speciality. Originally something like *bahba*, pastry stuffed with dates and a characteristically Middle Eastern sweet, they evolved, since India has no dates, to contain cheese instead. All food was fusion. Or rather everything in the family, like the family itself, was *chakla bakla*. As my aunts' instructions inform me, you can make *chakla bakla*, the spicy, fermented vegetable pickle, out of just about anything. And it will keep.

Even bland old Britain inflected our palette, the centre of empire mixing irreversibly with its far-flung imperial outposts. *Aloo chap*, a spicy meat filling covered with mashed potato and coated with breadcrumbs, must be a linguistic hybrid, I think, of Hindi and English, for 'potato chop'. And, of course, curry puffs, which Esther spent hours making and my grandfather loved, constitute perhaps the only truly delectable 'English' pasty. My mother sometimes manages to obtain curry puffs, with melt-in-your-mouth pastry and just the right combination of fillings from a Malaysian stallholder whom she's befriended in a London market. When she brings a huge bagful home for our lunches, her face says that she's pulled a rabbit from the hat.

Aviva says the food in our family is 'food for the soul'. Proust says something similar: if intellectual memory fails us, 'the smell and taste of things remain poised a long time, like souls, ready to remind us.' It is food that takes me back, from Singapore to India, and from there to Baghdad and beyond.

*

Before Singapore, there had been a previous *mahallah*, in Bombay. My great-grandfather Isaac lived in Bombay long enough for Jacob to be born there and to absorb the city into his soul, so that ever after he was known as 'Jacob Bumbai-Wallah' – that Jacob from Bombay; so that he loved Indian food, music and language most of all. I realise that when May, Jacob and family fled to Bombay as refugees during the war, they were returning not just to his birthplace but to the family's other stopping place. And they returned to the very neighbourhood: to Byculla, which I discover was the first Baghdadi Jewish area in Bombay. Byculla was the grinding stone that created the Indian-Jewish spice mix of the family fusion.

Byculla was developed by the Sassoons, who are everywhere credited with creating the Baghdadi Jewish community in Bombay, and whom I must therefore give a more prominent role to in this part of the story. In what was considered the then fashionable area of Byculla, immigrant to Bombay David Sassoon built the first Baghdadi Jewish synagogue, the beautiful Maghen David, and followed this with a Jewish school, a library, a hospital and a cemetery. All but the cemetery were named after him. Throughout the East, including in Shanghai and Hong Kong, I kept coming across buildings, roads and schools named after a Sassoon. I have to admit that when this happened, even as I struggled to put my family on the map and pin down their names in Asia, my heart sank with a 'not-another-Sassoon' feeling. I felt *Sassooned*.

Back in the UK, at exhibitions and talks my mother and I went to on Baghdadi Jews, we inevitably encountered someone who proudly explained their position in the Sassoon family tree. Many a Sassoon descendant has been hugely helpful to my own search. Yet our Eliases seemed to ride the coattails of the Sassoon empire and figure nowhere in Baghdadi Jewry. At these moments, my mother and I exchanged wry smiles. If *Sassooned* were actually a verb, it would mean to be outdone in your Baghdadi Jewish history, to be gazumped in telling your family tale.

The Sassoons' wealth was made initially in opium, a fact that books on the Sassoons by Sassoons themselves have only recently started to own. The Sassoons ran an opium empire, which stretched from Baghdad, Bombay and Calcutta; via Rangoon, Penang and Singapore; to Shanghai, Hong Kong and Kobe; and on to Amsterdam and London. So prominent and powerful were the family in China that I discover that the Shanghai Chinese also thought of *Sassoon* as a word with meaning. They thought that another name for all Jews was 'Sassoons'.

The Sassoons' success was harnessed to that of the British Empire. Hence Baghdadi Jews were known as the 'Empire's Jews'. When the American Civil War interfered with Britain's cotton supply and the Opium Wars outlawed the opium trade, the Sassoons switched their main trade from opium to textiles. David Sassoon built India's first textile mills in Byculla, and Britain consequently yoked its textile trade with India. Attracted by Sassoon mills, textile workers began to populate Byculla, and the area became poorer and less fashionable. It was the smell of these Sassoon cotton mills that my mother remembered from her refugee childhood in Byculla – something I'm only able to piece back together as I read the history and return to Byculla myself. There are still some old Sassoon mill signs just about readable on street corners.

Many of the mill workers were also Jews, but they were not from Baghdad or their descendants. These Jews were Bene Israel, meaning the 'children of Israel'. They had immigrated to India before the Baghdadis, and they came to be dependent on the mills and on the Sassoons.

India is often said to be the only country in the world that doesn't have a history of antisemitism. But what it might lack in prejudice from others towards Jews, I discover that it more than makes up for in divisions and exclusions practised within the Jewish community.

*

When I go back to India, I repeat the course of empire. I go first to Calcutta, where, at the Victoria Memorial on the Maidan, I read all about the East India Company, and of the subsequent influx into India of Eastern Jewish merchants and also of the Chinese in the eighteenth century. At the India Museum, I follow their trade routes and spice histories, and, in the botany section, inspect spice samples in glass cases and note their origins: cinnamon, cloves, cardamom; also the opium poppy. I learn of a new kind of camphor, a spice called *Cinnamon Camphora*.

From Calcutta, I fly to Bombay: nineteenth-century imperial metropolis and site of twenty-first-century religious and cultural divisions. During my flight between cities, there's a bomb in Bombay, at the Gateway of India. Over fifty people have been killed. The blame is laid firmly on Muslim protests against the upcoming election, and the press make dark connections to the global 'war on terrorism'.

When I arrive, my taxi takes me close to the site, near the docks – Sassoon Dock to be precise. I think about how this imperial arch is an incongruous site for terrorism. Meant to welcome King George on the British royals' first visit to the empire in India, the monument wasn't completed until the late 1920s, well over a decade after the royal visit, and when the city was already bubbling with anti-British, nationalist sentiment. The colonial building is very Mughal, with its arches and colonnades. It strikes me as out of place in today's Hindu nationalist India.

I have 'returned' to Byculla – the family home, but my own first time in India. I'm staying in a friendly Muslim hotel, named Heritage Hotel. It was the pun that clinched the booking for me. When I explain to the waiter what I'm doing here, he is interested, kind. He tells me that he's Muslim and that, when he was growing up here, his best friends were Jewish. But not anymore. They all left, with the creation of Israel.

One morning I'm invited to join an 'Arab' – his self-description – who turns out to be another Indian Muslim who was born in Bombay, but who now resides in Bahrain. He, too, grew up with Jewish friends; they used to live 'side by side'. He confirms my sense that there was more mixing then, fewer problems. His self-naming as 'Arab' – no longer Indian – is revealing. As if it's a struggle to be *both*: to be both Indian and Muslim; as it used to be Indian and Jewish. It's Indian Muslims who are being blamed for the Gateway of India bomb. Hindu nationalist banners are going up around Bombay, incited by the government and the press. The bomb attack is being used to stoke divisions in the upcoming election – which will be won again by the Hindu nationalist party.

That I meet mainly Muslim Indians in Byculla is no surprise. Inhabited by Jews in the past, Byculla is now a Muslim area and contains the largest number of Muslims I've yet come across in my travels around India. I feel an affinity with my breakfast companion and others I meet here. The men cover their heads and, like me, are bearded. The women dress in *shalwas*, long floaty dresses like those worn by Baghdadi Jewish women in the past. I visit the Sassoon High School. By the 1950s, this Baghdadi Jewish school took mostly Bene Israel, who were excluded when the school was set up by Sassoon. From the 1970s, the decline throughout the Jewish population was so great that it opened to all children from the local area – the majority of whom were by this point Muslim.

The irony of this mini 'population exchange' isn't lost on me. The parents hanging outside the school now, waiting to pick up their children, seem to me to blend into Byculla with their garb: their dishdashas or gabaliyas and *shalwas* of the East – Mizrahi – somehow. An old but clearly maintained sign displayed outside the school names the establishment's first objective as 'To Study Jewish religion and culture and Hebrew language.' Mine too, now, I think. And to my incredulity but great pleasure, I'm told that the children still number among their prayers in the morning some basic Hebrew, which means I can understand them, and they me. Using the stranger's tongue, mirror image of my Jewish grandfather speaking Arabic: what could be more loving, more *kadosh* and *abdalek* than this?

By this token, this Jewish-Muslim school is also meeting its seventh stated objective, in accordance with India's still – just about – multicultural society: 'To achieve national and international integration.' Outside the school I chat with a Muslim parent. 'Salaam', I say to him in greeting. He glances at my kippah (I've come straight from the synagogue next door): 'Shalom', he says back to me.

Jewish Bombay will open up to me only with the help of Muslims.

*

In part what I find in India in the treatment of the Bene Israel Jews by the Baghdadi Jews is a pattern of exceptionalism, separations, divisions – *clean* and *foul*, inside and outside – that is imprinted into the very self-concept of being a distinct people, of being 'chosen'. Chosen-ness has been the characteristic that made me most uncomfortable about Jewish history. It was a reason for *not* learning about my Jewishness, and an incentive

instead for following what I thought was the much more egal-
itarian and inclusive path of Buddhism. I was uncomfortable,
that is, until I began to understand what chosen-ness might
mean.

I'm learning in British Jewish circles today that the choice
of Jews in the Covenant with God means not being marked out
as better, as I initially thought, or contrasting yourself with others. It means instead being a 'light unto the nations', to quote
the Tanakh: being of benefit to others. It means inheriting an
expectation of doing good work, *tikkun olam* – for everyone. It's
exactly the opposite, in other words, of any prejudice I'd seen
within Jewish communities.

As I write about India, I read in *The Jewish Chronicle* that
the British Jewish Board of Deputies has set up (in 2020)
an enquiry into 'racial inclusivity in the Jewish community'.
Beyond the issue of antisemitism, of which there is wider press
discussion, the question of the Board's enquiry is whether British Jewry is marred by internal ethnic divisions, even whether
there is Jewish racism against non-white Jews. The enquiry is
the first of its kind in any Jewish community in the world, and
I find it a brave self-examination. It ends up making some powerful recognitions about not assuming that all Jews are white
or hail from Europe. It recommends that we mark those Jewish
histories, traumatic and otherwise, that do not centre on the
Holocaust. It reaches out particularly to Black, North African
and Middle Eastern Jews. My family.

I attend events and listen to stories from Jews of Afro-Ca-
ribbean descent, and of Middle Eastern origin like my family.
Individuals speak candidly about being made to authenticate
their Jewish identity in social encounters with other Jews, about

racially profiled security at Jewish institutions, even of being turned away from synagogues because of the darker colour of their skin and redirected to nearby Methodist churches. Their accounts are squirm-inducing. My mother is horrified when I tell her their stories. She believes it, and yet doesn't believe it. Her Orthodox synagogue in London has been open-arms welcoming to our family. But the personal testimonies in Britain today strongly echo the clashes in Jewish communities of the past in India.

I speak to a Baghdadi Jewish descendant in London, David Sopher, whose family like mine spent time in India. His grandfather also migrated from Baghdad to Bombay, where he set up a factory near Crawford Market, on Carnac Road, a street that divided another British ethnically segregated city. The factory churned out fezzes, the requisite headwear for all subjects of the Ottoman Empire. Like the Eliases, the Sophers had left the Turkish empire, of which Iraq was then a part, for the British Empire.

David tells me that, with regards to India – Jewishly – it's complicated. Yes, there was a degree of specific Jewish anxiety about kosher and lineage, about being and maintaining 'proper' Jewishness. But when they came to India, he says, Jews also absorbed something of India's own ancient caste system, and this unhappy pairing was then overlaid and fixed, like a second lot of dye printed onto fabric, with the new racial and class hierarchies of the British Empire.

Three types of people-dividing led to some pretty impassable and ugly walls. Under the British, he says, 'divide-and-rule' distinguished 'Anglo-Indian Jews' – in other words the Baghdadis, who hadn't a drop of Englishness in them but tended to be lighter skinned – who were 'Jews proper'; from the 'Indian Jews' – in other words the Bene Israel – who were by extension, therefore, not proper Jews. This fits with the narrative of Anglicisation that is mostly told of Baghdadi Jews as the 'Empire's Jews'. Names were changed: 'Abdulla' became 'Albert'; 'Abraham', 'Adrian'. Men shaved and suited up; women acquired the latest European fashions. And the languages switched, from Arabic to English, apparently, never transitioning through or adopting Hindi. Even the cemetery was divided. In 1836 one Sassoon wrote a petition to the British that he be allowed to build a wall to separate the Baghdadi Jewish dead from the Bene Israel dead. He wrote: 'Two distinct tribes of Jews inhabit this country; one having adopted the customs of the natives of India and the other faithful to their Arabian fathers.' When he was refused, he simply bought a new cemetery, excluding the Bene Israel.

The pattern repeats, indeed precedes, the splits in the *mahallah* in Singapore. Rules and customs emerged to prevent what was called 'intermarriage' between the different groups. Conversion was required of some Bene Israel, since the Baghdadis suspected them to have become too Indian, lovers of Indians, hence strangers to Judaism. Indeed, there was a suspicion that the Bene Israel might themselves be the product of intermarriage with non-Jewish Indians: half-castes, called strangers.

The Indian Jewish world split between British and Indian. The Baghdadi Jews assimilated to Britishness; the Bene Israel to Indianness. The end of the British Empire in India widened divisions. The Bene Israel supported Gandhi's call for a boycott of the British and the ousting of the empire and welcomed

Indian nationalism. Conversely, when it became clear that the British were going to withdraw from India, the Baghdadi Jews petitioned Parliament in London – another Sassoon – that they should be counted as British subjects or Europeans, in distinction from the other 'Indian' Jews.

At this point, some Baghdadis started to classify themselves as Sephardim, from *Sepharad*, Hebrew for 'Spain'. A crude distinction is often made between Sephardi, or Mediterranean Jews, and Ashkenazi, East European Jews. In this formula, my family is classified as Sephardi. But the label is a misnomer for the Eliases, among other Baghdadi or Eastern Jews, who are, more correctly, Mizrahi (from the Hebrew for 'from the East'), a term that, at least until the Board's report on racial inclusivity, was often elided within Jewish communities and still remains largely unknown to non-Jews.

When we sent my mother's genes for testing with Ancestry. com, the results were explained with a map that looked like the spice route. Her 'DNA story' plonked her substantially in the East. The sprinkling of 'European Jewish' genes puzzled us initially, but we worked out that this is shared DNA, rather than being derivative. May was certainly the first in her family ever to come to Europe. While she has always been 'the English one', she is immensely proud of her Eastern heritage, still, in her heart, 'a girl from the East'.

The Baghdadi Jews were at root Easterners, not British; not Spanish, not Europeans.

That the Eliases don't fit the template of the 'Empire's Jews' matters hugely to my return to Judaism. It also makes sense. I never felt myself to be fully British or European; did this unfamiliar Asian Jewishness explain something of my coming so late to my Jewish ancestry, when Jewishness, as the Board of Deputies' enquiry shows, has been so much equated with Europeanness? May, Jacob, Isaac too, identified with some degree of Britishness but not only; they adopted – and adapted – Indianness and other Asian stopping points in the journey. The fact that India has been kept alive at the heart of the Elias family Jewishness – that Jacob passed on to my mother his love of the language, the music, the food, and that she passed on at least the last two to me – gives me a counter-story to what I read in the histories.

*

I find Ripon Road, the location of the compound where May spent the war years. The street has been renamed Maulana Azad Road, obviously a Muslim name. I assume that this renaming is part of the city's effort to erase empire but the Muslim street name stands out in the current Hindu nationalist climate. I should at least acknowledge that I'm not in 'Bombay' at all but rather in 'Mumbai', although I can't bring myself to call this city by the name To do so would be to pretend that we can purify the city of its foundational cross-cultural past, extract and blend out the infusions of my family's and others' mixes.

Halfway down the Maulana Azad Road, I come across a compound – now for old men, but the only place that could fit my mother's descriptions. The streets around it are still full of fading old mill signs, though no working mills remain. The road backing onto Victoria Gardens displays a battered 'Sassoon Mill' plaque. There are many tailors at work. A neat, moustachioed man cuts carefully from a large roll of patterned cloth.

Many open-fronted stores are stacked with piles of sarongs and saris in the making. I can't smell the material, but there's so much else to absorb – the spices, the incense, occasionally clove cigarettes; urine, traffic fumes, sweat.

I spend a morning trying to find the Maghen David synagogue. I wander up and down Clare Road, where my map has it marked. I find the synagogue eventually, not on Clare Road but on Sir J. J. Road, named after a Parsi. The map seems to reflect the shiftingness and uncertainty that the inhabitants recognise is the nature of this city. Will the places be named the same? Will they even still be there? Whose city is it now?

Like its Baghdadi Jewish counterpart in Singapore, the Maghain Aboth, the Maghen David synagogue in Bombay is still beautiful, with evidence of the grandness it must have attained when it was fully attended. But when I visit, the synagogue is decrepit. The lovely yellow paint outside is peeling, and vegetation is growing on the roof. Inside, birds are nesting, and they fly from the arches to ceiling-hung candelabra. The Torah scrolls, locked in silver casing, and within that in their wooden ark, are in much better condition, the silver pure polished metal. The Muslim caretaker, wearing the perky Muslim prayer cap, opens the ark for me to kiss the Torah case. A Jewish couple are here also. She is clearly Bene Israel. He, I can't tell. A loudspeaker plays to an otherwise empty synagogue. The recordings are sermons – by an American rabbi? – about Jews in Israel.

In the office within the Maghen David, Flora Baruch is presiding. Sunk into an easy chair, she makes no attempt to rise. But I see that she's wearing a *ruppa* – one of the shapeless Arabic cotton dresses which Esther adopted. She also has my grandfather's long nose, straight but curled over at the end. Flora must be in her late seventies and, to me she seems, like the synagogue itself, in bad shape. She tells me that she would come with me to the other synagogue, the Kenesseth Eliyahoo, only she's too ill. But I need to go to this newer synagogue. All the records from Maghen David are now there.

On her directions, Mohammed, my driver, takes me to Kenesseth Eliyahoo synagogue in V. B. Gandhi Road. Mrs Symss, another Baghdadi Jew, has been looking after all the Bombay Jewish records here these past twenty years. In 1993, they moved everything that was left at Maghen David to combine with the archives here, a further condensing of the community.

I look through Maghen David's records. Though I don't find anything related to our family – nothing from my great-grandparents', grandparents', or my mother's stay – the ketubot make for fascinating reading and are beautifully hand engraved: Hebrew on one side, English on the other. They hold parallel family stories. Typically they start by certifying that both parents are of 'authentic' Jewish origin and parentage. The only mixed marriages that I find end in 'declarations of separation and release'. Mrs Symss consoles me by making some delicious ginger tea, masala chai, which is rich with milk and very sweet. She is a ball of motherliness coating a core of efficiency. We sit at long dark wooden tables. The fans whir high above my head and blow my papers onto the tiled floor.

I spend one final, sad, rainy afternoon in Bombay in the Jewish cemetery. I would never have found it, as my map gives up on road markings at this point and simply declares a large, blanked-out area 'Jewish'. But Flora Baruch gave Mohammed directions (in Jewish Hindi?), which the Muslim caretaker then elaborated (in Muslim Hindi?). The cemetery is bigger than I expected and, like everything else Jewish that I find in Bombay, in decay.

I hunt for any familial, or at least familiar, names amidst the overgrown weeds and cracked tombstones, as rats, raccoons and lizards scurry out of my path. Mrs Symss had said that the cemetery is always in a terrible state during monsoon season, that at Jewish New Year (one month away in September), the growth is cut back and tidied up and the graves will be clear. But I can't quite believe in regeneration. Headstones lie about in fragments. Moss is so overgrown that it makes many of them not only unreadable but organic again, and even the twenti-eth-century ones are covered over. A kind caretaker, another Muslim, walks around with me, patiently holding an umbrella to keep off the torrents of rain, while I scribble down what seems relevant. There are Judahs, Solomons (not many) – and Sassoons of course. There are few Eliases.

There is no place of recovery here, I think. In all my time in India, I don't meet a single Baghdadi Jew under sixty, although I'll meet many young Baghdadis elsewhere, particularly in Israel.

In Clare Road, while hunting for the elusive Maghen David, I come by accident upon the very first Jewish cemetery. This was the one that Jews used before the divisions grew up, before the second cemetery was acquired. A notice tells me that, in 1931, it became a 'recreation ground', on condition that the graves not be disturbed. The caretaker (who refuses a tip – 'no money', he insists) takes me to the sole grave left.

While I'm reading the headstone, about a Sillamon from Baghdad who died in 1828, he respectfully removes a plastic bottle lying on the grave. When I return later to spend some time there on my own, someone has placed a red flower on Sillamon's tomb. Though I know this to be a totally inappropriate memorial for a Jewish – or, for that matter, a Muslim – grave (no flowers in either religion; in Judaism only the finality and simplicity of stone), the gift strikes me as beautiful. A gesture symbolic of stranger love, it's perfect for Sillamon's resting place.

*

My name is Kassim Bhabha
renowned in North, South, East and West.
Constantinople, Turkey;
Baghdad, Yemen, Aden, Tripoli;
Bombai, Hindustan, Karikal, Pondicherry;
Hyderabad, Lahore, Afghanistan, Delhi.

I realise now that Haron's song from the Worlds *bangsawan* performances in Singapore is a riff and a gloss on the family business and the eastern trade routes. The spice trade had brought the family to Bombay. I think the family's business – an earlier version of the Elias Brothers – must have existed on or near Tamarind Lane, in the oldest part of the city, where the British Fort and the ramparts of military colonisation gave way to the cosmopolitan mix of the bazaars.

We think that my mother's grandfather, Isaac, left Iraq catalysed by the opening of the Suez Canal, in 1869, which dramatically shortened shipping routes from the Middle East, energising trade and migration, especially to India. My parents' letters, in the course of their journeys to England, describe going through the Suez Canal, both of them expressing surprise at its narrowness in places. May wrote to Keith from her boat: 'With arid desert on one side, and date palm, Egyptian structures, caravans in the distance and nomad tents on the other, I felt as though I were in another world, the world of Arabian Nights' stories.' Calcutta, Bombay, Aden, Gibraltar: I look at my tablecloth map. I realise that family journeys trace over each other.

*

Six years after my own visit to Mumbai, my parents took a cruise from Southampton to Singapore. They were inspired after they reread their love letters alongside me while I was working on the early part of this book – endearingly, inspired by their own words. Their ship embarked and disembarked at the same ports their ships had on their first journeys west fifty years previously but made additional, more touristy stops – Phuket as well as Bangkok, Petra as well as Cairo (the Suez Canal again), Ephesus and Athens, Barcelona and Rome. My mother sent me updates, via email from the ship, of their excursions and onboard activities.

Mumbai was the highlight. 'Bombay especially was very poignant for me', she wrote.

Seeing the coastline at dawn brought tears to my eyes, thinking of my Papa. It was all strange and yet familiar. Your notes and maps were crucial to our visit; we decided to go it alone (because the Jewish ship tour was cancelled) so we went by taxi.

During the morning we saw two synagogues (Maghen David & Knesset Elyahu) and the David Sassoon Library & School. We tried to find the exact spot in Ripon (now Maulana Azad) Rd where we had lived but it was impossible. It was all so crowded there & I have a feeling now that we actually lived along that road which at the time was so quiet I remembered it as a courtyard. There were cloth shops here & there still, but all those dwellings are now shanties occupied by very very poor Indian families as you know. It was sad to see them yet they went around with smiles on their faces.

We then took another taxi, which took us to Marine Drive, the Gateway, & drove along Chowpatty Beach to Colaba and Malabar Hill, then to the Hanging Gardens & Dhoby Ghat. He then took us back to Byculla to take one or two pictures.

He was a nice young man who sang whilst driving; Dad told him I could sing, which the driver made me do, so all the way, we sang in turn then found we were singing the same song together (in Hindustani of course!). It was such an uplifting experience. The driver was amazed I could sing & speak Hindustani!

I loved Bombay; not sure if I'll return but it was a very evocative experience and I thought of my Papa who talked so much about the different streets & I found them. It is amazing to think during the war it was the Jewish *mahallah* for the poorer Jews!

I think there's no place of return when I'm in Mumbai. And then I realise the return is here, in this dialogue with my mother, in the memorial going back that working with her on this book is prompting. True returns are not physical. They must be in the heart.

15. Babylon

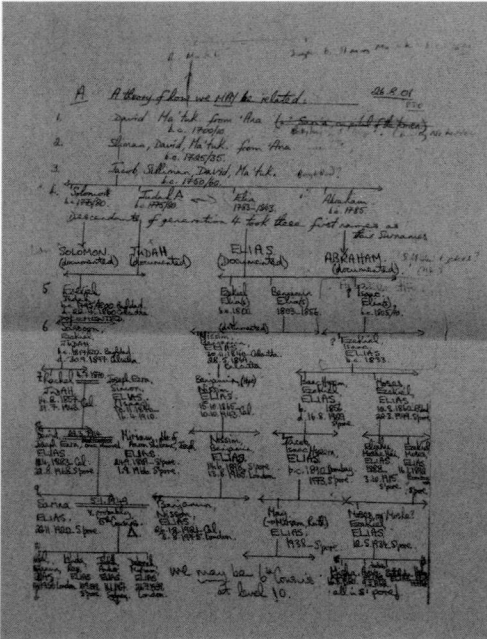

In blessed memory of Sarina Elias, mother of Linda. Died 24.5.2017. Sydney, Australia.

My mother and I are sitting side by side by the camphorwood chest, examining its most recent addition. This is an Elias family tree, created by a newfound cousin, who has been measuring her genealogy against my mother's side. Linda Elias came to us through our cousin Aviva, and she has sent us the document because she knows of my interest working on this book. Linda used to work in the Lloyds of London insurance market, drawing up and doing the sums on complex figures. She's still weighing the odds trying to figure out our degrees of relatedness. 'We may be sixth cousins at level 10', she notes on the back of the tree; alternatively, she could be another of our second cousin's 'fourth cousin once removed.' The tree is a process, a mixture of lives we are sure about and that have been documented, and guesswork to try and join up the dots with other lives. The work of ancestry cannot always be secured, particularly if your family migrated across countries and empires, particularly, as is the case with our lineage, if there was intermarriage and periods of poverty.

In any case, Linda's tree – which runs over several tabloid-sized pages – helps us to line up those who may have been our antecedents. There is Sliman David Ma'tuk: the scribe of Baghdad. Solomon Yakob, his grandson: a gem merchant who led the Baghdadi Jews to Bombay. Solomon's nephew, Ezekiel Judah, a wealthy indigo merchant in Calcutta. These are ancestors my mother has never heard of before, and she's startled to see how far her family might be shown to go back, and back to Baghdad. She's excited to find her father and her grandfather: 'Jacob Isaac Hyeem Ezekiel Elias, b.c. 1890 Bombay, died S'pore 73'; 'Isaac Hyeem Ezekiel Elias, b.c. 1856, Baghdad, died 16.8.1929, S'pore'. We figure out that 'b.c.' here means 'born circa', not, 'before Christ', which is at first what I think it means.

The tree traces all the way to my mother, then down to me. I look at the blank space below my name. I realise that, since I have no children – and my brother is not interested in our Iraqi Jewish ancestry nor in Judaism, and so is passing on nothing of these to my niece and nephew – I will be the very last in our line of the family. The very last in possibly thousands of years of a continuous Baghdadi Jewish ancestry. More tightly, I hold on to the pieces of paper.

'We've always been close, you and I', my mother says. 'But this book, what you've done – what you've found and created. It's special. Our relationship is now truly . . .'. It's unusual for my mother to be lost for words. But I know what she means, and she doesn't have to say it. She is saying that she knows this book is an act of love, for her and her family. That it's where we've worked together, become closest, for over a decade now. This book is really our co-creation.

I went backwards with my ancestors because I couldn't go forwards with children. In a way, this book is really my substitute child.

*

The furthest back we record is David Ma'tuk, from 'Ana, BC 1700/10: father of Sliman, *ben* David Ma'tuk, from 'Ana, BC 1725/35. Himself father of – I am tempted to write 'who begat' – Jacob, *ben* Silliman David Ma'tuk, BC 1745/60 (dates uncertain). At this point the Ma'tuks – like other Jews finding themselves in modernising empires (the Ottomans, then the British), particularly those who were more integrated or who mixed with non-Jews – were required to come up with surnames. And they did. This Jacob called his four sons Solomon, Judah, Elia and Abraham. From this point on, Linda writes, 'Descendants of generation four took these first names as their surnames'. Hence: Solomon, Judah, Abraham. And Elias.

To me it feels like a biblical moment – 'And so Jacob called his sons. . .'. It's so long ago, and the family has migrated so much, that it may as well be from the days of the Bible. No one can remember these ancestors, or Baghdad, or the arrival in Bombay, or the passage to Singapore, or where on earth 'Ana is. How do you trace the connections between roots and routes when you don't know – and can't ever accurately know – the exact 'stopping places'? How do I make sense of my place on this tree?

One way is history. You try to tell a cultural history of 'your people', however you draw the circumference of your tribe. This story is not personal. The other, more intimate, is rather like those *wayyiqtols* I'm learning about in the Torah: the 'And then this happened. . . And then another thing happened. . .' in the Bible. This other way doesn't even attempt to tell the background or the whole story. Instead it embraces the missing links and the repetitions, finds a kind of lived poetry in their patterns.

By no means are these two ways mutually exclusive. But I admit the task isn't easy. Which is why I've left these first ancestors, who are so key to our family plot, but about whom no one alive has any recollection, to last.

*

Isaac Hyeem Ezekiel Elias, my great-grandfather who had such trouble settling in Singapore, is our physical link to Baghdad. He was born there in 1856. Although again we have no dates, I think he must have emigrated to India sometime between the mid-1870s and 1880s, because he married his first wife, Sarah, in Iraq, and Jacob was born in Bombay ten years before the century ended. But while Isaac was the first in our direct Elias lineage to leave Iraq, via Linda's tree I discover constant traffic between Iraq, India and elsewhere in Asia, in earlier, more obliquely related family.

A distant ancestor – some multiplier of a cousin of Isaac's own great-grandfather – turns out to have been the very first Baghdadi Jew to settle in Bombay. The point is acknowledged by historian David Solomon Sassoon (grandson of the original David) in his history of Baghdadi Jews. I have been pipped at the post all along the Baghdadi Jewish ancestry trail by the precedence and pre-eminence of the Sassoons, so now I can't help a feeling of 'Ha! got there first!' at discovering this Indian forebear. But of much greater consequence is the fact that his way of being Jewish in India begins the mixed Asian family blend.

Solomon Yacob as he was called, or (the names become more Arabised the further back we go) Sliman ben Jacob Sliman, proves exactly what my childhood self wanted to find in an ancestor belonging in the camphorwood chest. A spice trader as well as a gem merchant and trader in Arabian horses, he was renowned for his line in rose water; a detail which I love, since I've used this distinctively Middle Eastern ambrosia for years in the annual making of my Iraqi apple jam (apples; rosewater; sugar; cardamom; cook for five hours on the lowest heat). Together with his brother Judah, Solomon had left Baghdad as part of the wave of early nineteenth-century mass emigration that would bring the Sassoons' India progenitor to Bombay.

That account of the Sassoon scion of the Baghdad Nasi (Jewish leader) fleeing persecution from the then Ottoman Turkish governor of Baghdad is told in every book on Baghdadi Jews. My family story, a story of the desires and attractions that acted as the pull of immigration, the other side of the push of emigration, is practically untold. It's more complex and there are missing links, but it's no less Jewish.

*

Sliman ben Jacob Sliman was a trader. He left Baghdad for Bombay. Sliman ben Jacob Sliman changed his name to Solomon Yacob.

Solomon Yacob merchandised hard stone hewn from the ground and petals plucked from the Garden of Eden. He trafficked sapphire and ruby jewels and ambrosial scents. He brought hot-blooded horses born of the desert wind. He sold spices. He trailed spices across the Indian Ocean.

He switched two cities beginning with 'B' and of two syllables. He transacted equally and unequally. He gave up some things and acquired others.

He negotiated between Asias. He did business with Indians and Arabs, Hindus and Muslims. He exchanged a city where his was the majority, for one in which his was the minority. He faced off the British, via the East India Company.

He sacrificed living with his extended family, for working alongside Ezekiel, his nephew, also a merchant, in indigo dye as purple as a moonless sky and muslin as fine as spider thread.

Solomon gambled an old home for a new home. He bartered twin rivers for a beautiful bay. He replaced head-to-toe dishdashas and forbidding abayas with diminishing lungis and inviting saris. He swapped veils and hijabs for nose studs and bindis. Turbans for turbans, sandals for sandals. A language that sticks to the sides of your throat for another that is a song from your heart.

But in his spirit Solomon continued to live in Baghdad. He imported acts of philanthropy to Baghdad and exported a Sefer Torah scroll by a Baghdadi scribe when someone in Bombay died. For the scroll he arranged a case of camphorwood to be brought from China.

He witnessed the eighteenth century becoming the nineteenth century. He experienced anxiety and curiosity, kindness and fear.

Solomon Yakob shared views with a European Jew. Rabbi David d'Beth Hillel had given up his Lithuanian citizenship for British naturalisation. He departed his new home for travels, writing these up as *Travels from Jerusalem, through Arabia, Koordistan, Part of Persia, and India, to Madras.* (I think Rabbi Hillel and Israel Cohen could easily occupy the same role in this story.) Rabbi Hillel recorded his thoughts on Solomon Yakob in his journal. Solomon's manner of life did not measure up, he wrote. The Bombay Baghdadi Jew had adulterated his Jewishness by mixing with 'Arabs and Hindoos', he wrote. Solomon had left off righteousness for 'bad disposition' and 'notorious character'. He had led in waywardness the Jews he was supposed to lead in narrowness. He had driven them off the path to 'unlawful usages which they have learnt from the Arabs and the Hindoos, and concerning which there is a prohibition in Leviticus 18.3.'

I scurry from Hillel to Leviticus 18.3. I read this: 'You shall not copy the practices of the land of Egypt where you dwelt, or the land of Canaan to which I am taking you; nor shall you follow their laws.' I read it as nothing other than a prohibition on deep communing with others.

And so, I tell you, I would not trade in this Solomon – not for all his jewels, rosewater, Arabian horses.

*

When the Ma'tuk name fell from the family tree and the sons of Jacob, ben Silliman David Ma'tuk, BC 1745/60 (dates uncertain) took their first names as their surnames, this act of renaming, taking the father's first name as a continuous surname, didn't resolve the confusion about roots. This is because the son's second name continued to remember the father's name, his third name thus remembering his grandfather's name. Names carried multiple previous generations, and this is a weight Jews continue to pass on in naming their children by using grandparents' initials. Except when a father died before the child was born, in which case the child was given his father's first name. So we can end up with a double name – 'Saul Saul' – as well as (endlessly) recycled names. 'Up until our generation (level ten),' Linda's notes inform us as my mother and I struggle with our cousin's oversize papers, 'Jewish naming was according to set pattern/custom, *not* an arbitrary or random choice of names.' Endogamous marriage – cousins marrying cousins, most often – compounded the confusion.

Our attempt to sort out names and the family tree papers prompts a new memory in my mother. 'You know, for a long time that's true, because we used to be known as the Jacobs,' she says, as she reads Linda's explanation. 'My sister was "Sally Jacob." I was "May benti Jacob." I never realised the history or reason behind this.'

As *ben* is 'son' in Hebrew, and *bin* is daughter, *benti* is 'girl-child' in Arabic. My head spins. Anglo (Chinese?), Jewish, Arabic? May, and sisters June and Julie ('July'; though as I've said none of them was born in these months) were not given Jewish names. My mother didn't receive her official Jewish names, Miriam Ruth, until her conversion, in her own 'Book of Ruth'. Names indicate the problem of origins, as I've discovered with Koh-wei/Esther. The names tell of the inseparability of roots from routes.

What made necessary both the remembering of the father in the son's name and the creation of the surname? Until the end of the eighteenth century, it was unknown among Jews to adopt family names. But with urbanisation and more movement among the Jewish population, and especially when Jews relocated for trade to empires with systematic records, the son (or daughter) could no longer be relied upon to stay in the same place as the father. This meant, in effect, that the *ben*, son (or *bat*, daughter) would not carry back to a known, fixed, rooted, stem. Yet whose child you were continued very much to matter, in order to keep that balance of inside (endogamy) and outside (exogamy) to ensure 'enough' Jewishness without inbreeding. So surnames were magicked in a number of ways, as in our biblical moment of naming from the Ma'tuk rhizome. The new names remembered place of origin (*Hillawi*, 'from Hillah'); or profession (*Sopher*, 'scribe'); or place in the community (*Cohen*, of course 'priest'); or, as in our case, the patronym – the name of the father (Elia) now fixed as surname (Elias).

Elias, I think, must be from *el yas*, which is Arabic for 'myrtle' (*hadassah* in Hebrew). Elias is not a Hebrew name. Myrtle had a special significance for Baghdadi Jews, who strongly identified the prophet Elijah – 'Khidr Elyas' – with *el yas* because of the homonym, the echoing name. At Friday night dinners, they adorned Elijah's chair with *el yas*. And since the time of Solomon's Temple and their exile, Baghdadi Jews decorated the Torah in the synagogue with *el yas* during spring, one of the four blessed types of foliage at the festival of sukkot. Coinciding with spring awakening, the leaf was symbolic of Elijah's ability to transform dead landscapes into fruitfulness and awaken the dead; Elijah, who in the Tanakh never died a natural death but 'went up by a whirlwind into heaven'. The custom was transported to synagogues in India and made it to Singapore.

So when Jacob gave May some myrtle from his visits to the synagogue in Waterloo Street, and when he said to her, 'here is some *yas* for you, *abdalek*', I now see that he was giving her this very ancient piece of Baghdad and re-enacting a symbolic naming. Whether he knew it or not, I don't know, but my learning about this ritual brings Jewish antiquity right into this moment of family intimacy.

Elijah was a traveller in the wilderness, a poor man and a visionary. The family name 'Elias' takes me back to an origin myth, but immediately travels. It takes me right back not to home, but before the Promised Land.

*

Iraq – Baghdad – is the one place in the family story I've not been able to get back to. In the long years in which I've been travelling, digging through various archives and writing this book, Iraq has undergone invasions, wars, killings, new exoduses. Baghdad especially has become what one recent historian of the city calls 'a cauldron of killing'. During this time, my mother and I have been keeping track of the effects on present-day Iraqi Jews, with whom we feel affiliation, as we unearth the family's long historical past. We go to an exhibition, concerts, talks on Babylonian Jews, which draw interest precisely because of the current unrest in Iraq appearing in our newspapers. People are astounded. Did Iraq, such an extremist, violent, sectarian, totalitarian state, really have Jews?

My mother and I send each other clippings from newspapers on the plight of Iraqi Jews today. I send an article by one of the descendants from our family tree, about his visit to war-devastated Iraq and his inability to identify with this bombed-out place. The articles mostly take a valedictory, mournful stance, lamenting the 'last Jews of Iraq'. My mother and I also count down the Babylonian Jews left: from forty at the time of Saddam Hussein's defeat at the hands of the Americans and British; to thirty in the subsequent year; most recently to less than five. The number is insufficient to muster a minyan, though there's still a synagogue, now in the poorest part of Baghdad, with no signs to indicate its Jewishness, not even a Magen David. To talk to the leader of the community, journalists need permission from the Iraqi Ministry of Information, and then they're told that the synagogue no longer exists.

During the War on Terror, Israel seeks to airlift out the 'last Jews' in an Operation dubbed 'Help from Zion'. One ninety-year-old, once he's in Israel, is quoted as saying he wanted to end his life in Baghdad; Iraq was his home. He came to Israel only because the Israelis were very kind, 'for their sake'. Another, a woman, is insistent on remaining in Baghdad. She says she's first of all Iraqi; Jewish second. She remains inextricably tied to those around her. Tangled roots indeed.

One startling irony of the camphorwood chest archive is that the further back in time I go, the more I find it connects to what's current. Origin stories are always written in their moment, of course, can't be told any other way. Looking at it now, I feel that the story of the Babylonian Jews over history – in their beginning and their end – couldn't be more symptomatic of the divisiveness, and also opportunities, of our own age.

*

I'm in the Hebrew collections of the British Library, looking for the manuscripts of another, even more distant, relative. The grandfather of Bombay Solomon, Sliman ben David Ma'tuk was the first migrant: the one who upped roots for Baghdad in the early eighteenth century. Up to that point, the family dwelled in 'Ana, north of Baghdad and on the Euphrates.

I test my feet out in the giant footsteps of this forebear. The only writer I can find in the family, Sliman was, like me, a scholar. He was a voracious reader, with a library of over seven thousand volumes. I feel like I've had to read almost as much to find out about him and this Iraqi period. But Sliman was famous first and foremost as a poet, a composer of Hebrew religious poems, called piyyutim, and it's these I've come to the library to see. Many of his piyyutim are still recited by Iraqi Jews, though the prayers gradually became more secular and about all kinds of topics. They fused Hebrew with Arabic, a hybrid language called Judeo-Arabic. And I find that this mixed yet rooted form of the piyyut is making a comeback now in Israel, in the contemporary Middle Eastern music I love. From the 1700s, it's amazing that Sliman's poems have survived at all.

As I put in my catalogue request, I can't resist another moment of ancestor-bragging or -bagging. 'A distant relative. . . on our family tree. . . the original Baghdadi', I tell the librarian, an unwanted explanation of why this item. She gives me an Israeli shrug. 'They're not here', she says. 'The manuscripts were sold off to private collectors as part of the Sassoon Collection.'

Sassooned again. Disbelief. I won't get to touch the hand of my ancestor through any handwritten scroll. But five minutes later the curator is handing me the microfilms that the library made of the piyyutim, before the original manuscripts were sold.

Scrolling through the flimsy reels and peering into the micro-lens, I can barely make out the script, particularly given this unfamiliar fusion form, particularly when I'm still struggling with Hebrew just by itself. And when I do manage to decipher parts, the writing seems formulaic. 'My enemies are surrounding me'. Isn't this a quote from the psalms?

But if I could converse with this first Baghdadi Jew, meet this fellow writer face to face instead of chasing his vanishing trace, what would we say to each other? How might we connect?

*

I come from a family that comes from a city that for over a millennium was the centre of world Jewry. I come from a city that will name our family as Baghdadis, whether we are in Singapore, London, India, Israel.

I come from a city of four gates, three walls, and a river acting as a fourth wall not a wall. I come from where Jewishness was built into the stones of the city, brick by brick, by Jewish slaves. I come from the Gardens of Babylon, Eden, palms, dates, plantations. I come from the Tigris and the Euphrates. A river wide as a lake, capturing sunsets and moon risings in pictorial stills. I come from barbecued fish by the river and date pastries. From rooftop-sleeping, dove-flying, kite-flying.

I come from the first epic, *Gilgamesh*, from the home of Harun in *One Thousand and One Nights*. I come from a synagogue open to Eden's spices. From Song of Solomon. Myrtle. Camphor. From owl, gazelle, ass, horse. I come from 2600 years. I come from a Jewish homeland in exile, when Palestine was the diaspora. From 'the father of mysteries' and the origins of Kabbalah. From the belief that Jews, all human beings, are star-atoms of an exploded God; that we are all, at once, strangers and lovers.

I come from the Great Synagogue with the stone that spoke, *Even me-Erets-Yisrael*: 'a stone from the land of Israel'. I come from walking circles around synagogues, as Buddhist monks are also doing around stupas, in countries in my future. A city of circles and returning and no return. Langston Hughes, my soul will not grow deep like rivers; I will not bathe in the Euphrates. I come from renewal and destruction and reinvention. Refugees. Ruins, rebuilding. Flood, famine, plague.

I come from Babylon, Mesopotamia (meaning 'twin rivers'), Iraq. I come from an 'emanation' of British policy: 'a make-believe kingdom, built on false pretences and kept going by a British design and for a British purpose' (Elie Kedourie, Iraqi Jew, also from here). I come from city of peace, city of war, rivers red with blood. From enslavement, conquest, torture. Empire after empire after empire. From religious sectarianism and foreign invasions, from dictators, emperors, ideologues. I come from the death of children, orphans and amputations and terrible grief. Prisons and gallows and jeering crowds at televised public hangings. From IEDs and car bombs. From fairy tales and news atrocities. From 'shock and awe'.

I come from neighbours attacking and protecting. From Abraham and Ibrahim and Abram. From Elijah, Ezekiel, or El-Kifil. From Muslim or Jew, and others. From a common tongue. I come from shared shrines, Muslims shutting shops to respect the Jewish Shabbat, from Jews lauded as Arabic musicians, from Arabic writers composing in Hebrew. From the Venn centre of the overlapping circles of the Jewish world and the Arab Empire, the centre of Islam and Jewry. I come from Judeo-Arabic.

I come from the souk and the street. From cafes and politics and bookshops and libraries. Houses with courtyards, balconies curved. I come from the oud and 'kili-lili-lili-lili' ululation at weddings, *shashah* and throwing melon skins and pistachio shells. I come from superstition, from feeding cobras to placate them; from a great-grandmother who brought this ritual with her to tame the snakes in Singapore and left it with my mother. From handwashing two, three, four times; from don't step over legs, don't pick up your own glove, upright overturned shoes, never open an umbrella indoors.

I come from bridges between times, worlds, writers. I come from a poem indivisible from a city.

*

Before they arrived in Baghdad with the poet Sliman, the ancestors of David Ma'tuk (I learn from Sassoon's book) 'had lived

362

for centuries' in the town of 'Ana. Linda wonders on the back of her family tree if 'Ana is really San'a, the capital of Yemen. But Google maps allows me to pinpoint an 'Ana within Iraq. It's in northern Iraq, close to the Syrian border. Appropriately given what we've been reading in our news about this part of the world for the last twenty years or so, that city was named after Anat, the goddess of war.

Historian Sassoon specifies that the 'Ana the Ma'tuks came from rose on the site of the ancient former city of Nehardea, when Iraq was part of the Babylonian Empire. But like many subsequent family members, the place was moved, renamed and reinvented.

The Jews of Nehardea (later 'Ana) are thought to be the oldest in Iraq, having been brought to Babylonia as slaves by the Babylonian Emperor Nebuchadnezzar after the destruction of the Temple in Jerusalem in 597 BCE. Those first Jewish settlers built a synagogue from stones and earth they brought with them from the fallen Temple. They called their synagogue – I note again the literalism around land and movement – 'Removed and Settled': *Shaf-ve-Yativ*. This reconstruction was itself destroyed in 259 CE, rebuilt and *re*destroyed a century later, in an echo of what the previous generations of exiles had witnessed happening in Jerusalem. At the end of the fourth century CE, Nehardea once again became a centre of Judaism. It's repeatedly mentioned in the Talmud, and there's a proverb by the Babylonian Talmudist Samuel that said, 'The paths of heaven are as familiar to me as the streets of Nehardea.' But given all the renaming and removing, the destruction and rebuilding, this seems to me to put heaven and even a safe home at a further distance.

And yet I find it was here, in Babylonia, that Jewishness flourished. The practices and canon that are now taken as underwriting Jewishness were born in exile, not in Judah/Israel. It was in Babylonia that the Talmud and its intricate legal discussions took shape. It was in Babylonia that the Hebrew script was invented – as if now, away from any sense of home, it became all the more important for Jews to record their story. This is a revelation to me given the displacement of Iraq in the Jewish world and the focus now on Israel. It was among strangers, then, that Jews gained a greater sense of identity.

There are archaeological sites in the Middle East where, standing just in one place, I've been able to look down and see the successive waves of empires recorded in the strata of the rock. Jaffa old city is one example: a Jewish extension of Tel Aviv now, but before that an Arab city, and before that. . . We tend to see the top layers best, the moment closest to our present. But excavation exposes history in cross section. Assyrian, Babylonian, Persian, Greek, Roman, Christian, Islamic, Mongol, Ottoman, British, pan-Arabist, Islamist. In this order, empires rose and fell, rose and fell across what was once called 'Babylonia'. With each empire, the Jewish diaspora spread from Babylonia, throughout the Middle East, and eventually into Europe.

Under all the systems, Jews were always treated differently from their compatriots. They were all empires' Jews, archetypal strangers. But what did this mean in practice? I wade through research that gives me two oppositional narratives. Jews thrived in the Middle East; many became successful and wealthy, and served within courts or government. Jews were victimised in the Middle East. They were required to mark themselves out as Jewish in their dress and they were made to give way, even physically in the street, to Muslims. Ample evidence is provided for both sides. What the alternatives don't say is that there are probably as many sides as there are lives of our ancestors, and actually many more again, given that we can't help writing their biographies from where we stand, reconstructing the strata of past lives from our place in the present.

If the Eliases/Ma'tuks were mostly traders/brokers, this was likely a necessary occupation. In being forbidden many other professions as Jews, they were compelled into trade. Plus with migration, often forced, Jews created family networks and acquired skills such as languages that helped their trade. My family couldn't work and stay put. Instead they tried to use each displacement to expand their business. The most iconic global trade routes in history, including my family's spice route, were supported by diaspora Jews. Jewish traders became catalysts of the movement of cultures, languages, religions, ideas, as much as material goods. In China, I discovered that Jews settled as far east as Kaifeng, where a memorial stone that once marked a synagogue remembers them in a mix of Chinese and Hebrew scripts. Rather than return to Babylon, these 'Chinese' Jews also took Chinese wives and set up home in Kaifeng. There's an awfully long precedent for Jacob's and Isaac's loves.

*

Love of home and alienation from home arising from this most travelled and estranged of peoples is an archetypally Jewish tension. In long-held mythologies, and too much in politics today, I think, Jews are equated with ideas of return and a homeland, and with a particular country, of course – Israel. What I find troubling about this identification is not only the collapsing of Jewishness into Israel, a key error of antisemitism, but also the assumption that any one of us can simply go back to the origins of our earliest ancestors and erase the aeons of mobility and mixing undertaken by subsequent generations. My family's Jewishness was not formed in Israel but in diaspora: in Babylon, Iraq, India, Singapore. Their story, I realise as I near its end, has been overwhelmed by another, centring on homeland, Israel and return, which too often emphasises Jewish difference from those with whom Jews mix. Given our family's shaping in displacement, it's not surprising that I'm coming 'home' late to Jewishness.

In one ancient example, the Book of Psalms, the Sefer Tehellim, produces the trope of longing for home. After the fall of Jerusalem and the capture of the Jews by the Babylonian Emperor, the psalmist depicts the exiled Jews as sitting down between Mesopotamia's rivers (Iraq), remembering lost Zion, and weeping:

> By the rivers of Babylon,
> there we sat and we also wept,
> when we remembered Zion.
> Upon the willows in its midst, we hung our harps.
> For there our captors demanded of us words of song,
> and our tormentors asked of us with mirth;
> 'Sing to us from the songs of Zion.'
> How shall we sing the song of Adonay on alien soil?

It's lyrical, for sure. Loss of home; acute nostalgia; an inability to sing or praise the Lord (*Adonay*) on foreign soil. It makes for a poignant picture. How can one resist this plucking on meta-phorical heartstrings, with literal willow-harp strings?

Yet despite the lament about how *can* we sing, the psalmist *does* have the Jews singing in exile, even if it's a self-conscious dirge wondering *how* can we do that. I think about the degree to which desire for otherness and migration generated my grand-father's songs. I think of how love songs were the lifeline hold-ing my parents together across 7000 miles. The words helped people from very different worlds connect across religious, cul-tural and physical gaps. With my family history, I realise that the Jewish story is about celebrating and singing the distances, rather than mourning home and seeking singularity.

I'm learning that portability, the extraordinary capacity to transport cultures, peoples, a religion, is right there at the beginnings of Jewishness. In the Temple, the Covenant that bound this God to these people was first of all placed in an Ark, a wooden chest. And every time I see the Sefer Torah (Torah Scroll) removed from the *Aron* (wooden cupboard) in any syn-agogue, I can't help thinking of the camphorwood chest; to me, a sacred object that as my mother's, containing her family, will always be associated with my Jewish history. What I hadn't realised is that Jews likewise began with an identity that could be transported quickly and easily, in a piece of furniture used by countless migrants over the millennia, for precious things when on the move.

*

I visit the Babylonian Heritage Museum in Or Yehuda, near Tel Aviv. The one museum devoted to Iraqi Jewry, with its wonderfully animating exhibition and research library, also only gives one side of the story. The displays recount the time in Iraq as exile from homeland, the weeping-by-the-waters psalm given due prominence. The plot ends with the creation of modern Israel in 1948 and the triumphant rescue of the Iraqi diaspora back home to the promised land, the ingathering of the tribe. The last section of the exhibition is entitled 'Zionism and Ali-yah' ('lifting up' to Israel).

But what the exhibition nowhere mentions – perhaps not surprisingly since the museum is in Israel – are the Jews who chose to remain in Iraq. Written out of the narrative from the politically charged present and the historical archive are those Jews who preferred to be among strangers.

Some fifty years or so after the destruction of the First Temple, a Persian King conquered Babylonia and permitted the exiled Babylonian Jews to return to Jerusalem to rebuild the Temple. But the *majority* of Jews chose to remain in Babylon, in exile; a fact that I find very hard to uncover. Ezra and Nehemiah were the prophets who came to lead the Babylonian Jews back to the Promised Land, back to Judah/Israel. Ezra was horrified by the practices of what he found among the Judaeans, as recorded in the Book of Ezra. They 'have not separated themselves from the people of the lands, doing according to their abominations'. Some of them 'had taken strange wives': and by some of these wives they had children. They had broken those laws against 'copying the practices' of the other land again. They had mingled languages; they had fused their foods; they had intermarried, and they had loved. Jews had not kept themselves apart from strangers.

Ezra saved his greatest vitriol for mixed relationships, and the children that had resulted. *Half-castes.* I hear, from my schooldays, the voice between the walls in the bathroom: a reverberation of this ancient biblical history. Ezra demanded that those couples already married be separated, that families be split apart.

And this is where, in the end, I find my family and myself: among the majority of Jews who never left Iraq, until my great-grandfather; among those Jews – the majority – who didn't heed Ezra's call to 'return home'; among those who didn't want to give up whatever affiliations they had formed. At first it feels like too much of a stretch to use my family's history to try to get inside the exiles' choice. But then I realise I'm descended from this remaining majority. I carry their 'DNA story'. Having been in Babylon for some fifty years, they too had made a life among strangers. They had obtained recognition, even status in Babylonian society. What for Ezra were 'abominations' were for them simply the ways of their neighbours – the clothes, food, music, and yes, even lovers. For some, it was the only life they had known.

And this life was also in the Torah, in that most rule-bound – and hence legally Jewish – of Jewish books, Leviticus. For I find it there in the Covenant, the most repeated commandment in the Torah, in the words of God in his contract with the Jews:

When a stranger resides with you in your land, you shall not wrong him. The stranger who resides with you shall be to you as one of your citizens; you shall love him as yourself, for you were a stranger in the land of Egypt.

Definitely there were costs. A legacy that was not immediately obvious or that could be taken for granted. A Jewishness that would have to be consciously retraced and recovered in the intersection with other stories. I would not be writing this book without the questions demanded by this history. I would not have to remake my Jewishness.

*

Once I began writing this book, I also started trying to learn Hebrew seriously. I wanted to move on from my stumbling uncertainty when standing on the bimah in my mother's synagogue. I wanted to translate some of the research I knew I'd need to do for this book. But I also wanted, the more I progressed with discovering the family story, to get closer to Jewishness. I thought initially that this was to our family's Jewishness, although I've learned now that Hebrew was never a language spoken or written in the family or read outside of synagogue. So learning Hebrew has been not a return to a lost Jewishness but my making of a newly arrived Jewishness.

Nevertheless, through Hebrew, I wanted to get inside, or back to the basics of, Jewishness. Etymology – tracing the roots and family history of words – is a technique I use a lot for explaining difficult concepts to students, since I think it allows you to go back to beginnings.

I spent one summer in Ulpan – Hebrew crash-course language school – in Tel Aviv. Since then, I've been taking classes online via the Hebrew University of Jerusalem. Right now, I'm in the process of transitioning from modern Hebrew to Biblical or Torah Hebrew.

I'm still uncertain in Hebrew, but I've loved it from the beginning. The language feels to me ancient, but expansive enough to include the newest words and concepts. It has a logic that challenges what you normally think belongs with what. This is in good part because every word has a root, and that same root will bring together a diversity and multiplicity of meanings that you wouldn't have associated.

Take the word קֶדֶם *cadem*, for example. 'front', 'east', but also 'the past'. I knew that moving into a Jewish future demanded that I unpack and lay out the kind of Jewishness my ancestors lived. That going forwards meant going into the past.'

As I write this I have a recurrent dream.

I am taking a bus journey with my mother. She is old and tired. She leans her head against the bus window. I say, to her, to the bus driver – do you mind if I stop off home to see my baby?

My son is about four months' old. Inexplicably, my wife has left him home alone.

I go to his room. I pick him up and hold him. I show him to my mother. I want her to see him, to take him in. The sense of fulfilment and pride are so intense and beautiful, they wake me up from my dream.

In reality, in waking life, I have no son. I have no wife. There are decisions I've made in my life that mean that when I could have had children, I didn't, and once I wanted them, I couldn't.

And so now I wonder, who will take on this story?

*

The word *Hebrew* itself comes from עבר , *eber/ever, avar/abar.* עבר has these multiple connotations:

(as a verb) to pass, to advance, to go by; to cross (a street, border, bridge); to transfer; to traverse; to go over, to study; to undergo; to surpass; to violate, to transgress, to breach;

(as a noun): the past; past, history, record; past tense; criminal record; side, direction, way; foetus; embryo;

(in compound words, adjectivally): last, past (week, month, year).

Why this association with passing, crossing, the past, birthing, advancing, undergoing, violating, transgressing, transferring, transversing, at the very root of the Hebrews/Jews? עבר derives from the Aramaic for 'the other side' – which is the other side of the river of the Euphrates. In Abraham, the first Jew in the Torah, Jews originated from this other side, the eastern side of the river: Iraq. Hence *eber*/Hebrew.

עבר is also the root that runs through and brings into commonality – and here's where you really see the richness of the root, its proliferation into possible routes you wouldn't have thought compatible – both 'Hebrew' and 'Arab': *'eber'* and 'arab', עבר, 'God's most treasured pun', as the American poet Ammiel Alcalay quips. Abraham was the root and father of the Jews, of course, the first Jew. But he was also father of the Arabs, which turns us into affiliates, in words and origin stories. Another family story, of sorts.

The common root is tantalisingly resonant before Abraham changed his name. Originally, before he was Jewish, he was *Abram*. The root was *av aram,* 'father of Aram'. Abram came from the 'other side': literally, geographically, Ur in Iraq. Abram/

Abraham left his old culture, religion and country to become Jewish. With his name change, Abraham also became not simply a father to his son, Aram, *av aram*, but a father to nations: *av hamon*. And so you can read that Abraham too was a convert – the first Jew and the first convert. Although this is an origin story not much told, in the Babylonian Talmud Abraham is referred to as 'the first of the proselytes'. For this reason, converts to this day take 'Abraham' as the name of their father. This childless man who left home in order to become Jewish then becomes the ancestor of all those who also leave home and become Jewish. To convert is to journey from your father's house; to journey from your father's house is to cross to the other side.

And as the ancestors in my family story, in the Torah, when he gets to the Promised Land, Abraham doesn't leave his past behind so that he forgets or buries it in his new home. His crossing is an act of creative transformation, a myth which is all the more magical because it reworks and keeps alive the history that came before.

When his wife who came with him from this Iraq dies – also called Sarah, like my mourned great-grandmother – Abraham asks of the Canaanites (the children of Heth) for a burial plot for her in this Canaan, this Israel. Not because this is his land by right; but rather precisely because he is a visitor, a foreigner, an immigrant, a stranger.

Here is the passage:

And Sarah died in Kirjath-arba; the same is Hebron in the land of Canaan; and Abraham came to mourn for Sarah, and to weep for her. And Abraham rose up from before his dead, and spoke unto the children of Heth, saying: 'I am a stranger and a sojourner with you: give me a possession of a burying-place with you, that I may bury my dead out of my sight.'

'A stranger and a sojourner': גֵּר־וְתוֹשָׁב (*Ger ve toshav*).

It's exactly the wording that appears in Leviticus, in God's Covenant with the Jews, and includes that term for convert used in my mother's and grandmother's conversion certificates.

This original stranger, even as he's burying his dead, never loses sight of the fact that he came from elsewhere; and that he – or his descendants – are very likely soon to be headed elsewhere.

*

Ten years after I was first called to the bimah, I'm back in my mother's synagogue. In honour of Jacob's yahrzeit again, now the fiftieth anniversary of his death, and also to raise money for the synagogue's maintenance, together my mother and I have organised an event. We have called it 'An evening of Iraqi Jewish music, food and culture'. The line-up collates bits of the family legacy I've found and people who've helped me discover it. I host a conversation with chef and cookery writer Linda Dangoor about her memories of Baghdad. She is charming and nostalgic, and she makes us feel hungry. The food for the evening is cooked by my Saffron chef cousin, Aviva: *mahasha, sambusak, kubbah*. We ask musician Sara Manasseh, born in Bombay of Iraqi Jewish descent, to perform with her band Rivers of Babylon. They mix in Bollywood classics with liturgy and popular songs from the Babylonian tradition. People are clapping along and tapping their feet, even much more than they normally do in a synagogue. A song my mother recalls and sings for one of the musicians – she can't remember the words; are they Aramaic? – turns out to be in their repertoire.

In an audience of friends, family and synagogue members, there are two men my age whom nobody knows. We learn they're Iraqis. Are they Jews or non-Jews? Refugee Christians or Muslims? Nobody asks. They sit quietly at the back of the synagogue. They know the tunes to most of the music, although not the words. Joining in, they hum and 'clack' their fingers. It's not a clicking but a shaking of the whole hand, so that the index and fourth finger seem to hit against each other, producing a wooden beat. I turn to my mother and find her eyes shining with wonder and what seems to be love.

She hasn't seen anyone do this since Jacob used to clack along to the music of his heart – another one of those memories that she had forgotten until this moment. These men, welcome and surprising guests at the synagogue, appear as if from another world and another time. I think that they're not so much Elijah at the Passover seder. They're more like reverse Ezra and Nehemiah, or the two travellers on the camphorwood chest who make the return journey back, not quite the same people they were before. They are interfaith prophets, strangers who bring curiosity and openness. They give us hope.

As the evening comes to a close, I study the bimah. I think about how I'll feel when they next call me to the platform in this synagogue – in any synagogue. I hope I'll feel more confident. They'll ask for my Jewish name. I can now retrace the whole of this journey to my Jewish inheritance: Jay, *ben* May/Miriam, *ben* Jacob, *ben* Isaac, *ben*. . . I'd certainly want to include Sim

Koh-wei, her conversion and the other crossings that made our Jewish continuity possible. But now that I'm getting into Biblical Hebrew, I could just say simply, *ben* Abraham, because I know that the end of my story is also this beginning. And when they open the doors of the wooden ark and take out the scroll for me to read, I'll now know that this, this legacy of loving strangers, is how I belong.

Increasingly these days, my mother tells me, in texts, in phone calls, 'love you always and forever', 'love you to the end of time'. She has always shown this limitless, forever love but it's only now that she's in her mid-eighties that she's started articulating it with a naked clarity that moves me to tears.

Recently we were sitting opposite each other in a restaurant celebrating my parents' sixtieth-first anniversary. My father was by her side, enjoying his food. We had travelled to Malaysia and Singapore, on what I imagine, given my parents' age and in particular my father's frailty, will be my parents' last trip back together, and possibly my last trip back with my mother.

My mother looked into my eyes more directly than I felt she'd ever done before. Or maybe I just saw that look for the first time. 'You know I will always be with you', she said.

And yes, I think that now I know.

*

Except it's not quite the end, because after I put everything back in the camphorwood chest – all the treasures I've unearthed to gift me this story – I have another dream.

Years after some catastrophe in which everyone was lost, my brother and I go to an underground place. It's an archive, only with bodies perfectly unspoiled in the very gestures held at their moment of death, frozen in their last moment of living. My brother and I descend to their level and see them in formation, one after the other, like the Terracotta Warriors. They are marching, walking; moving on, the dream me thinks. Something – a chemical? another substance? or the fact of being underground? – has preserved the scene for a very long time.

My brother and I perform what feels like a violation. We rifle through the pockets of some of the dead, finding personal effects – letters and cards among them. But we take nothing. Someone disturbs us in our searching – the curator of this archive of the dead – and my brother and I run back towards the land of the living. When the curator reaches us, I see that he is my age, also with glasses, short. He is a version of myself.

He doesn't chide us. Instead, he takes from his pocket some of the items that we were looking for. A postcard from my father; a letter from my mother. There is the looping, full-of-hope-and-ideals forward slope of my mother's handwriting; the neat military marching-out imprint of my father.

Holding these things, my dream self weeps.

A Note on Sources

Beyond the camphorwood chest cache, in the research for *Loving Strangers* I read many books and articles and consulted many documents in archives. Below I list some of my principal sources. Where I have used items across chapters, I do not repeat their citation.

4. Some Enchanted Evening

Freud, Sigmund, 'Family Romances' (1909), *The Standard Edition of the Complete Psychological Works of Sigmund Freud*, Vol. IX (London: Hogarth Press, 1975), 235-42.

Gioia, Ted, *Love Songs: A Hidden History* (New York: Oxford University Press, 2015).

Suyin, Han, *A Many-Splendoured Thing* (1952; London: Chatto, 1985).

5. MC; CT

Gleave, John, *The Jungle War, With the First Battalion, The Cheshire Regiment* (The *Chester Chronicle* and Associated Newspapers, Ltd, 1958).

Hale, Christopher, *Massacre in Malaya: Exposing Britain's My Lai* (Stroud: History Press, 2013).

Jackson, Robert, *The Malayan Emergency: The Commonwealth's Wars, 1948-1966* (London: Routledge, 1991).

Lyn, Martin, *The British Empire in the 1950s: Retreat or Revival?* (Basingstoke: Palgrave Macmillan, 2005).

Stubbs, Richard, *Hearts and Minds in Guerrilla Warfare: The Malayan Emergency, 1948-1960* (Singapore: Oxford University Press, 1989).

Suyin, Han, *And the Rain My Drink* (London: Cape, 1956).

7. The Menorah

Angel, Marc D., *Choosing to be Jewish: The Orthodox Road to Conversion* (Jersey City: Ktav Publishing, 2005).

Bieder, Joan, *The Jews of Singapore* (Singapore: Suntree, 2007).

Chan, Heng Chee, *A Sensation of Independence: A Political Biography of David Marshall* (Oxford: Oxford University Press, 1984).

Lee, Kuan Yew, *The Singapore Story* (Singapore: Times Editions, 1998).

Marshall, David, Oral History Interview, 24 September 1984, Reel 8, National Archives of Singapore.

Parfitt, Tudor, *The Thirteenth Gate: Travels Among the Lost Tribes of Israel* (London: Weidenfeld and Nicolson, 1987).

Tan, Kevin Y. L., *Marshall of Singapore: A Biography* (Singapore: ISEAS Publishing, 2008).

Turnbull, C. M., *A History of Singapore 1819-1988* (Oxford: Oxford University Press, 1989).

8. The Worlds

Elias, Moshe, *The Messiahs of Princep Street* (Woodstock: Writersworld, 2014).

Farrell, J. G., *The Singapore Grip* (London: Phoenix, 1978).

Koh, Tommy, 'The Worlds?', *Singapore: The Encyclopedia* (Singapore: Editions Didier Millet, 2006), 380.

'Singapore's New Playground', *Singapore Free Press and Mercantile Advertiser* (27 April 1937), 1.

Tan, Sooi Beng, *Bangsawan: A Social and Stylistic History of Popular Malay Opera* (Singapore: Oxford University Press, 1993).

Wise, Michael, ed., *Travellers' Tales of Old Singapore* (Singapore: Times Books International, 1985).

Wong, Yunn Chi, and Tan, Kar Lin, 'Emergence of a Cosmopolitan Space for Culture and Consumption: The New World Amusement Park-Singapore (1923–70) in the Inter-war Years', *Inter-Asia Cultural Studies*, 5.2 (2004), 289-90.

Yen, Phan Ming, 'Three Worlds and a Time When Life was a Cabaret', *Straits Times* (9 June 1995), 8.

9. The Ankle Bells

Brooke, Geoffrey, *Singapore's Dunkirk* (London: Leo Cooper, 1989).

Chou, Cindy, *Beyond the Empires: Memories Retold* (Singapore: National Heritage Board, 1995).

Elphick, Peter, *Singapore, The Pregnable Fortress: A Study in Deception, Discord and Desertion* (London: Hodder and Stoughton, 1995).

Nathan, Eze, *The History of Jews in Singapore 1830-1945* (Singapore: Herbilu, 1986).

Warner, Lavinia, and Sandilands, John, *Women Behind the Wire* (London: Hamlyn, 1982).

WO 361/448, 'Casualties at sea, Far East: SS Felix Roussel, bombed at Singapore, 5 February 1942', National Archives, Kew.

10. Jacob and Esther

Davison, Julian, *One for the Road and Other Stories: Recollections of Singapore and Malaya* (Singapore: Topographica, 2001).

Si, Jing, *Down Memory Lane in Clogs: Growing Up in Chinatown* (Singapore: Asiapac Books, 2002).

11. Girl Moses

Baschet, Eric, ed., *China 1890-1938 from the Warlords to World War: A History in Documentary Photographs* (Germany: Swan, 1989).

Johnson, Kay Ann, *Women, the Family, and Peasant Revolution in China* (Chicago: University of Chicago Press, 1985).

Pan, Lynn, *Sons of the Yellow Emperor: The Story of the Overseas Chinese* (London: Mandarin, 1991).

Wolf, Arthur P., and Huang, Chieh-shan, *Marriage and Adoption in China: 1845–1945* (Stanford: Stanford University Press, 1980).

12. Shema

Campo, J. N. F. M. à, *Engines of Empire: Steamshipping and State Formation in Colonial Indonesia* (Leiden: Hilversum Verloren, 2002).

Corn, Charles, *The Scents of Eden: A History of the Spice Trade* (New York: Kodansha, 1998).

Czarra, Fred, *Spices: A Global History* (London: Reaktion, 2009).

Keay, John, *The Honourable Company: A History of the English East India Company* (London: HarperCollins, 1993).

Keay, John, *The Spice Route: A History* (London: John Murray, 2005).

Stein, Gertrude, letter to Thorton Wilder, in *The Letters of Gertrude Stein and Thornton Wilder*, ed. Edward M. Burns (New Haven: Yale University Press, 1996), 364.

Stein, Gertrude, *The Autobiography of Alice B. Toklas* (New York: Vintage, 1990), 239.

13. The House at the Crossroads

'An Unsavoury Case', *Straits Times* (10 May 1909), 7.

Cohen, Israel, *The Journal of a Jewish Traveller* (London: John Lane, 1925).

'Father and Son: Trouble in a Jewish Family', *Singapore Free Press and Mercantile Advertiser* (16 June 1908), 5.

'Medicine or Beverage? Singapore Jew Charged with Selling Illegal Intoxicants', *Straits Times* (2 March 1912), 9.

'Sergeant Payne's Case: Perils of the Police', *Eastern Daily Mail and Straits Morning Advertiser* (1 August 1907), 3.

14. Heritage Hotel

Dangoor, Linda, *Flavours of Babylon: A Family Cookbook* (London: Waterpoint Press, 2011).

Proust, Marcel, *Swann's Way*, trans. C.K. Scott Moncrieff (London: Penguin, 1957).

Roland, Jean G., *Jews in British India: Identity in a Colonial Era* (London: University of New England Press, 1989).

Roth, Cecil, *The Sassoon Dynasty* (London: Hale, 1941).

15. Babylon

Alcalay, Ammiel, *After Jews and Arabs: Remaking Levantine Culture* (Minneapolis: Minnesota University Press, 1992).

Hillel, David d'Beth, *The Travels of Rabbi David d'Beth Hillel from Jerusalem, through Arabia, Koordistan, Part of Persia, and India, to Madras* (Self-printed: Madras, 1832).

Kedourie, Elie, *The Chatham House Version and Other Middle Eastern Studies* (Chicago: Ivan R. Dee, 2004).

Marozzi, Justin, *Baghdad: City of Peace, City of Blood* (London: Penguin, 2015).

Rejwan, Nissim, *The Jews of Iraq: 3000 Years of History and Culture* (Weidenfeld and Nicolson: London, 1985).

Sassoon, David Solomon, *A History of the Jews in Baghdad* (Welwyn Garden City: Letchworth, 5700/1949).

Sassoon, David Sassoon, and David, Ohel, *Descriptive Catalogue of the Hebrew and Samaritan Manuscripts in the Sassoon Library* (Oxford, Oxford University Press, 1932).

Snir, Reuven, trans. and ed., *Baghdad: The City in Verse* (Cambridge, MA: Harvard University Press, 2013).

Stillman, Norman A., ed., *Encyclopedia of Jews in the Islamic World* (2013: Brill Online).

ACKNOWLEDGEMENTS

To my family, for their generosity with their memories and mementos: May Prosser, Keith Prosser, Moshe Elias, Aviva Elias, Linda Elias, Sunny Elias (of blessed memory), Rita Elias, Michelle Elias, Hannah Owen (of blessed memory), June Chua, Katie Elias Edginton, Julie Neerman and Hannah Campbell. To others close to me, for their love and faith: Helen Pleasance, Dave Prosser, Jenny Prosser, Rosa Prosser, Sam Prosser.

To readers of earlier drafts, for their comments, critiques, dialogue: Tahneer Oksman, Lily Dunn, Agi Erdos, Judith Russell, Carol Skuse, John Kahn, Lauren Maltas, Anthea Fraser Gupta, Sally Atkinson, Mick Gidley, Tracy Hugill, Georgia Hennessy Jackson, Shirley Chew, Mandy Bolster, Jutta Vetter, Donna Carter, Sandrine Boehm, Sarah Hubbard, Rabbi Elisheva Salamo. To my reading and writing groups, especially Andrew Kauffman, Joyia Fitch, Caroline Phillips.

To friends and colleagues for their example and support: Nancy K. Miller, Victoria Rosner, Marianne Hirsch, Leo Spitzer, Sami Zubaida, Margaretta Jolly, the late David Parker, Denis Flannery, Rachel Bower, Jess Richards, Kimberly Campanello, Nick Ray, John Whale, John McLeod, Pam Rhodes. To my students, from whom I've learned.

To Leslie Hakim-Dowek, for her photographs of objects from the camphorwood chest and her conversation. To those who acted as tour guides, whether physically or virtually: Flora Baruch, Mavis Symms, David Sopher (of blessed memory), Wu Liang-yu. For help with manuscripts and/or translations: Ilana Tahan, Eva Frojmovic, Ananya Jahanara Kabir. To Todd Swift, for his passionate belief in this book from the moment I contacted him, and to my BSPG proofreaders/editors Evelyn Rowan and Todd Swift.

I dedicate this book to my mother, with love always and forever.